JOHN CONSTANTINE, HELLBLAZER: REASONS TO BE CHEERFUL

JOHN CONSTANTINE, HELLBLAZER:

REASONS TO BE CHEERFUL

Mike Carey
Writer

"Event Horizon" and
"Reasons to be Cheerful"
Leonardo Manco
Artist

"Cross Purpose"
Giuseppe Camuncoli
Penciller

Lorenzo Ruggiero
Inker

Lee Loughridge
Colorist

Jared K. Fletcher
Phil Balsman
Letterers

Tim Bradstreet
Original Series Covers

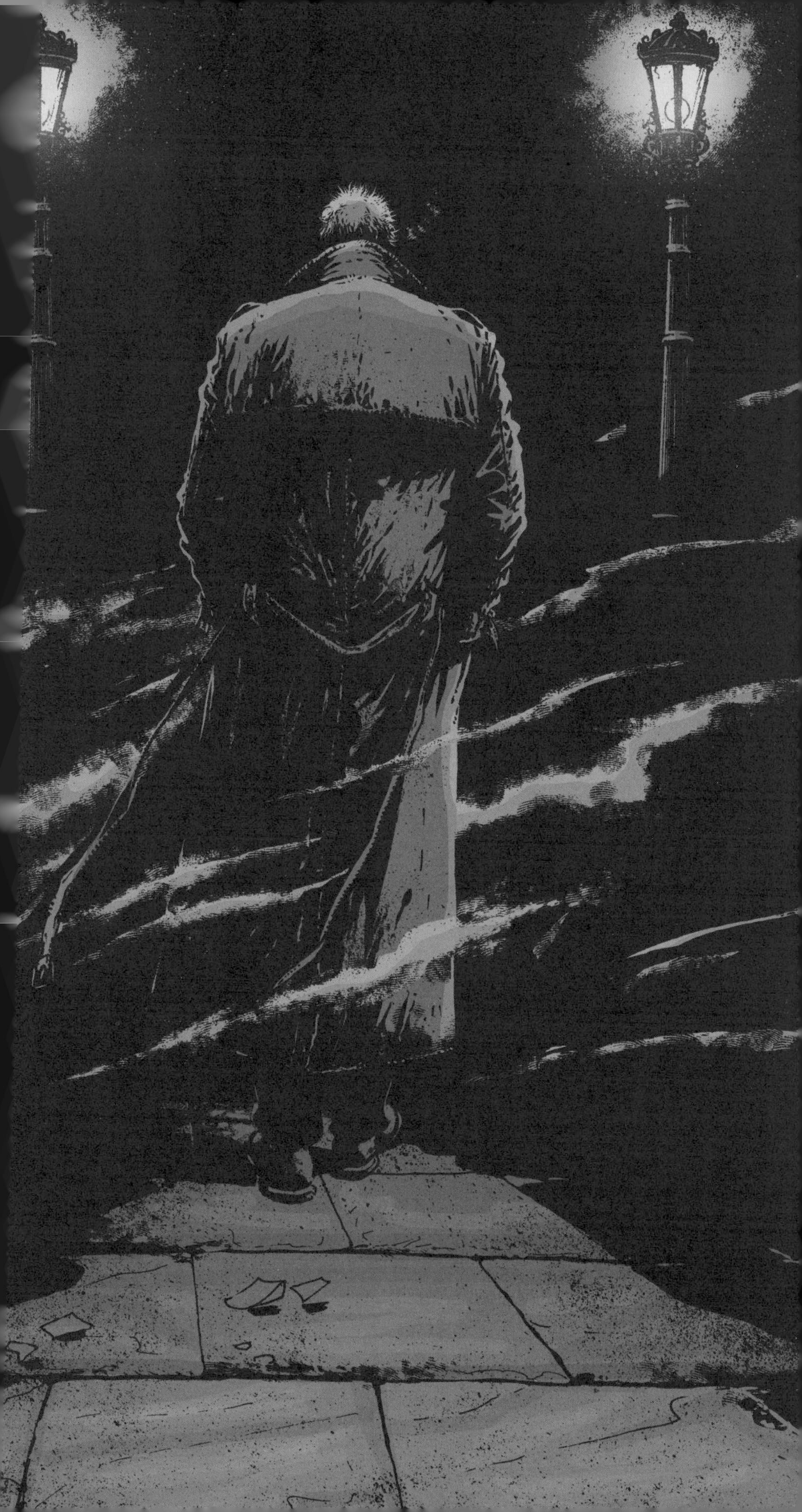

Karen Berger	Senior VP-Executive Editor
Jonathan Vankin	Editor-original series
Casey Seijas	Assistant Editor-original series
Bob Harras	Editor-collected edition
Robbin Brosterman	Senior Art Director
Paul Levitz	President & Publisher
Georg Brewer	VP-Design & Retail Product Development
Richard Bruning	Senior VP-Creative Director
Patrick Caldon	Executive VP-Finance & Operations
Chris Caramalis	VP-Finance
John Cunningham	VP-Marketing
Terri Cunningham	VP-Managing Editor
Alison Gill	VP-Manufacturing
Hank Kanalz	VP-General Manager-WildStorm
Jim Lee	Editorial Director-WildStorm
Paula Lowitt	Senior VP-Business & Legal Affairs
MaryEllen McLaughlin	VP-Advertising & Custom Publishing
John Nee	VP-Business Development
Gregory Noveck	Senior VP-Creative Affairs
Sue Pohja	VP-Book Trade Sales
Cheryl Rubin	Senior VP-Brand Management
Jeff Trojan	VP-Business Development, DC Direct
Bob Wayne	VP-Sales

Cover illustration by Tim Bradstreet.
Logo design by Nessim Higson.

JOHN CONSTANTINE, HELLBLAZER: REASONS TO BE CHEERFUL

DC Comics, 1700 Broadway, New York, NY 10019
A Warner Bros. Entertainment Company
Printed in Canada. First Printing.

ISBN: 1-4012-1251-4
ISBN 13: 978-1-4012-1251-3

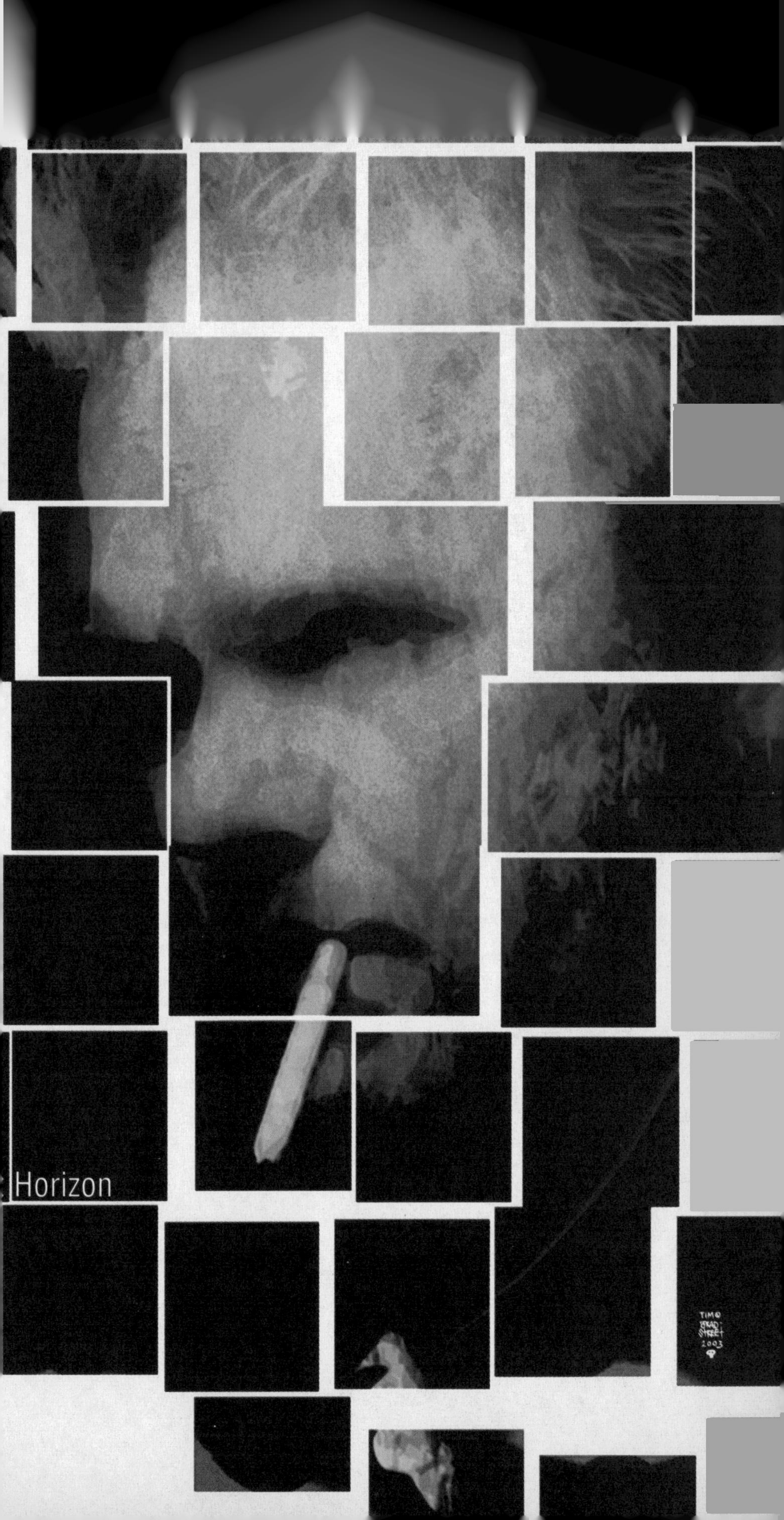
Horizon
TIM BRADSTREET 2003

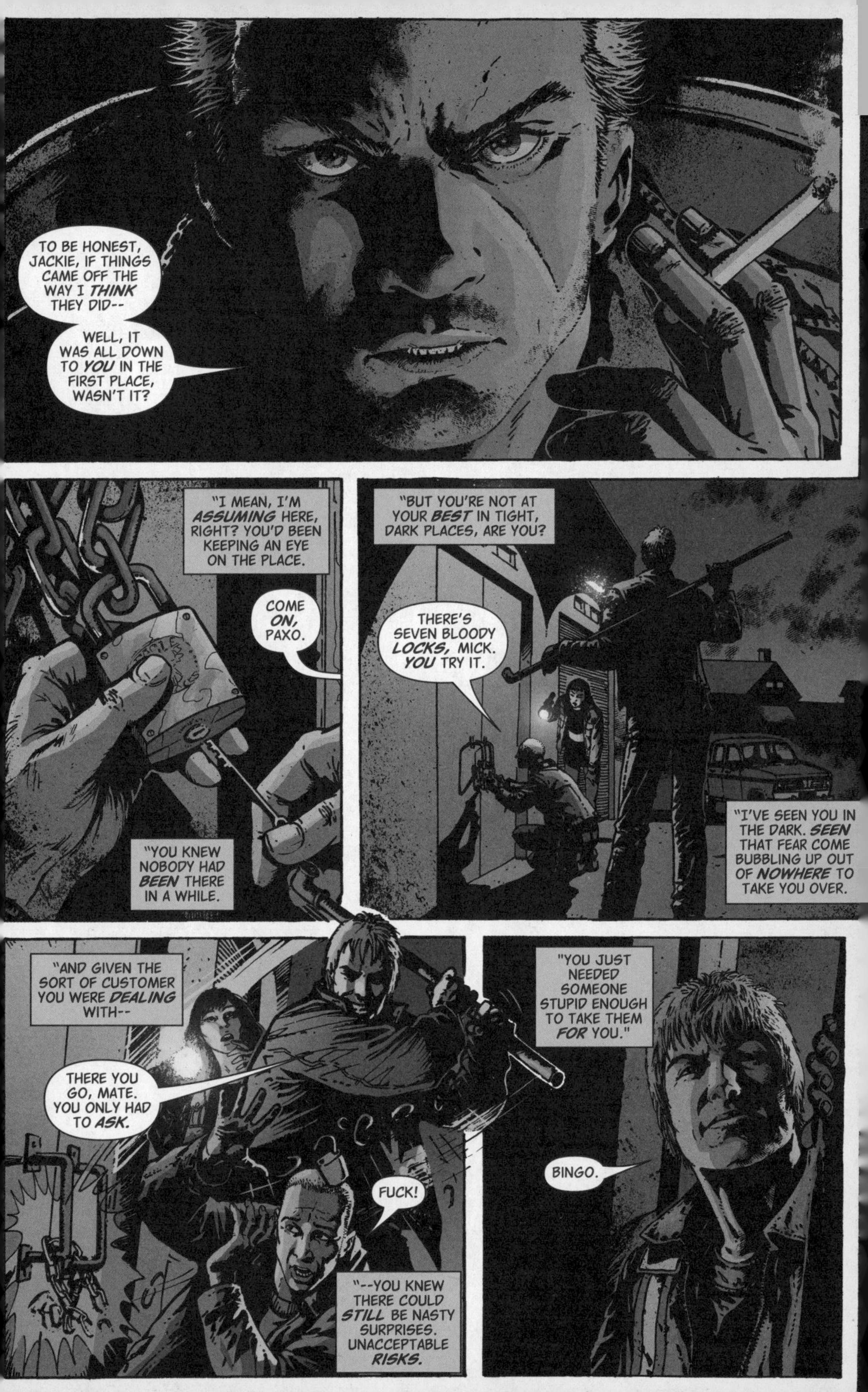
TO BE HONEST, JACKIE, IF THINGS CAME OFF THE WAY I *THINK* THEY DID--
WELL, IT WAS ALL DOWN TO *YOU* IN THE FIRST PLACE, WASN'T IT?
"I MEAN, I'M *ASSUMING* HERE, RIGHT? YOU'D BEEN KEEPING AN EYE ON THE PLACE.
COME *ON,* PAXO.
"YOU KNEW NOBODY HAD *BEEN* THERE IN A WHILE.
"BUT YOU'RE NOT AT YOUR *BEST* IN TIGHT, DARK PLACES, ARE YOU?
THERE'S SEVEN BLOODY *LOCKS,* MICK. *YOU* TRY IT.
"I'VE SEEN YOU IN THE DARK. *SEEN* THAT FEAR COME BUBBLING UP OUT OF *NOWHERE* TO TAKE YOU OVER.
"AND GIVEN THE SORT OF CUSTOMER YOU WERE *DEALING* WITH--
THERE YOU GO, MATE. YOU ONLY HAD TO *ASK.*
FUCK!
"--YOU KNEW THERE COULD *STILL* BE NASTY SURPRISES. UNACCEPTABLE *RISKS.*
"YOU JUST NEEDED SOMEONE STUPID ENOUGH TO TAKE THEM *FOR* YOU."
BINGO.

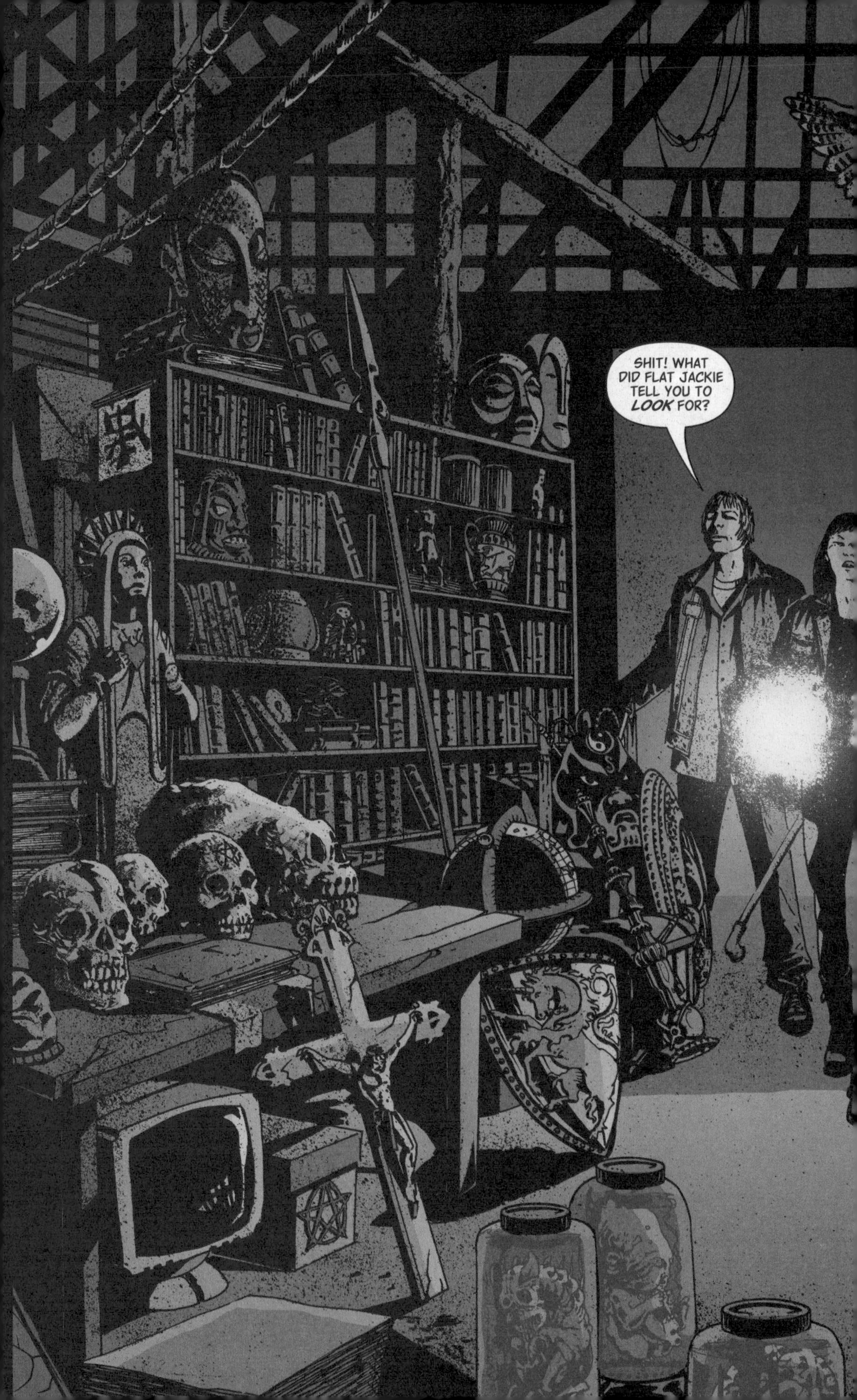
SHIT! WHAT DID FLAT JACKIE TELL YOU TO *LOOK* FOR?

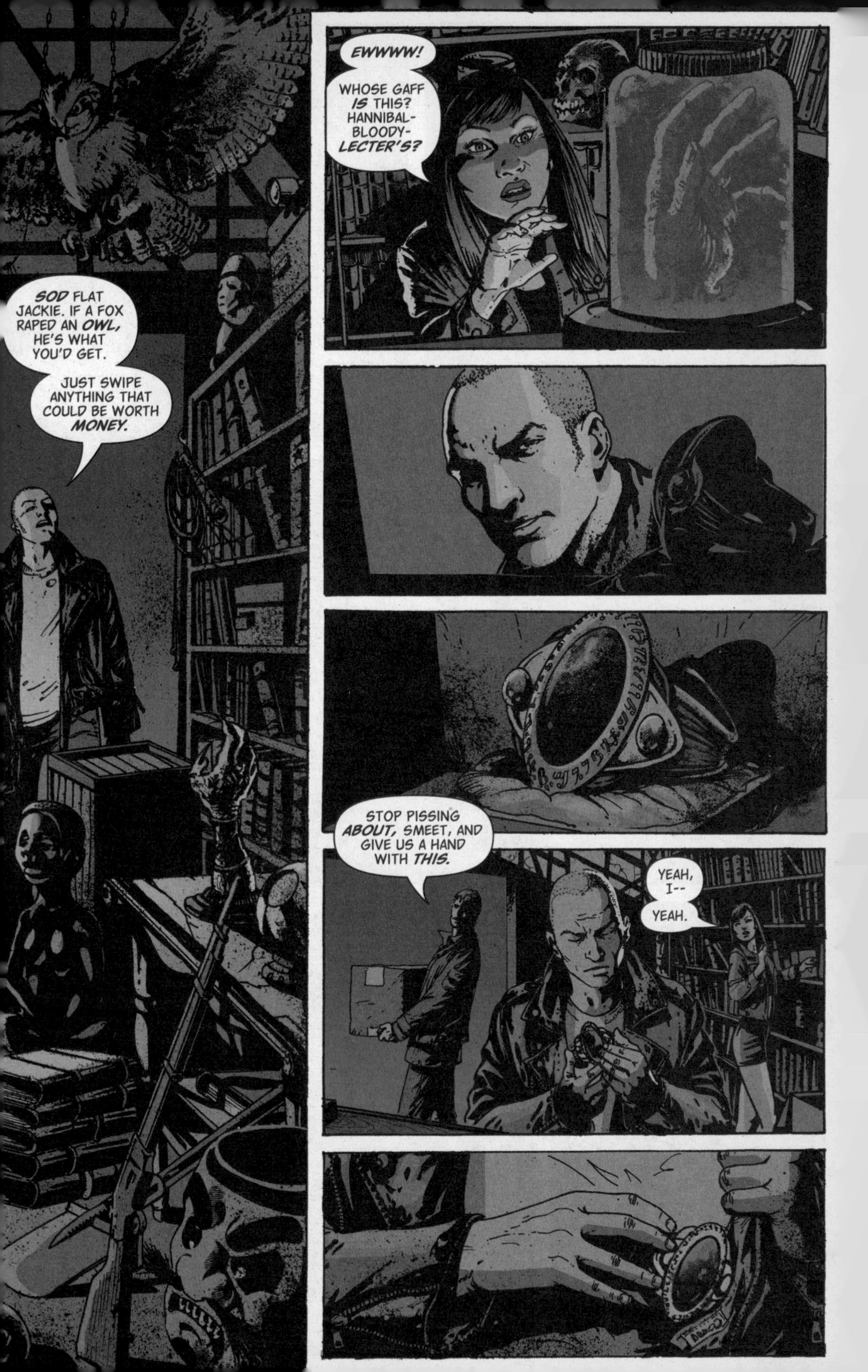
SOD FLAT JACKIE. IF A FOX RAPED AN OWL, HE'S WHAT YOU'D GET.
JUST SWIPE ANYTHING THAT COULD BE WORTH MONEY.
EWWWW!
WHOSE GAFF IS THIS? HANNIBAL-BLOODY-LECTER'S?
STOP PISSING ABOUT, SMEET, AND GIVE US A HAND WITH THIS.
YEAH, I--
YEAH.

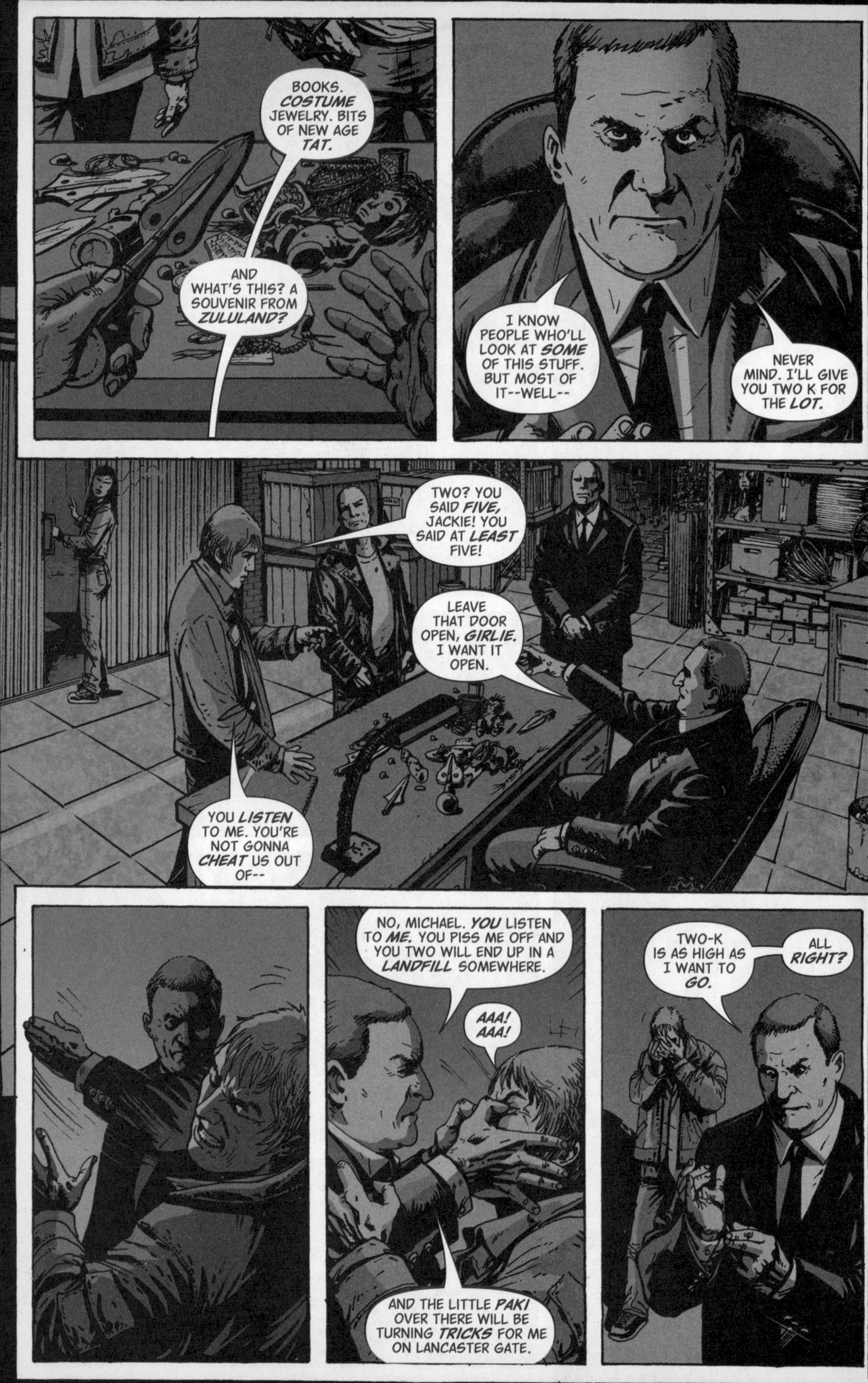
BOOKS. COSTUME JEWELRY. BITS OF NEW AGE TAT.
AND WHAT'S THIS? A SOUVENIR FROM ZULULAND?
I KNOW PEOPLE WHO'LL LOOK AT SOME OF THIS STUFF. BUT MOST OF IT--WELL--
NEVER MIND. I'LL GIVE YOU TWO K FOR THE LOT.
TWO? YOU SAID FIVE, JACKIE! YOU SAID AT LEAST FIVE!
LEAVE THAT DOOR OPEN, GIRLIE. I WANT IT OPEN.
YOU LISTEN TO ME. YOU'RE NOT GONNA CHEAT US OUT OF--
NO, MICHAEL. YOU LISTEN TO ME. YOU PISS ME OFF AND YOU TWO WILL END UP IN A LANDFILL SOMEWHERE.
AAA! AAA!
AND THE LITTLE PAKI OVER THERE WILL BE TURNING TRICKS FOR ME ON LANCASTER GATE.
TWO-K IS AS HIGH AS I WANT TO GO.
ALL RIGHT?

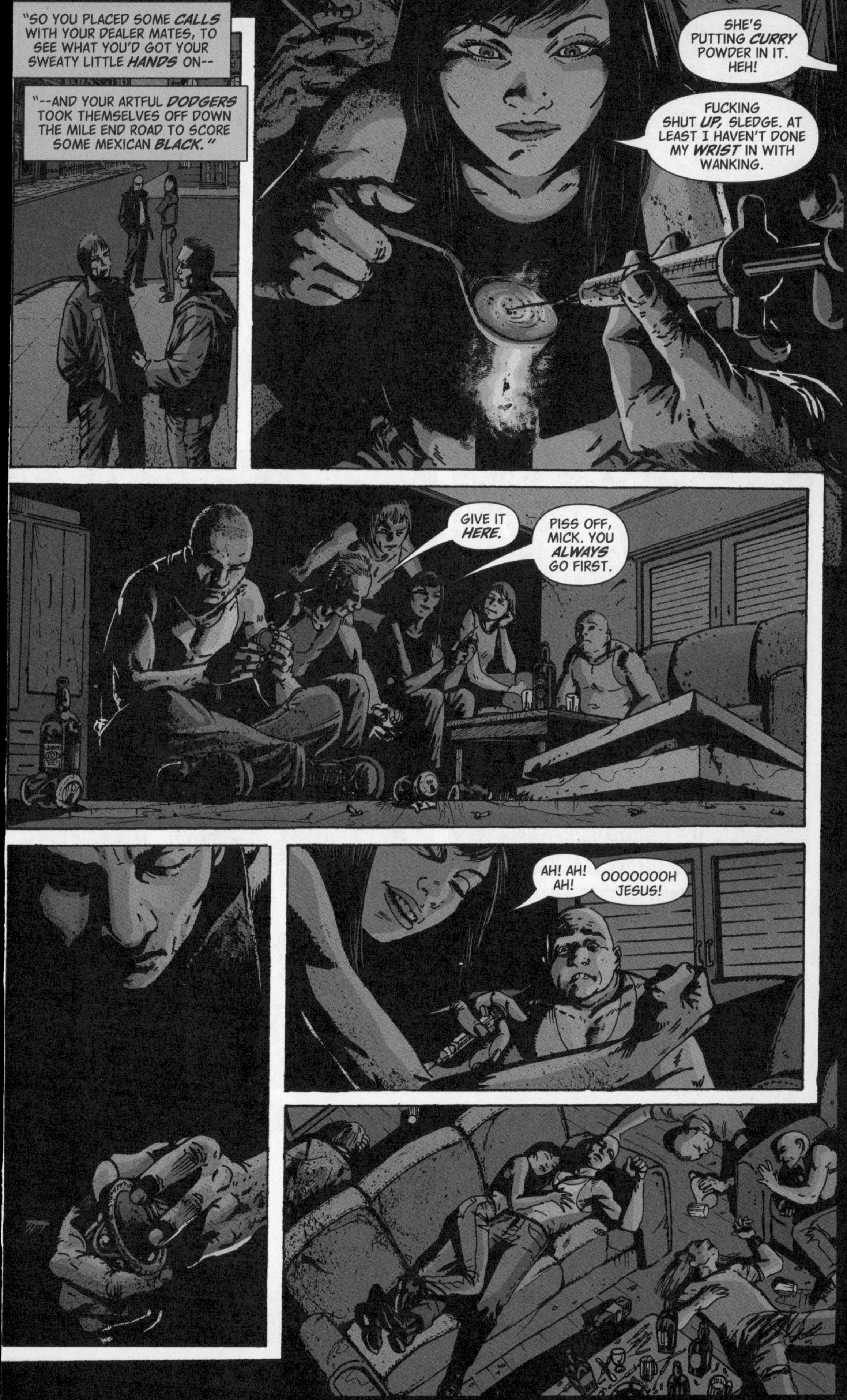
"SO YOU PLACED SOME CALLS WITH YOUR DEALER MATES, TO SEE WHAT YOU'D GOT YOUR SWEATY LITTLE HANDS ON--
"--AND YOUR ARTFUL DODGERS TOOK THEMSELVES OFF DOWN THE MILE END ROAD TO SCORE SOME MEXICAN BLACK."
SHE'S PUTTING CURRY POWDER IN IT. HEH!
FUCKING SHUT UP, SLEDGE. AT LEAST I HAVEN'T DONE MY WRIST IN WITH WANKING.
GIVE IT HERE.
PISS OFF, MICK. YOU ALWAYS GO FIRST.
AH! AH! AH!
OOOOOOOH JESUS!

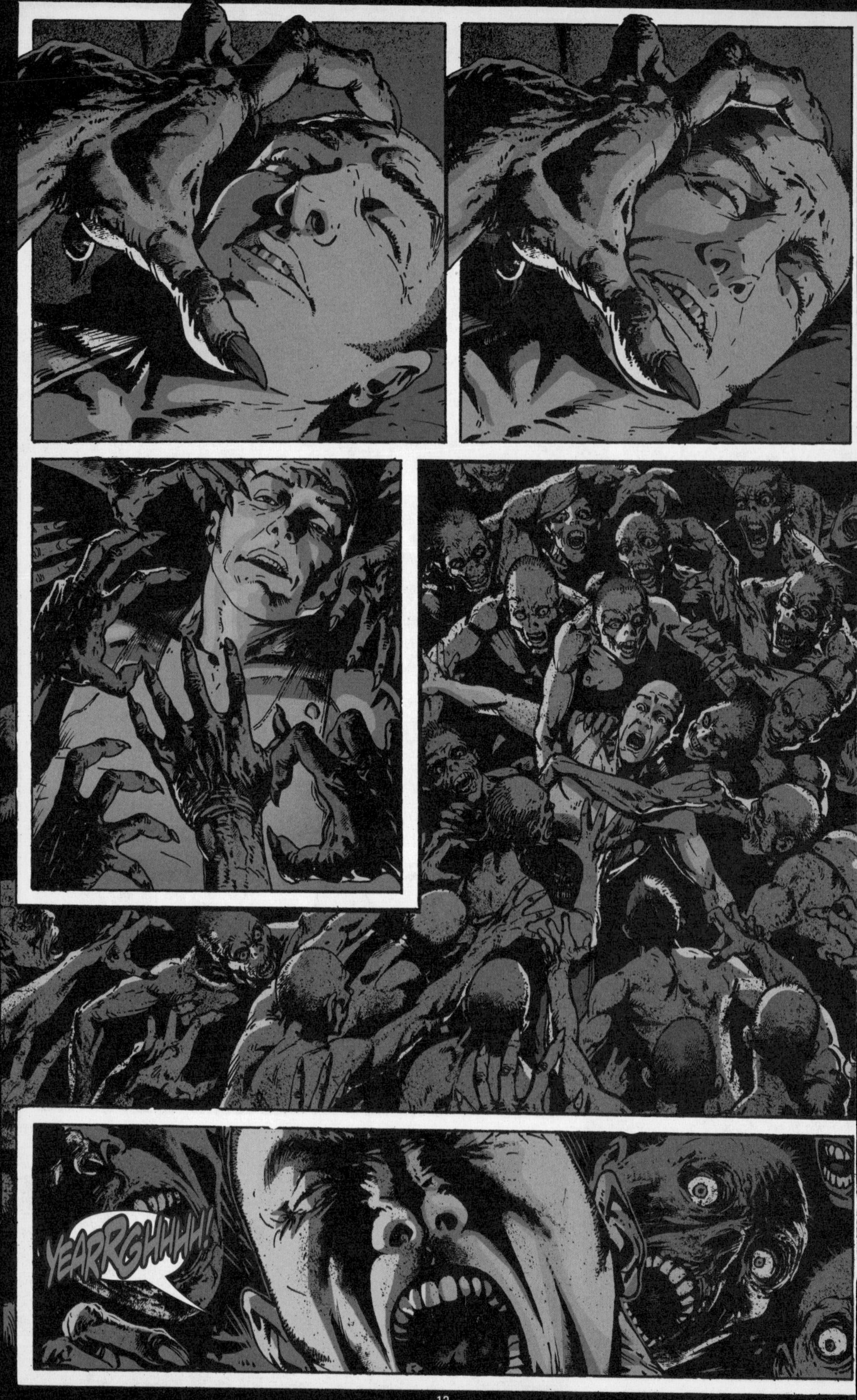
YEARRGHHHH!

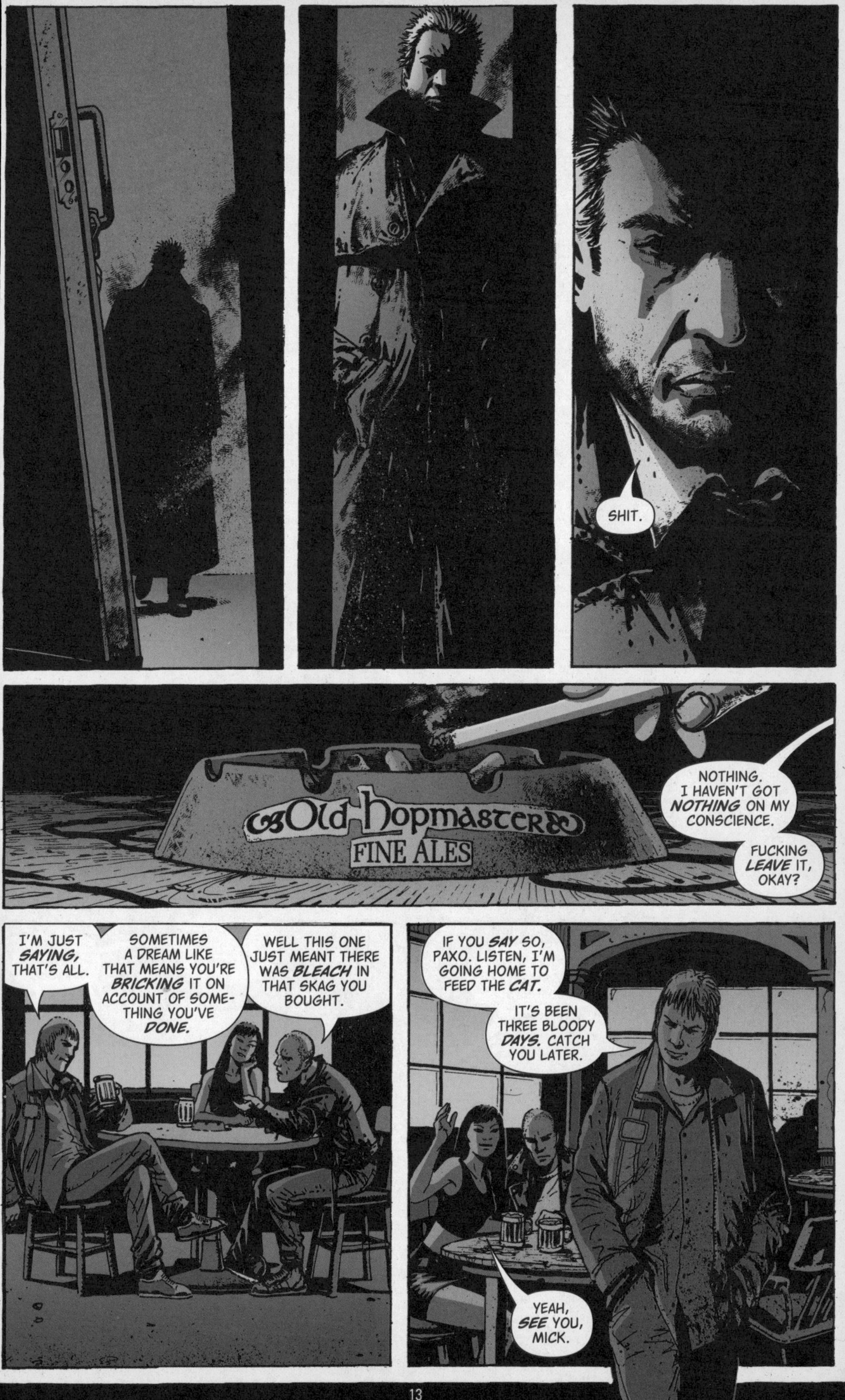
SHIT.
OLD HOPMASTER FINE ALES
NOTHING. I HAVEN'T GOT NOTHING ON MY CONSCIENCE.
FUCKING LEAVE IT, OKAY?
I'M JUST SAYING, THAT'S ALL.
SOMETIMES A DREAM LIKE THAT MEANS YOU'RE BRICKING IT ON ACCOUNT OF SOMETHING YOU'VE DONE.
WELL THIS ONE JUST MEANT THERE WAS BLEACH IN THAT SKAG YOU BOUGHT.
IF YOU SAY SO, PAXO. LISTEN, I'M GOING HOME TO FEED THE CAT.
IT'S BEEN THREE BLOODY DAYS. CATCH YOU LATER.
YEAH, SEE YOU, MICK.

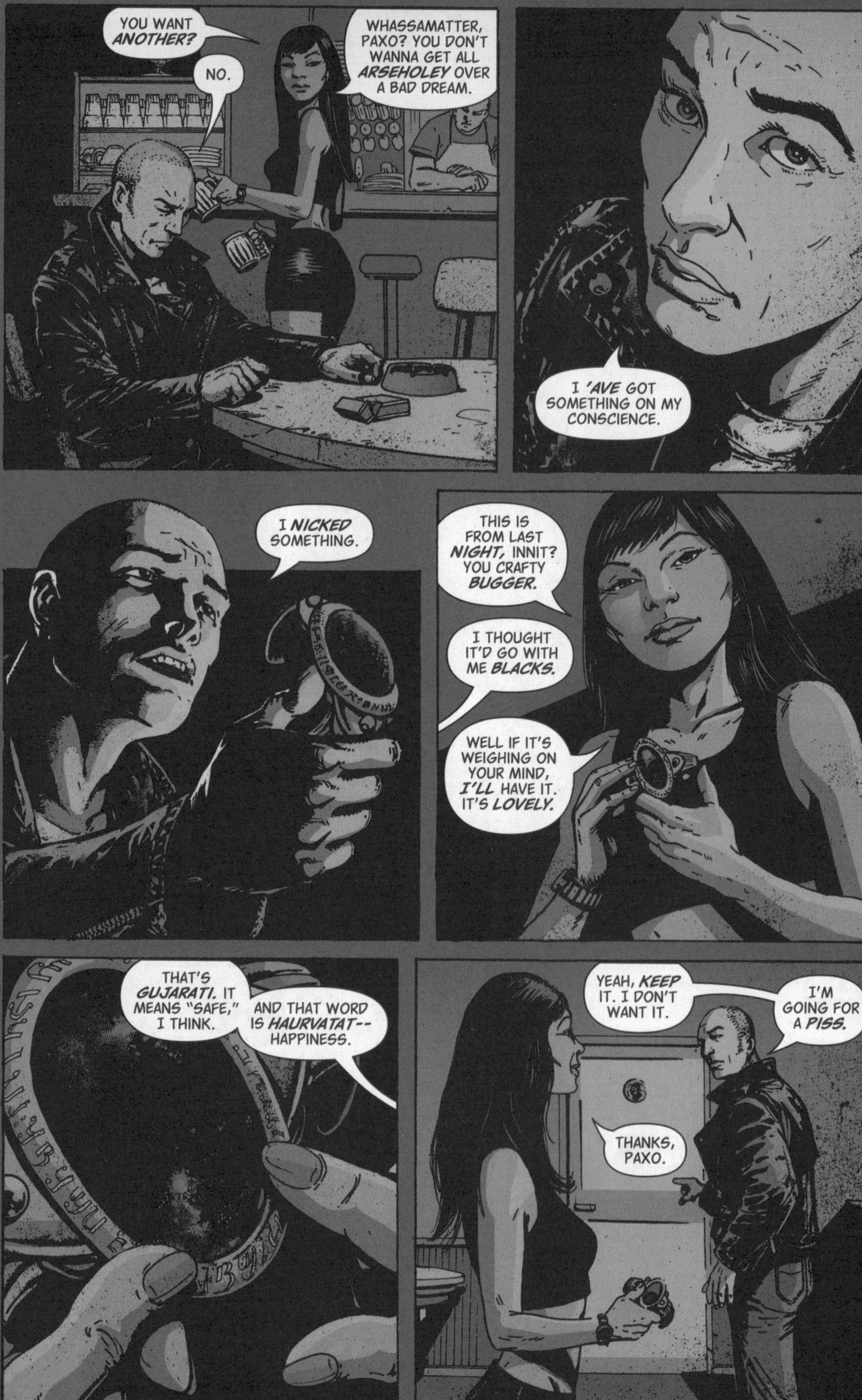

YOU WANT ANOTHER?
NO.
WHASSAMATTER, PAXO? YOU DON'T WANNA GET ALL ARSEHOLEY OVER A BAD DREAM.
I 'AVE GOT SOMETHING ON MY CONSCIENCE.
I NICKED SOMETHING.
THIS IS FROM LAST NIGHT, INNIT? YOU CRAFTY BUGGER.
I THOUGHT IT'D GO WITH ME BLACKS.
WELL IF IT'S WEIGHING ON YOUR MIND, I'LL HAVE IT. IT'S LOVELY.
THAT'S GUJARATI. IT MEANS "SAFE," I THINK.
AND THAT WORD IS HAURVATAT-- HAPPINESS.
YEAH, KEEP IT. I DON'T WANT IT.
I'M GOING FOR A PISS.
THANKS, PAXO.

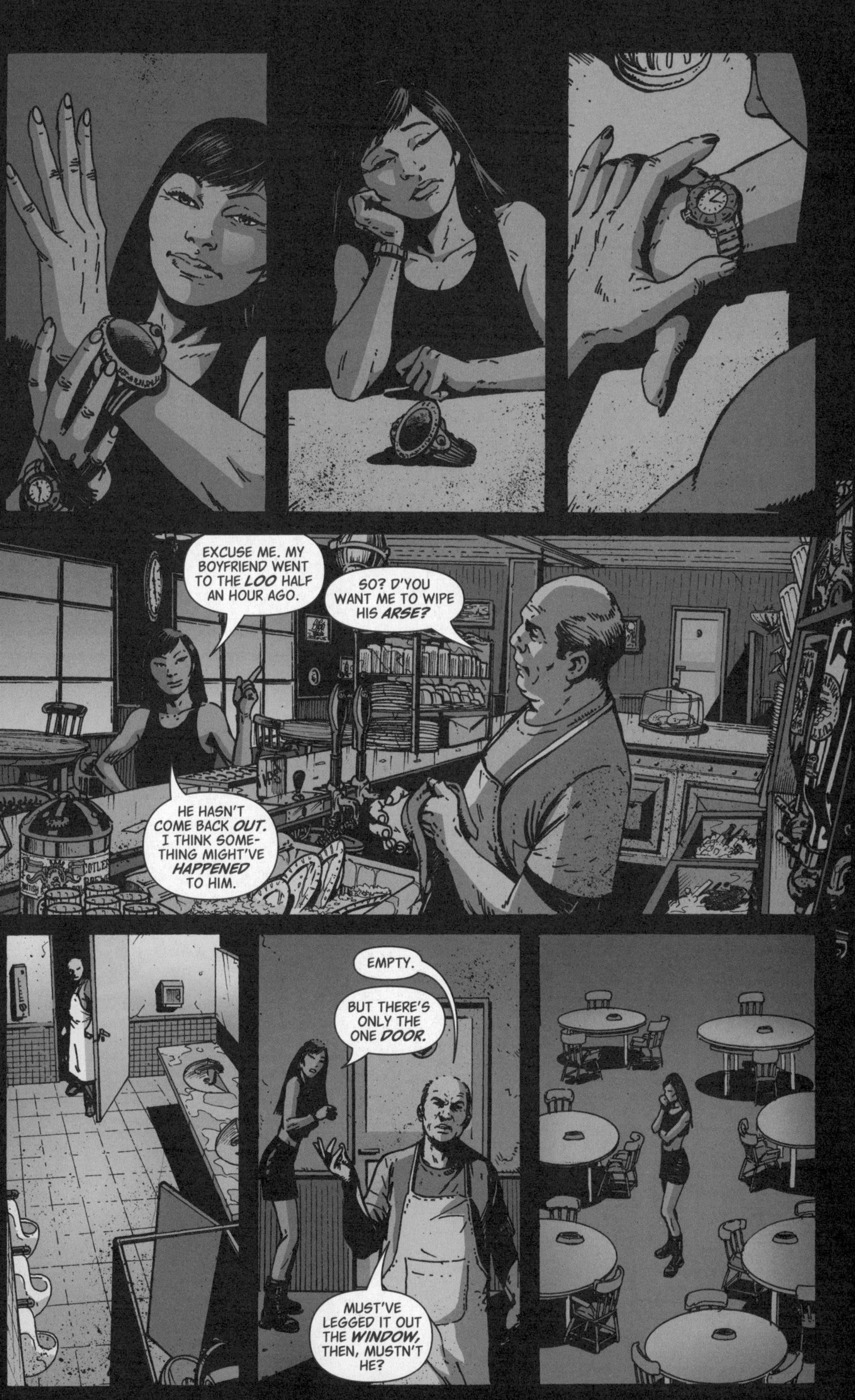

EXCUSE ME. MY BOYFRIEND WENT TO THE LOO HALF AN HOUR AGO.
SO? D'YOU WANT ME TO WIPE HIS ARSE?
HE HASN'T COME BACK OUT. I THINK SOME-THING MIGHT'VE HAPPENED TO HIM.
EMPTY.
BUT THERE'S ONLY THE ONE DOOR.
MUST'VE LEGGED IT OUT THE WINDOW, THEN, MUSTN'T HE?

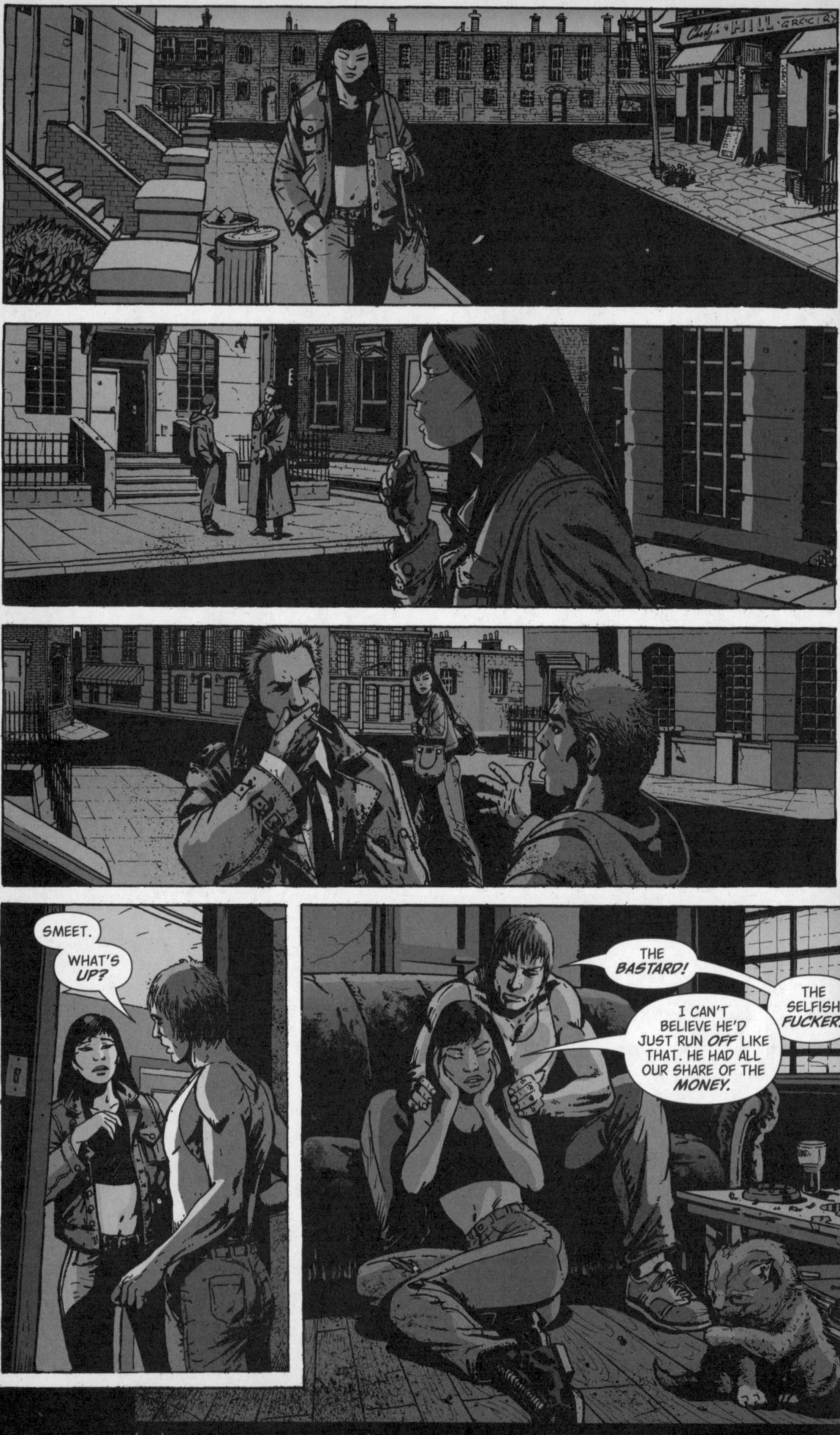

Chealy's
HILL GROCERY
SMEET.
WHAT'S UP?
THE BASTARD!
I CAN'T BELIEVE HE'D JUST RUN OFF LIKE THAT. HE HAD ALL OUR SHARE OF THE MONEY.
THE SELFISH FUCKER.

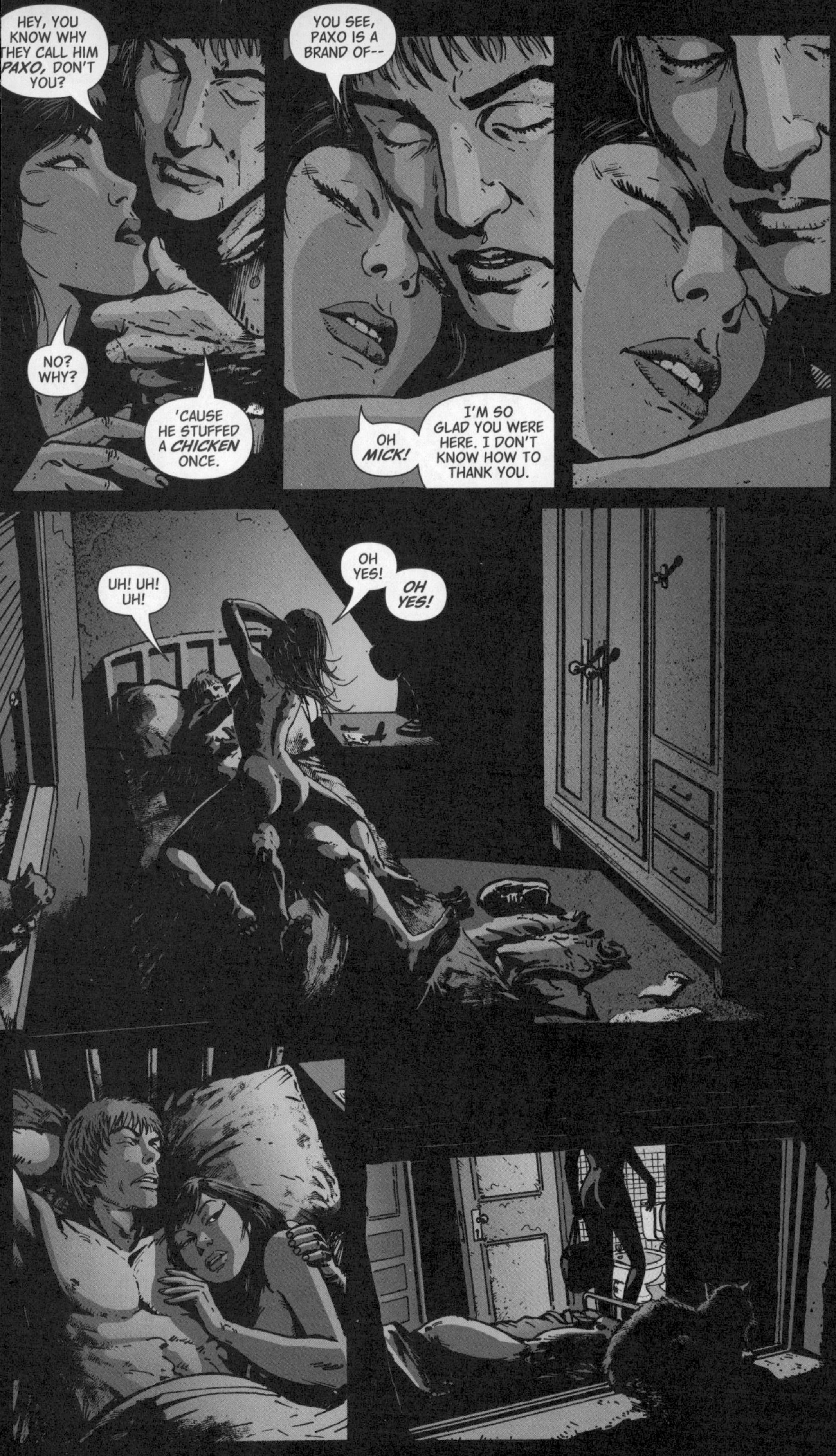
HEY, YOU KNOW WHY THEY CALL HIM PAXO, DON'T YOU?
NO? WHY?
'CAUSE HE STUFFED A CHICKEN ONCE.
YOU SEE, PAXO IS A BRAND OF--
OH MICK!
I'M SO GLAD YOU WERE HERE. I DON'T KNOW HOW TO THANK YOU.
UH! UH! UH!
OH YES!
OH YES!

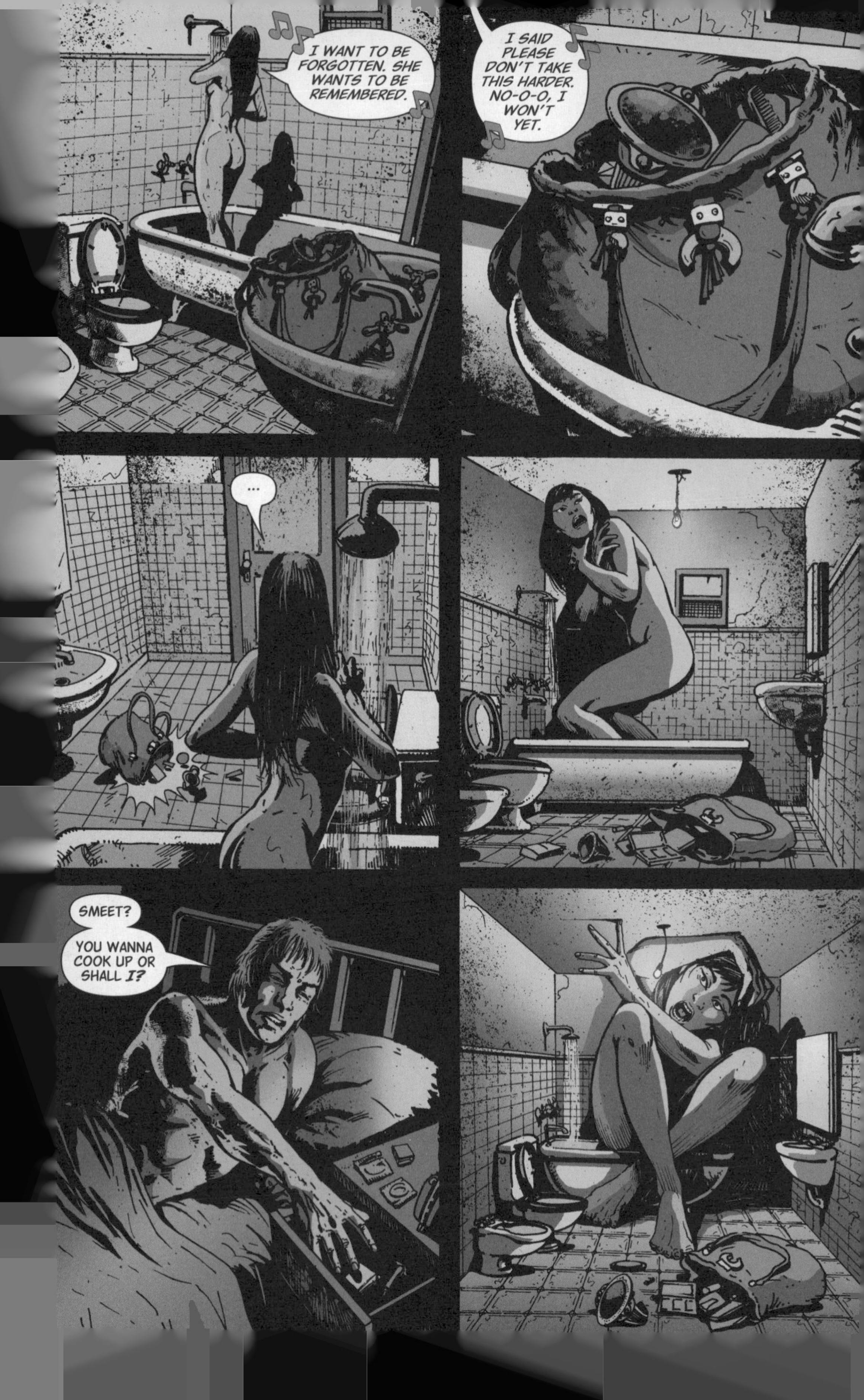
I WANT TO BE FORGOTTEN. SHE WANTS TO BE REMEMBERED.
I SAID PLEASE DON'T TAKE THIS HARDER. NO-O-O, I WON'T YET.
...
SMEET?
YOU WANNA COOK UP OR SHALL I?

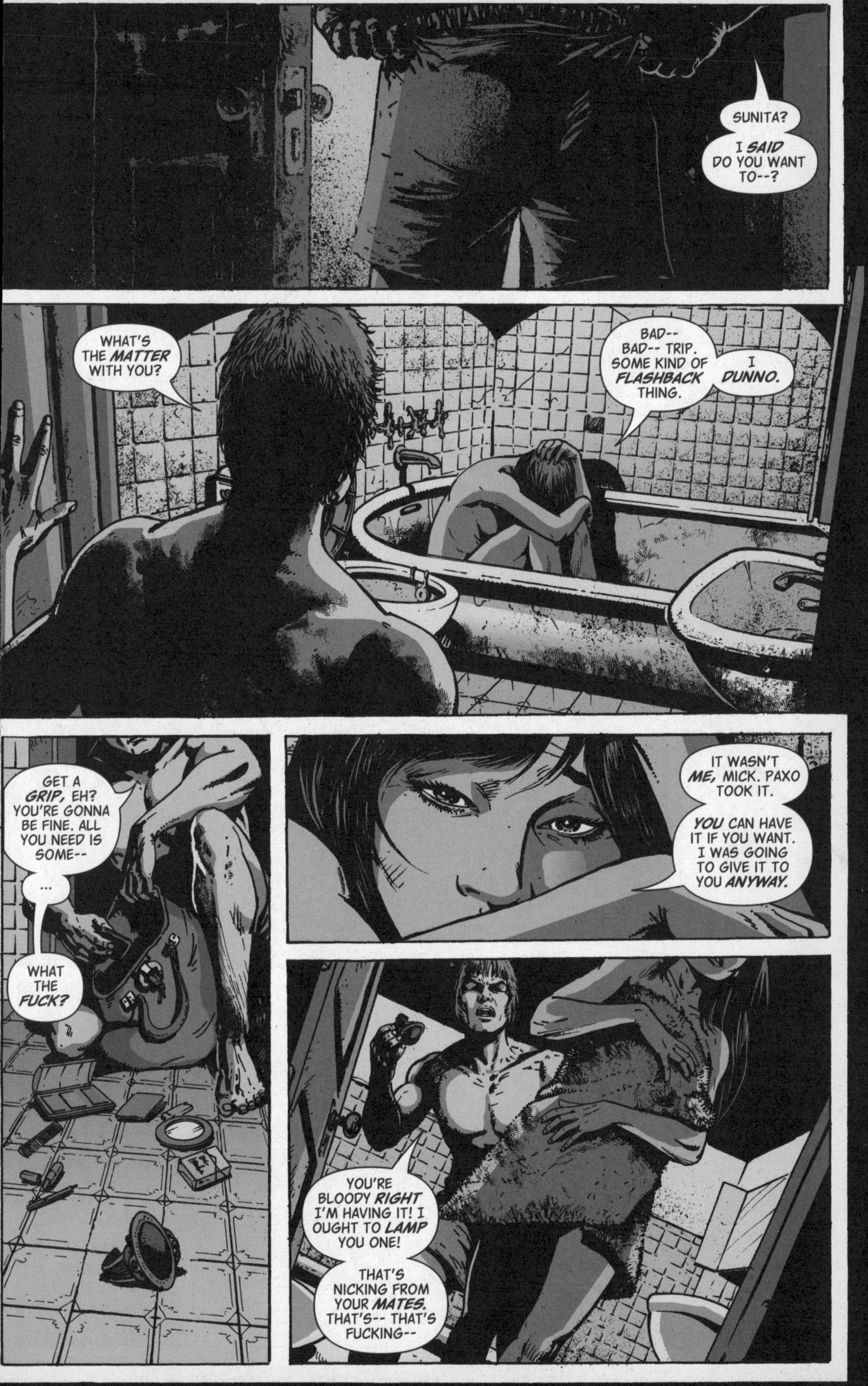
SUNITA?
I *SAID* DO YOU WANT TO--?
WHAT'S THE *MATTER* WITH YOU?
BAD-- BAD-- TRIP. SOME KIND OF *FLASHBACK* THING.
I *DUNNO.*
GET A *GRIP,* EH? YOU'RE GONNA BE FINE. ALL YOU NEED IS SOME--
...
WHAT THE *FUCK?*
IT WASN'T *ME,* MICK. PAXO TOOK IT.
YOU CAN HAVE IT IF YOU WANT. I WAS GOING TO GIVE IT TO YOU *ANYWAY.*
YOU'RE BLOODY *RIGHT* I'M HAVING IT! I OUGHT TO *LAMP* YOU ONE!
THAT'S NICKING FROM YOUR *MATES.* THAT'S-- THAT'S FUCKING--

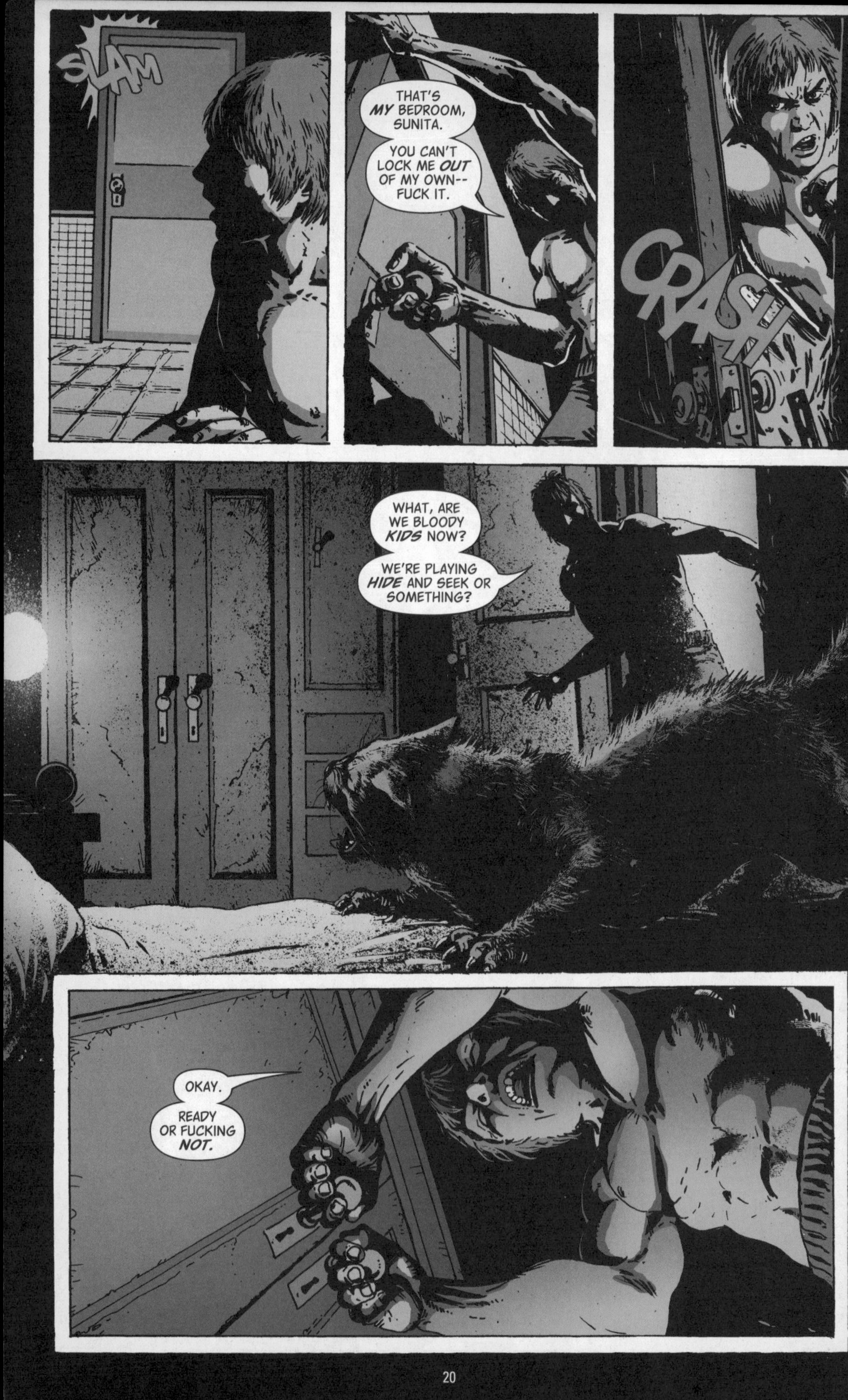
SLAM
THAT'S *MY* BEDROOM, SUNITA.
YOU CAN'T LOCK ME *OUT* OF MY OWN-- FUCK IT.
CRASH
WHAT, ARE WE BLOODY *KIDS* NOW?
WE'RE PLAYING *HIDE* AND SEEK OR SOMETHING?
OKAY.
READY OR FUCKING *NOT.*

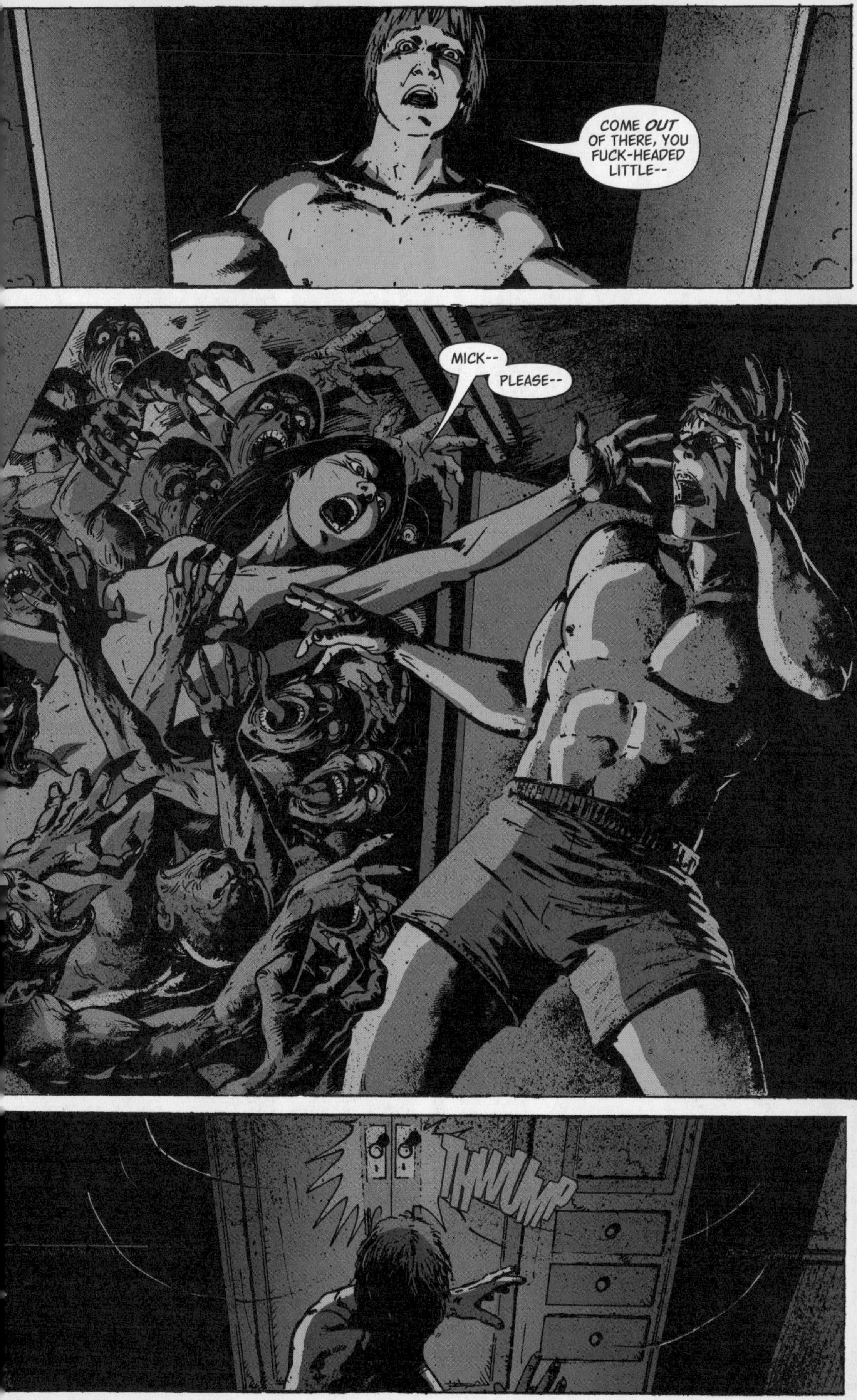
COME OUT OF THERE, YOU FUCK-HEADED LITTLE--
MICK--
PLEASE--
THWUMP

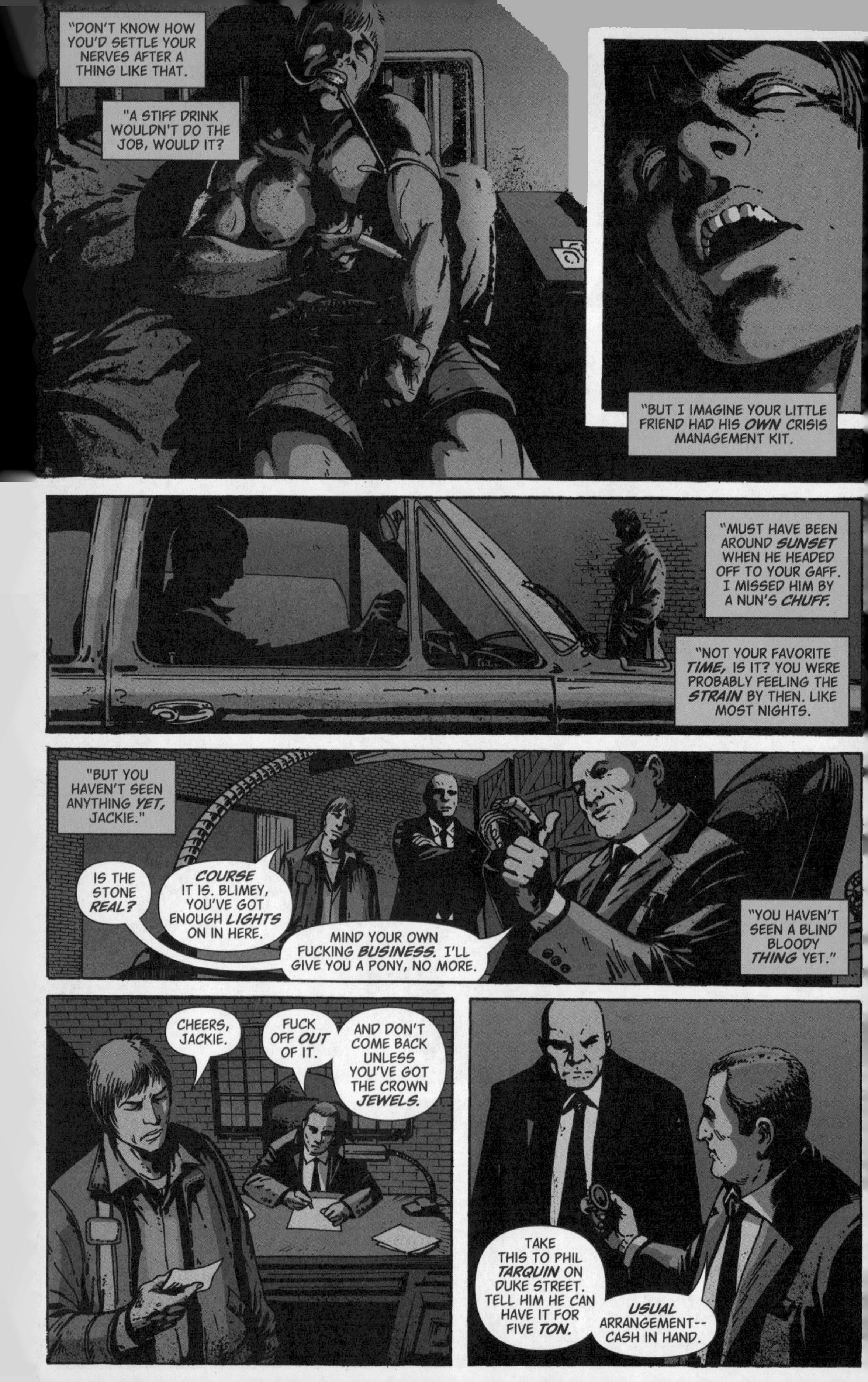
"DON'T KNOW HOW YOU'D SETTLE YOUR NERVES AFTER A THING LIKE THAT.
"A STIFF DRINK WOULDN'T DO THE JOB, WOULD IT?
"BUT I IMAGINE YOUR LITTLE FRIEND HAD HIS OWN CRISIS MANAGEMENT KIT.
"MUST HAVE BEEN AROUND SUNSET WHEN HE HEADED OFF TO YOUR GAFF. I MISSED HIM BY A NUN'S CHUFF.
"NOT YOUR FAVORITE TIME, IS IT? YOU WERE PROBABLY FEELING THE STRAIN BY THEN. LIKE MOST NIGHTS.
"BUT YOU HAVEN'T SEEN ANYTHING YET, JACKIE."
IS THE STONE REAL?
COURSE IT IS. BLIMEY, YOU'VE GOT ENOUGH LIGHTS ON IN HERE.
MIND YOUR OWN FUCKING BUSINESS. I'LL GIVE YOU A PONY, NO MORE.
"YOU HAVEN'T SEEN A BLIND BLOODY THING YET."
CHEERS, JACKIE.
FUCK OFF OUT OF IT.
AND DON'T COME BACK UNLESS YOU'VE GOT THE CROWN JEWELS.
TAKE THIS TO PHIL TARQUIN ON DUKE STREET. TELL HIM HE CAN HAVE IT FOR FIVE TON.
USUAL ARRANGEMENT-- CASH IN HAND.

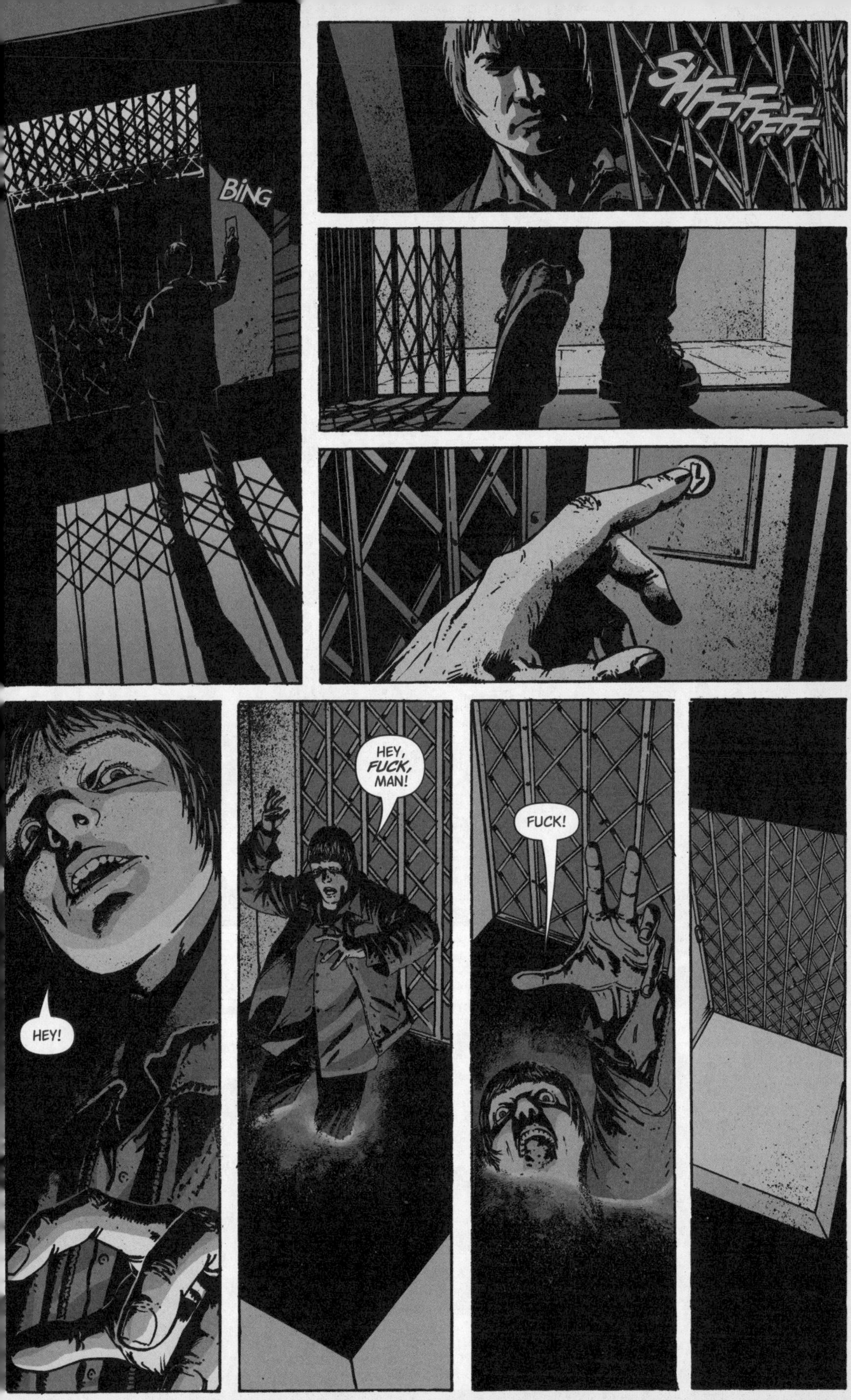
BING
SHFFFFFF
HEY!
HEY, FUCK, MAN!
FUCK!

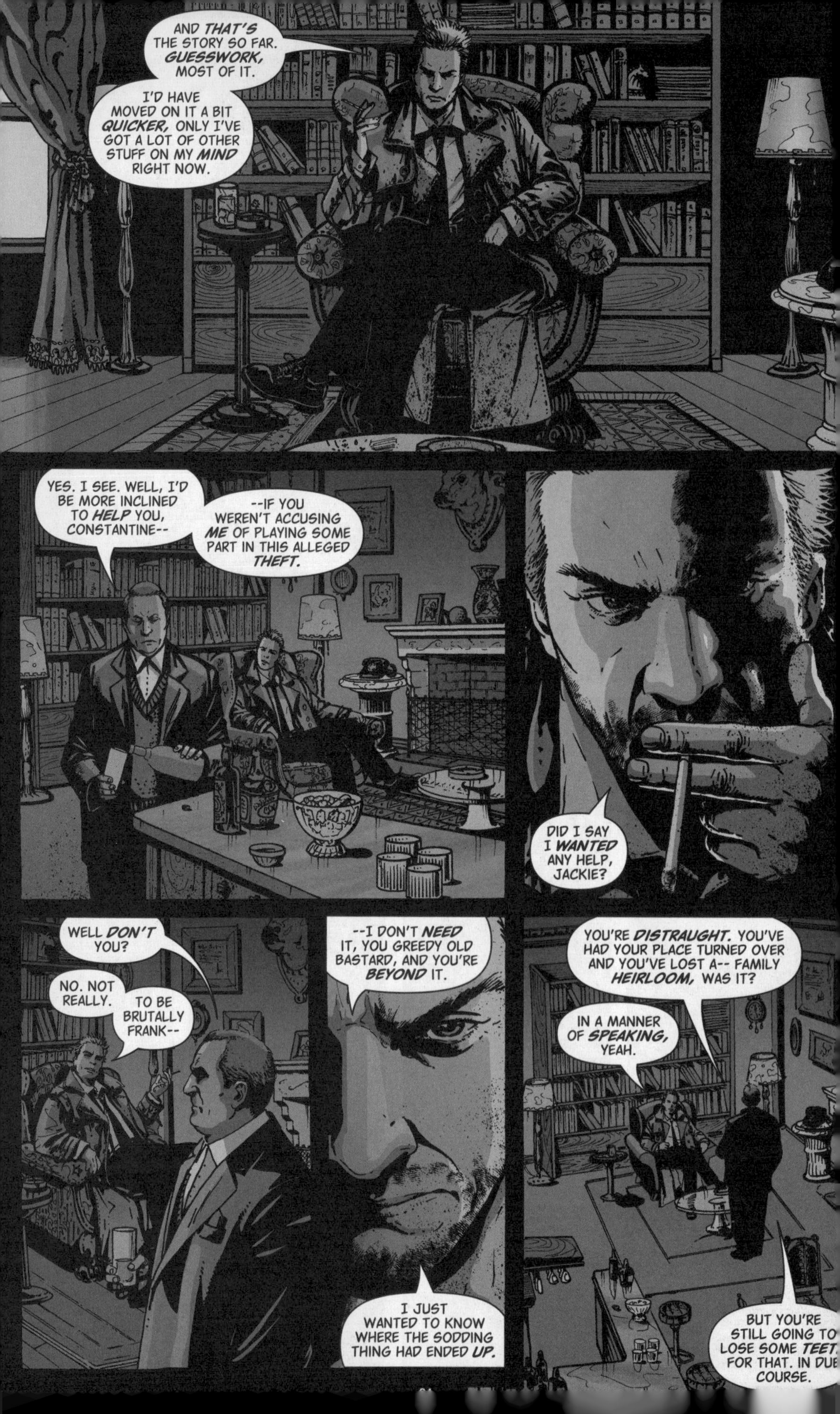
AND THAT'S THE STORY SO FAR. GUESSWORK, MOST OF IT.
I'D HAVE MOVED ON IT A BIT QUICKER, ONLY I'VE GOT A LOT OF OTHER STUFF ON MY MIND RIGHT NOW.
YES. I SEE. WELL, I'D BE MORE INCLINED TO HELP YOU, CONSTANTINE--
--IF YOU WEREN'T ACCUSING ME OF PLAYING SOME PART IN THIS ALLEGED THEFT.
DID I SAY I WANTED ANY HELP, JACKIE?
WELL DON'T YOU?
NO. NOT REALLY.
TO BE BRUTALLY FRANK--
--I DON'T NEED IT, YOU GREEDY OLD BASTARD, AND YOU'RE BEYOND IT.
I JUST WANTED TO KNOW WHERE THE SODDING THING HAD ENDED UP.
YOU'RE DISTRAUGHT. YOU'VE HAD YOUR PLACE TURNED OVER AND YOU'VE LOST A-- FAMILY HEIRLOOM, WAS IT?
IN A MANNER OF SPEAKING, YEAH.
BUT YOU'RE STILL GOING TO LOSE SOME TEET FOR THAT. IN DUE COURSE.

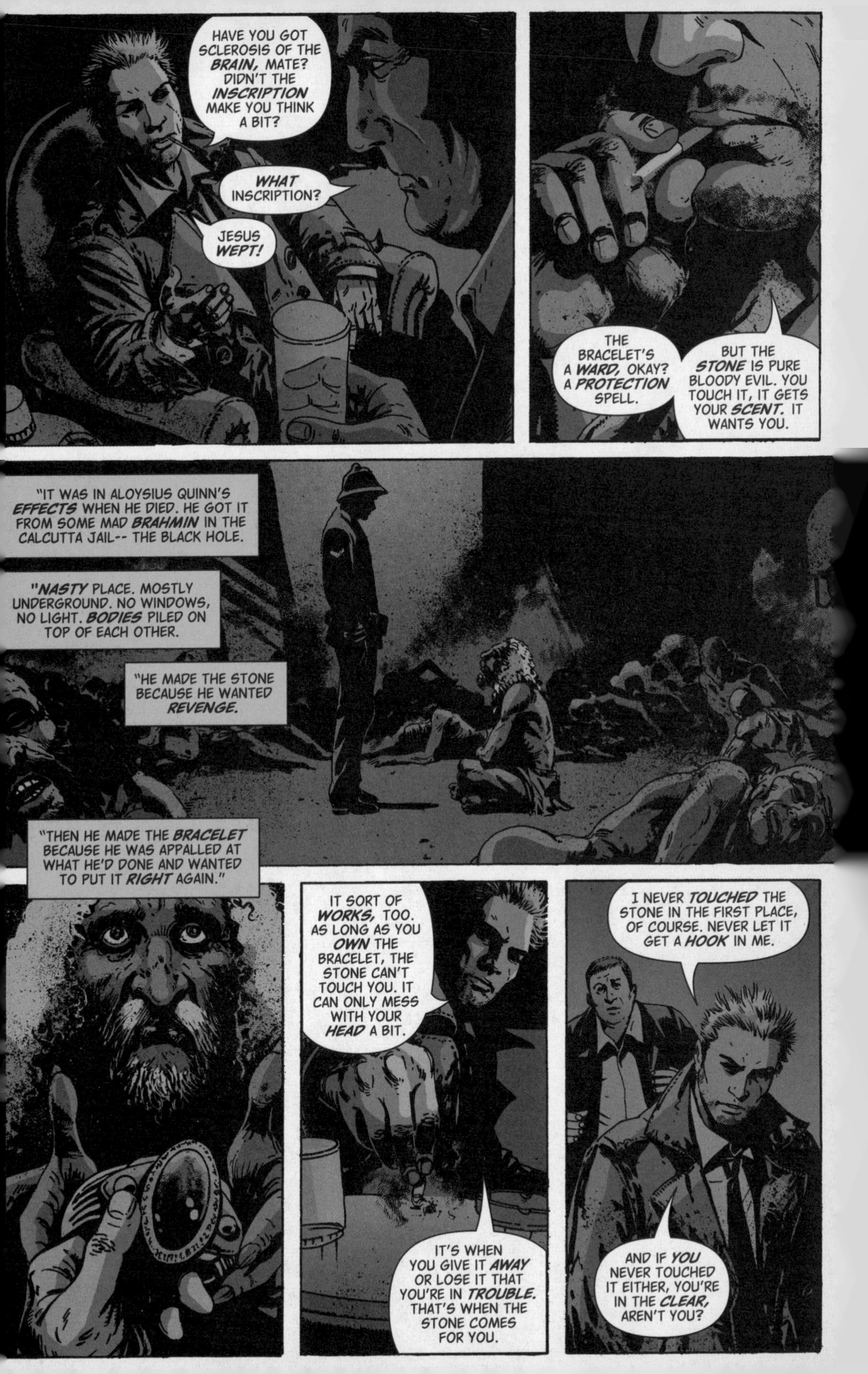
HAVE YOU GOT SCLEROSIS OF THE BRAIN, MATE? DIDN'T THE INSCRIPTION MAKE YOU THINK A BIT?
WHAT INSCRIPTION?
JESUS WEPT!
THE BRACELET'S A WARD, OKAY? A PROTECTION SPELL.
BUT THE STONE IS PURE BLOODY EVIL. YOU TOUCH IT, IT GETS YOUR SCENT. IT WANTS YOU.
"IT WAS IN ALOYSIUS QUINN'S EFFECTS WHEN HE DIED. HE GOT IT FROM SOME MAD BRAHMIN IN THE CALCUTTA JAIL-- THE BLACK HOLE.
"NASTY PLACE. MOSTLY UNDERGROUND. NO WINDOWS, NO LIGHT. BODIES PILED ON TOP OF EACH OTHER.
"HE MADE THE STONE BECAUSE HE WANTED REVENGE.
"THEN HE MADE THE BRACELET BECAUSE HE WAS APPALLED AT WHAT HE'D DONE AND WANTED TO PUT IT RIGHT AGAIN."
IT SORT OF WORKS, TOO. AS LONG AS YOU OWN THE BRACELET, THE STONE CAN'T TOUCH YOU. IT CAN ONLY MESS WITH YOUR HEAD A BIT.
IT'S WHEN YOU GIVE IT AWAY OR LOSE IT THAT YOU'RE IN TROUBLE. THAT'S WHEN THE STONE COMES FOR YOU.
I NEVER TOUCHED THE STONE IN THE FIRST PLACE, OF COURSE. NEVER LET IT GET A HOOK IN ME.
AND IF YOU NEVER TOUCHED IT EITHER, YOU'RE IN THE CLEAR, AREN'T YOU?

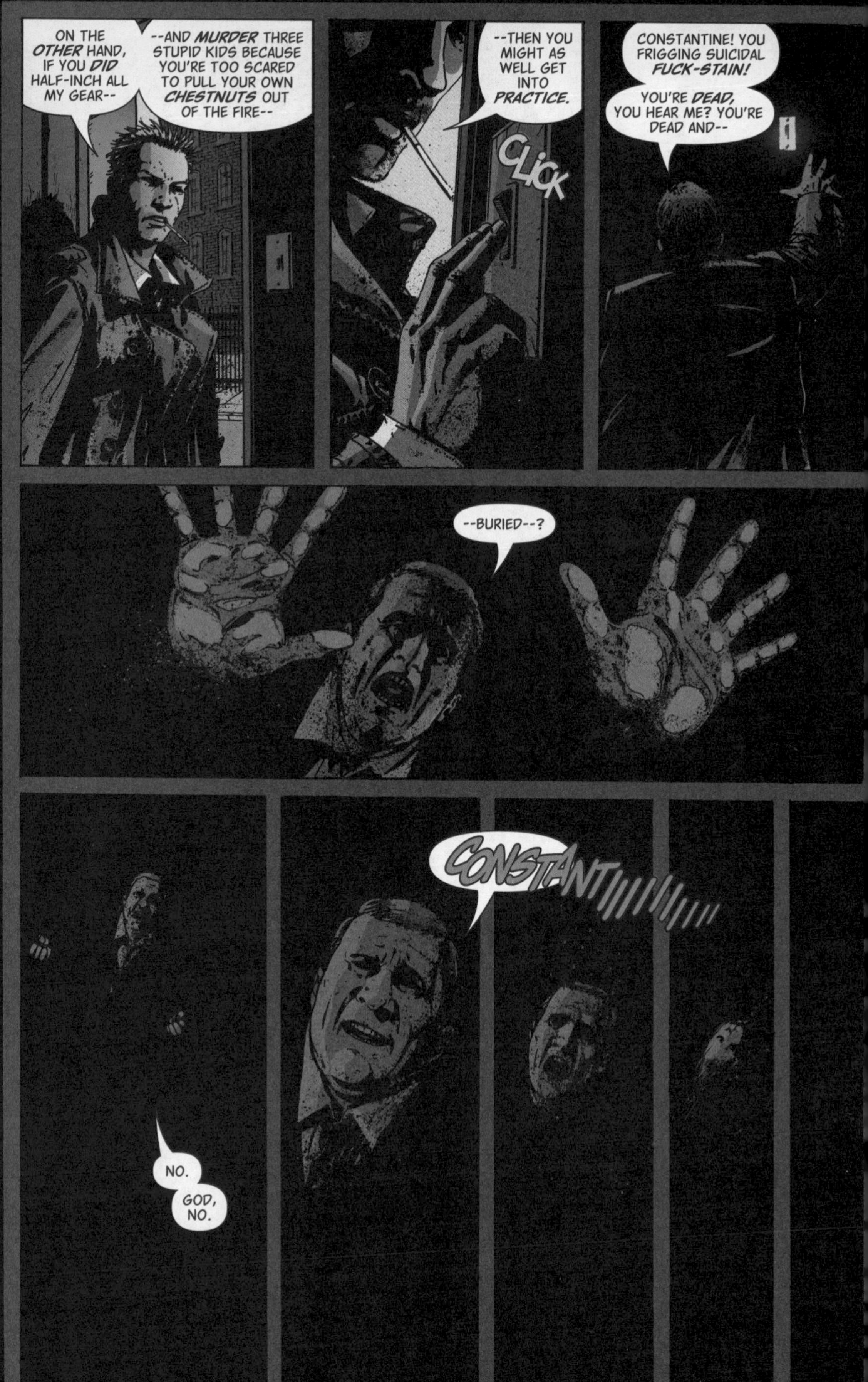

ON THE OTHER HAND, IF YOU DID HALF-INCH ALL MY GEAR--
--AND MURDER THREE STUPID KIDS BECAUSE YOU'RE TOO SCARED TO PULL YOUR OWN CHESTNUTS OUT OF THE FIRE--
--THEN YOU MIGHT AS WELL GET INTO PRACTICE.
CLICK
CONSTANTINE! YOU FRIGGING SUICIDAL FUCK-STAIN!
YOU'RE DEAD, YOU HEAR ME? YOU'RE DEAD AND--
--BURIED--?
NO.
GOD, NO.
CONSTANTIIIIIIIIII

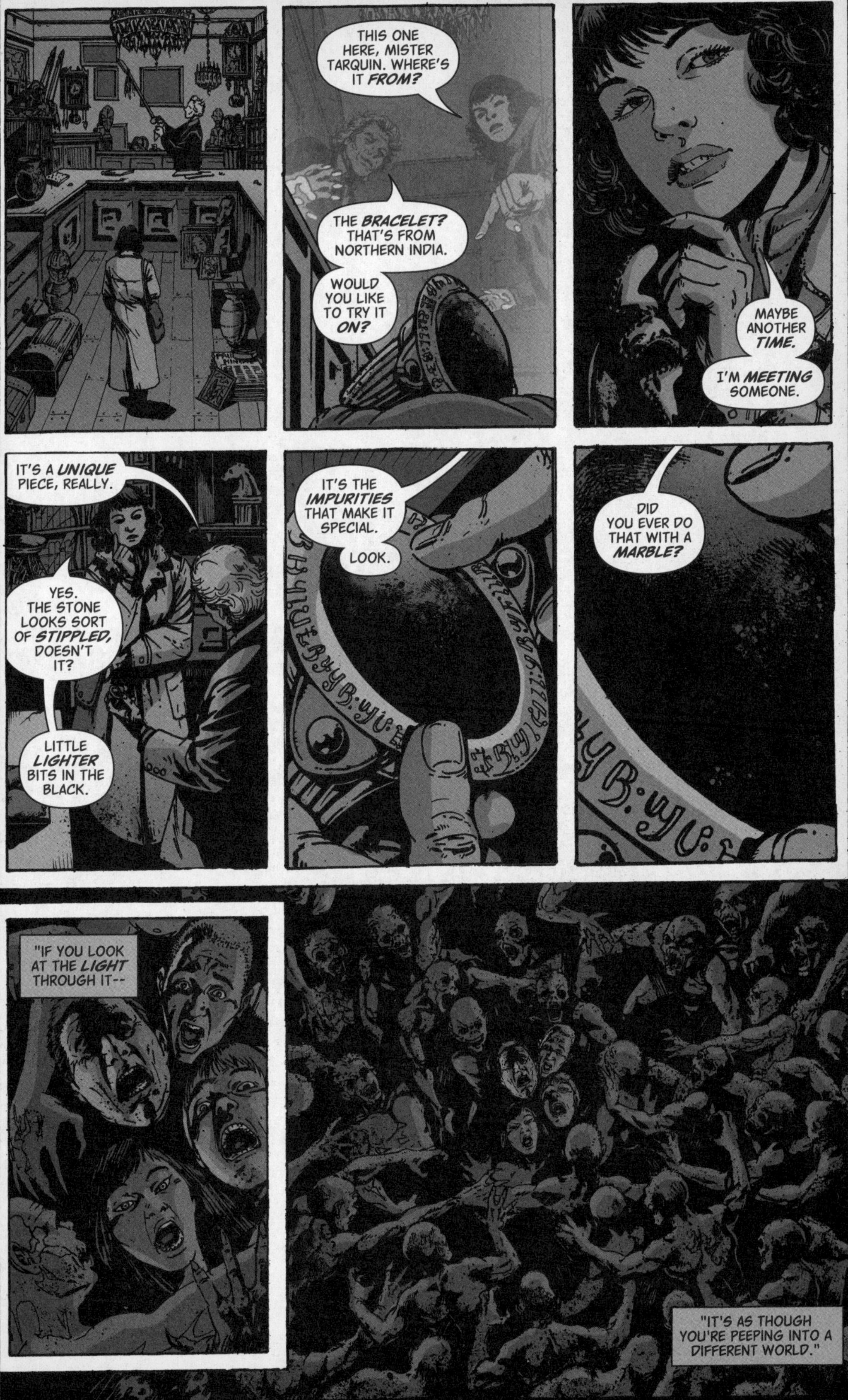
THIS ONE HERE, MISTER TARQUIN. WHERE'S IT FROM?
THE BRACELET? THAT'S FROM NORTHERN INDIA.
WOULD YOU LIKE TO TRY IT ON?
MAYBE ANOTHER TIME.
I'M MEETING SOMEONE.
IT'S A UNIQUE PIECE, REALLY.
YES. THE STONE LOOKS SORT OF STIPPLED, DOESN'T IT?
LITTLE LIGHTER BITS IN THE BLACK.
IT'S THE IMPURITIES THAT MAKE IT SPECIAL.
LOOK.
DID YOU EVER DO THAT WITH A MARBLE?
"IF YOU LOOK AT THE LIGHT THROUGH IT--
"IT'S AS THOUGH YOU'RE PEEPING INTO A DIFFERENT WORLD."

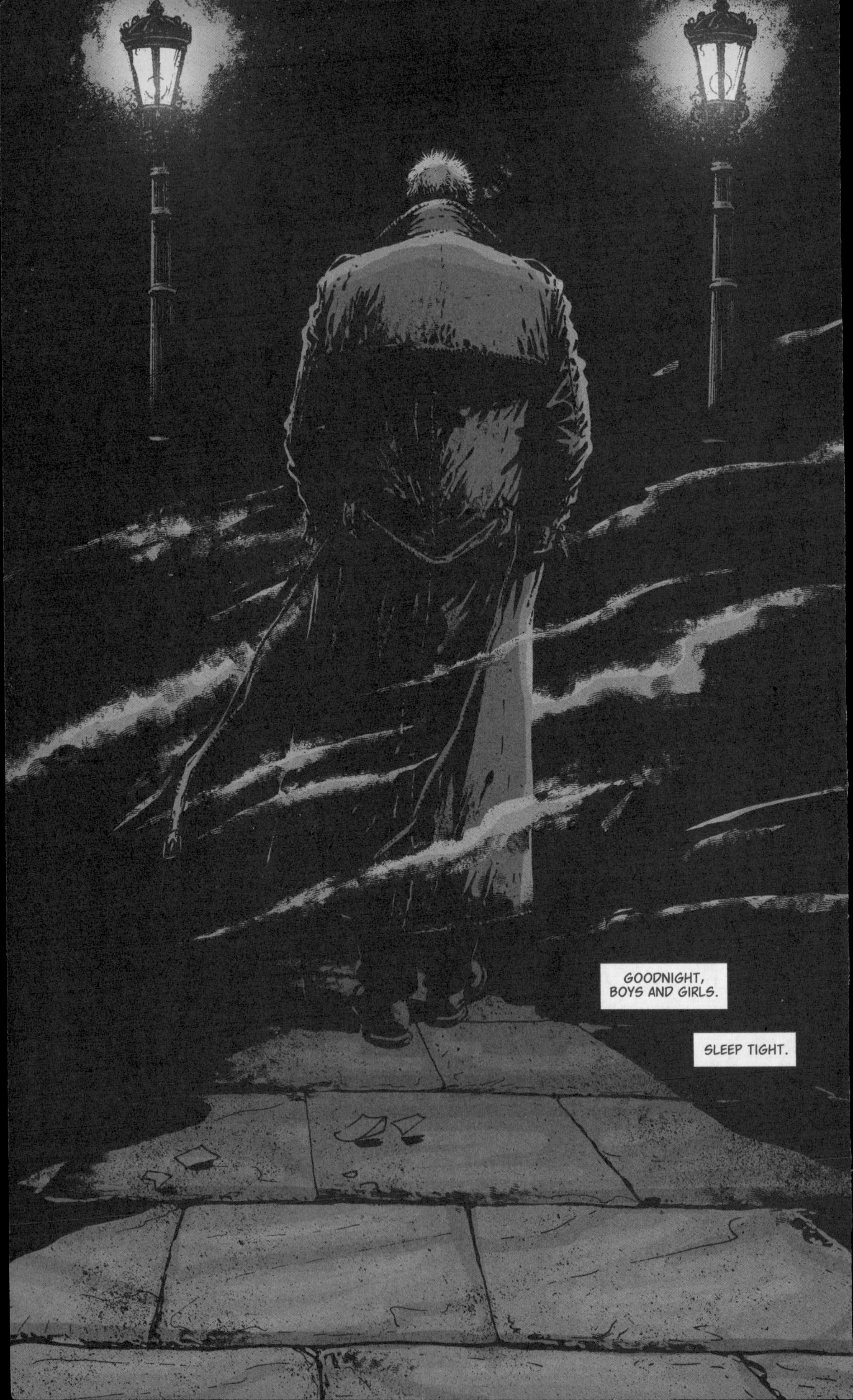
GOODNIGHT, BOYS AND GIRLS.
SLEEP TIGHT.

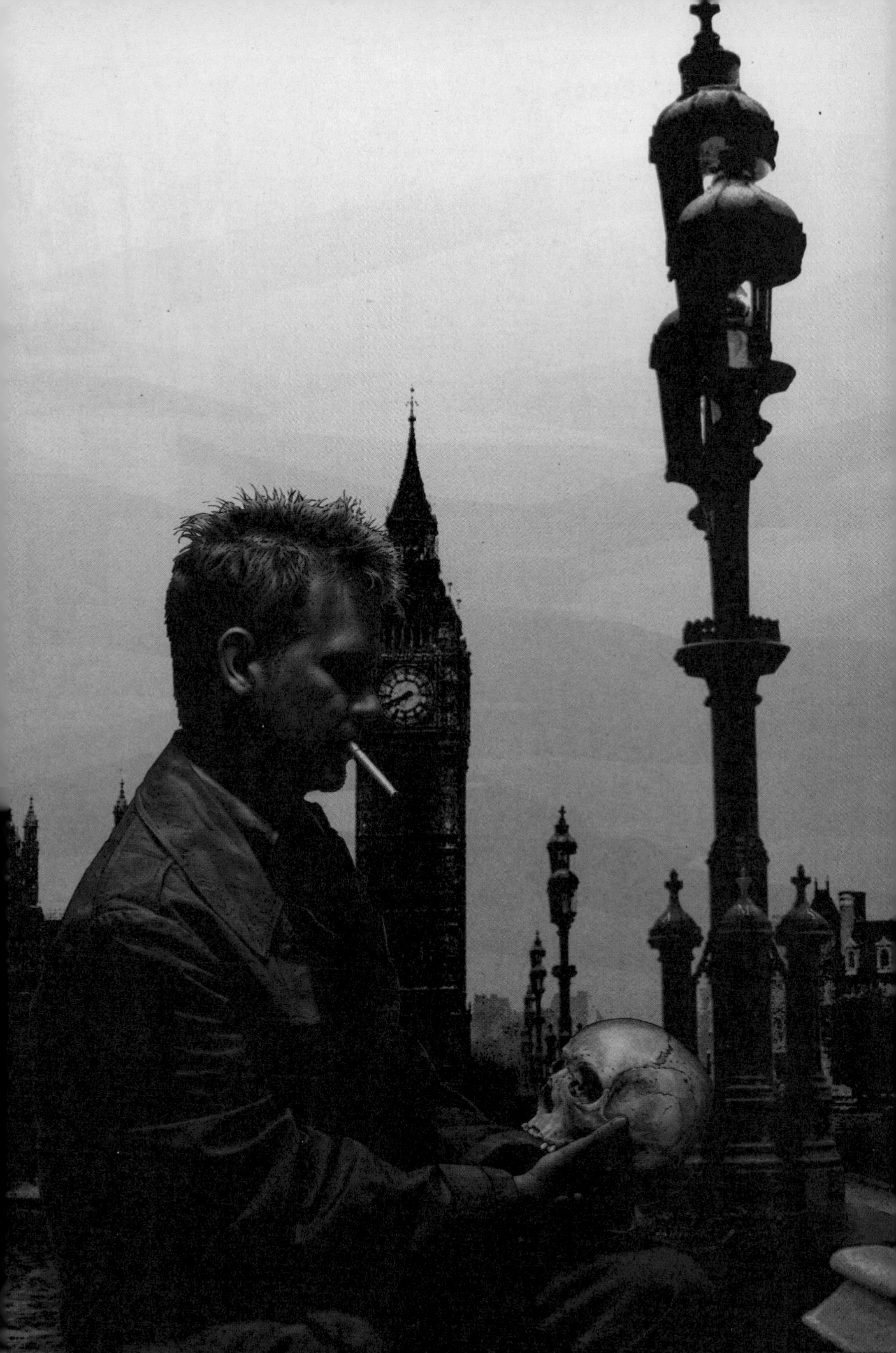

Reasons to be Cheerful CHAPTER ONE

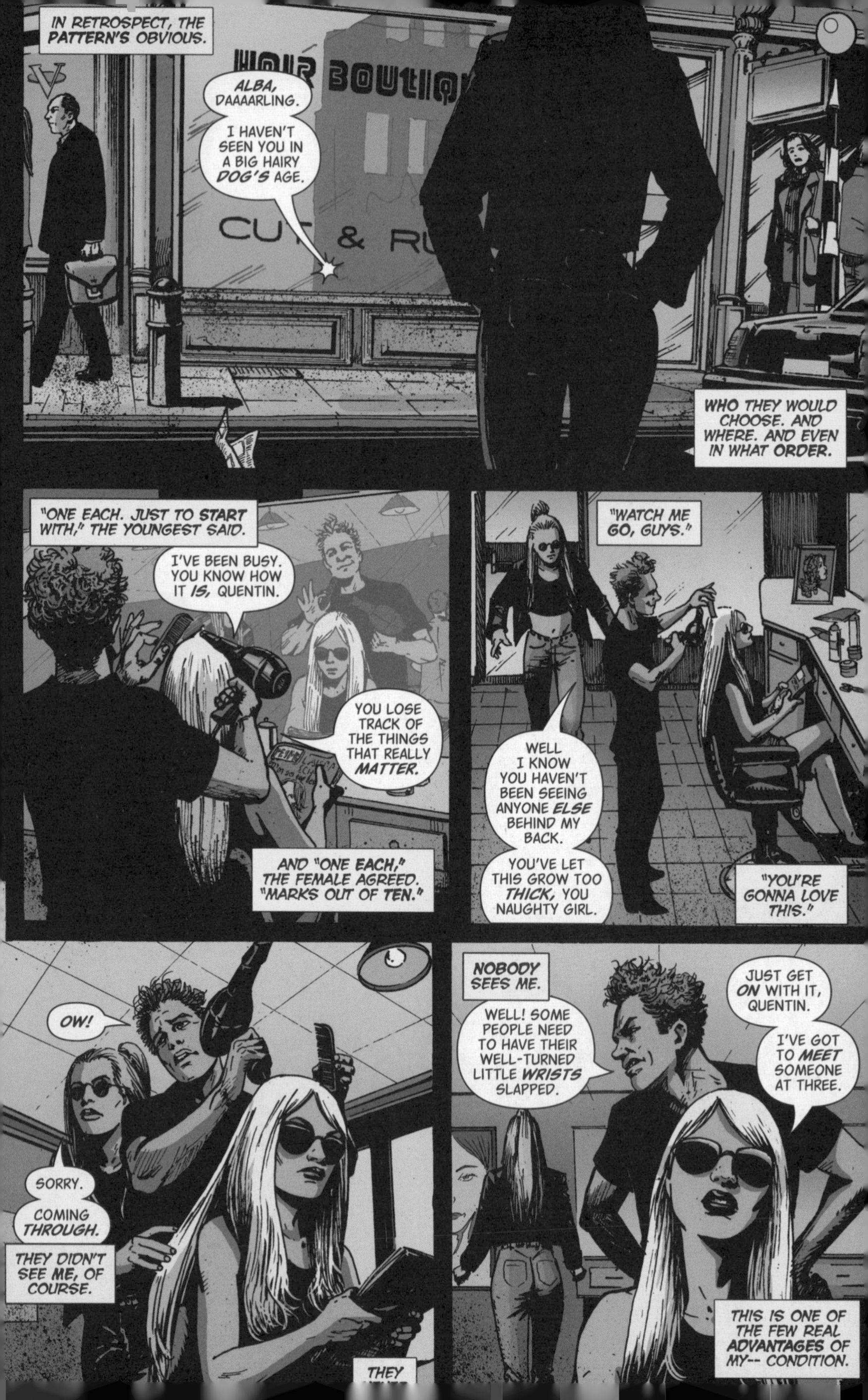
IN RETROSPECT, THE PATTERN'S OBVIOUS.
ALBA, DAAAARLING.
I HAVEN'T SEEN YOU IN A BIG HAIRY DOG'S AGE.
CUT & RU
WHO THEY WOULD CHOOSE. AND WHERE. AND EVEN IN WHAT ORDER.
"ONE EACH. JUST TO START WITH," THE YOUNGEST SAID.
I'VE BEEN BUSY. YOU KNOW HOW IT IS, QUENTIN.
YOU LOSE TRACK OF THE THINGS THAT REALLY MATTER.
AND "ONE EACH," THE FEMALE AGREED. "MARKS OUT OF TEN."
"WATCH ME GO, GUYS."
WELL I KNOW YOU HAVEN'T BEEN SEEING ANYONE ELSE BEHIND MY BACK.
YOU'VE LET THIS GROW TOO THICK, YOU NAUGHTY GIRL.
"YOU'RE GONNA LOVE THIS."
OW!
SORRY.
COMING THROUGH.
THEY DIDN'T SEE ME, OF COURSE.
THEY
NOBODY SEES ME.
WELL! SOME PEOPLE NEED TO HAVE THEIR WELL-TURNED LITTLE WRISTS SLAPPED.
JUST GET ON WITH IT, QUENTIN.
I'VE GOT TO MEET SOMEONE AT THREE.
THIS IS ONE OF THE FEW REAL ADVANTAGES OF MY-- CONDITION.

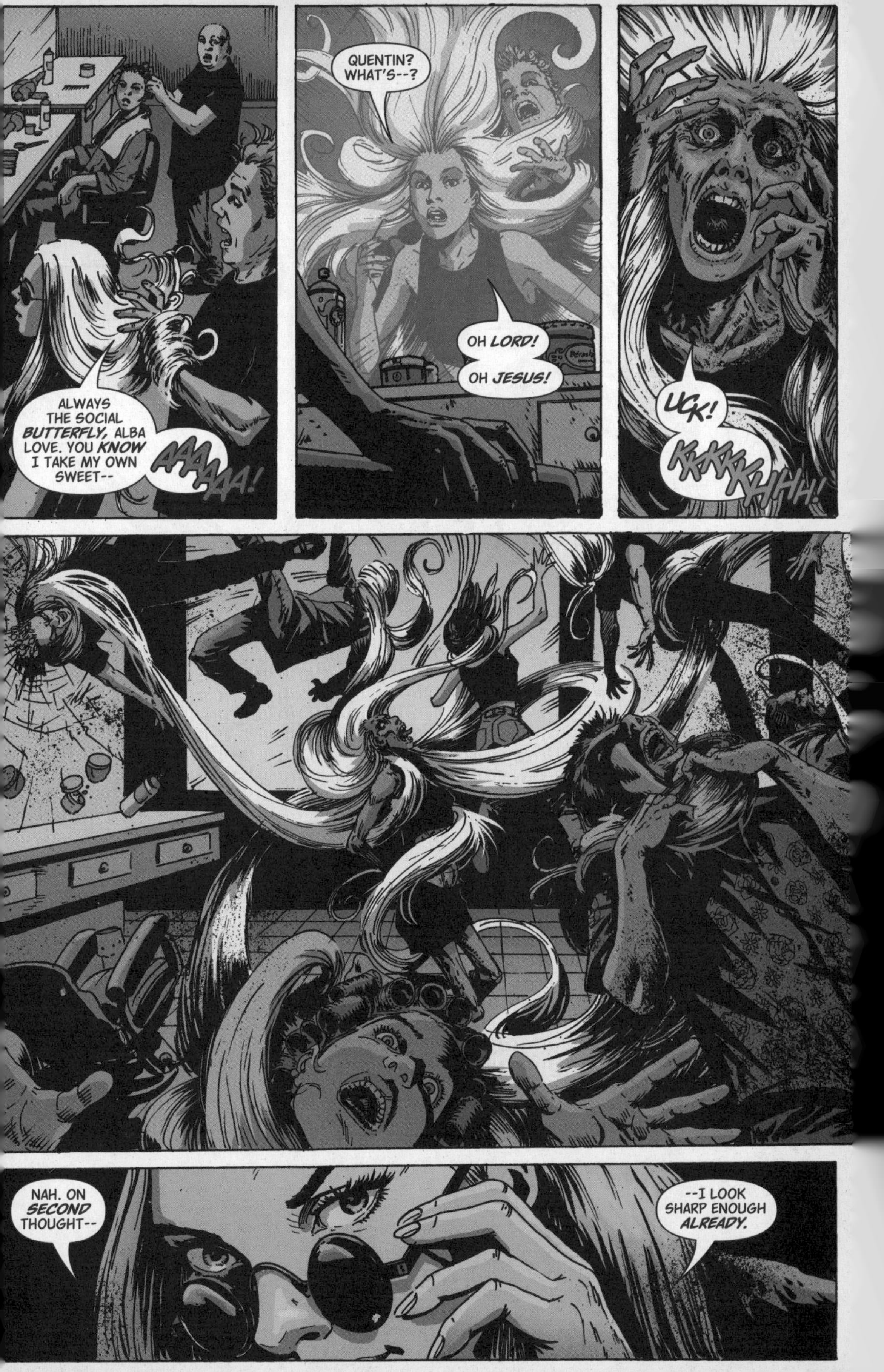
ALWAYS THE SOCIAL BUTTERFLY, ALBA LOVE. YOU KNOW I TAKE MY OWN SWEET--
AAAAAA!
QUENTIN? WHAT'S--?
OH LORD!
OH JESUS!
UCK!
KKKKKKHHH!
NAH. ON SECOND THOUGHT--
--I LOOK SHARP ENOUGH ALREADY.

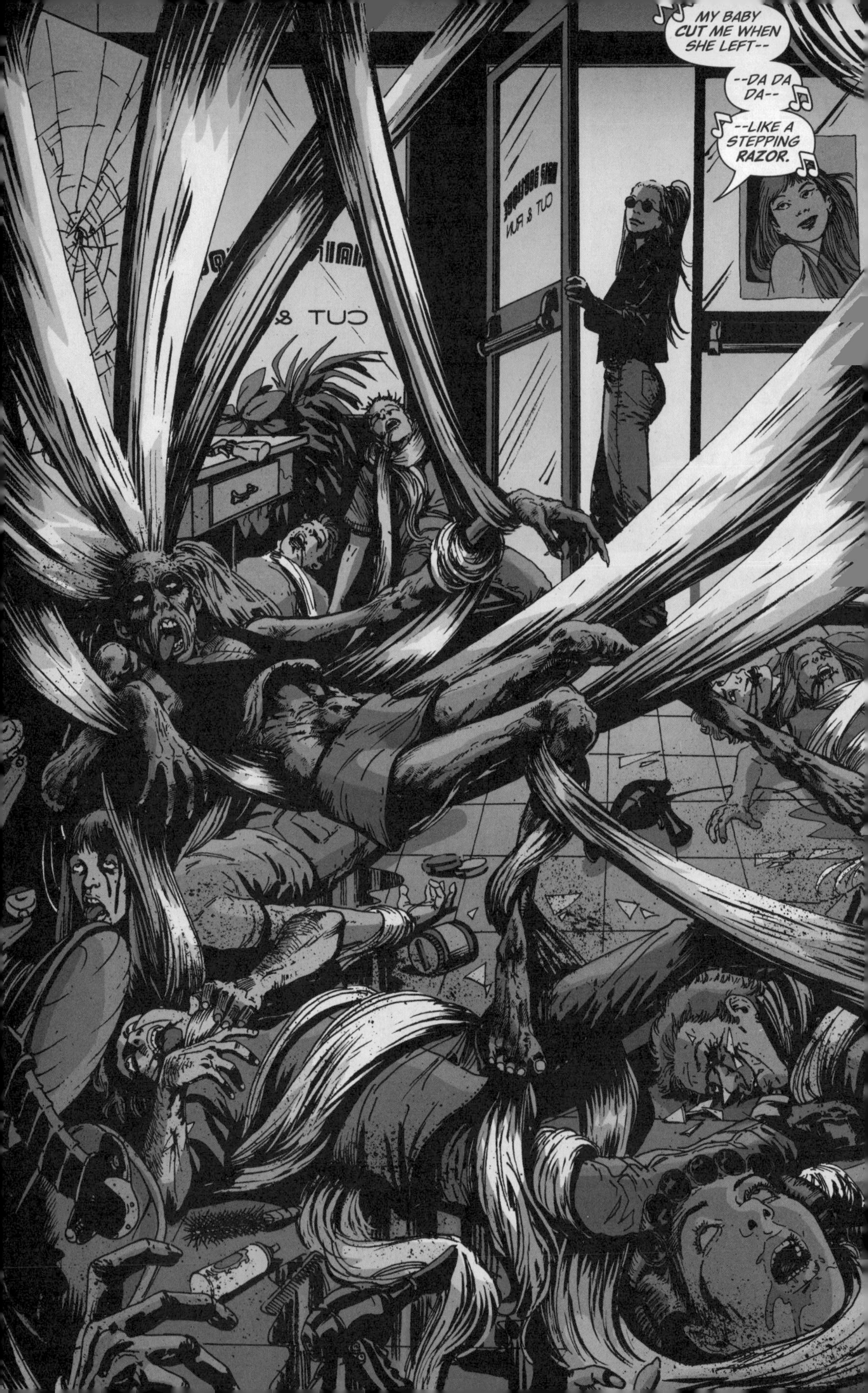
MY BABY CUT ME WHEN SHE LEFT--
--DA DA DA--
--LIKE A STEPPING RAZOR.

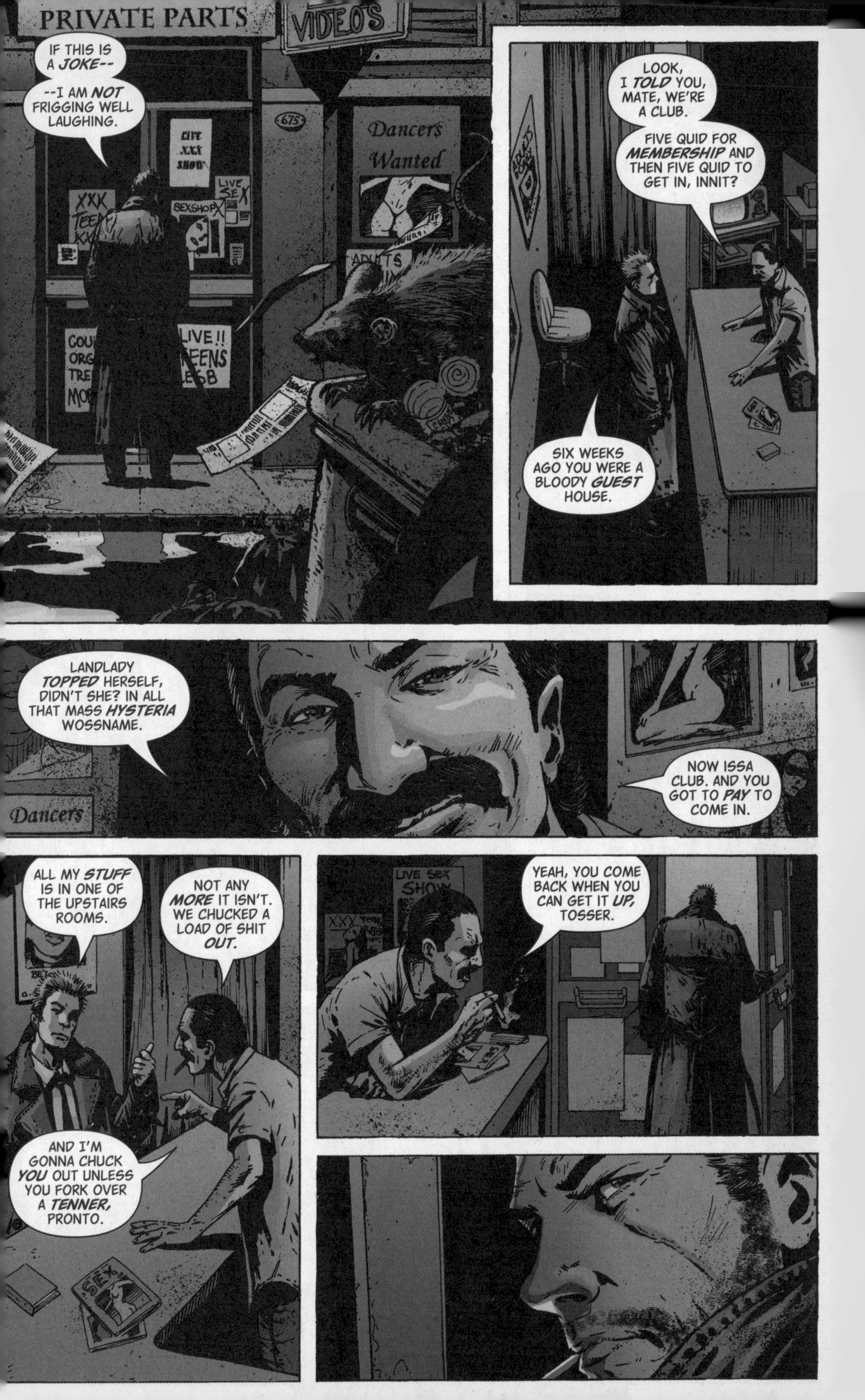
PRIVATE PARTS
VIDEOS
IF THIS IS A JOKE--
--I AM NOT FRIGGING WELL LAUGHING.
Dancers Wanted
LIVE SEX
SEXSHOP
XXX TEEN
LIVE!! TEENS LESB
ADULTS
LOOK, I TOLD YOU, MATE, WE'RE A CLUB.
FIVE QUID FOR MEMBERSHIP AND THEN FIVE QUID TO GET IN, INNIT?
SIX WEEKS AGO YOU WERE A BLOODY GUEST HOUSE.
LANDLADY TOPPED HERSELF, DIDN'T SHE? IN ALL THAT MASS HYSTERIA WOSSNAME.
Dancers
NOW ISSA CLUB. AND YOU GOT TO PAY TO COME IN.
ALL MY STUFF IS IN ONE OF THE UPSTAIRS ROOMS.
NOT ANY MORE IT ISN'T. WE CHUCKED A LOAD OF SHIT OUT.
AND I'M GONNA CHUCK YOU OUT UNLESS YOU FORK OVER A TENNER, PRONTO.
SEX
LIVE SEX SHOW
XXX
YEAH, YOU COME BACK WHEN YOU CAN GET IT UP, TOSSER.

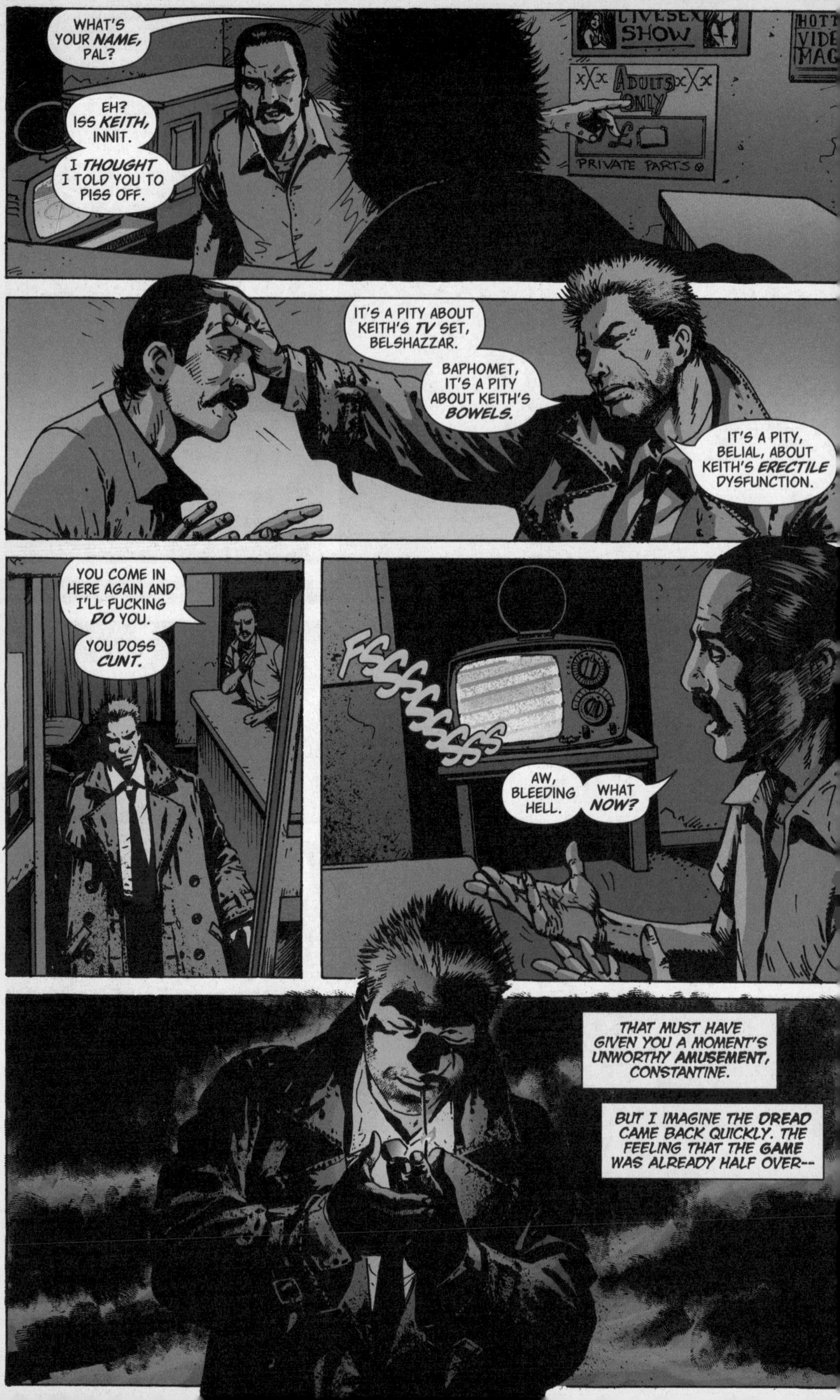
LIVE SEX SHOW
HOT VIDE MAG
XXX ADULTS ONLY XXX
PRIVATE PARTS
WHAT'S YOUR NAME, PAL?
EH? ISS KEITH, INNIT.
I THOUGHT I TOLD YOU TO PISS OFF.
IT'S A PITY ABOUT KEITH'S TV SET, BELSHAZZAR.
BAPHOMET, IT'S A PITY ABOUT KEITH'S BOWELS.
IT'S A PITY, BELIAL, ABOUT KEITH'S ERECTILE DYSFUNCTION.
YOU COME IN HERE AGAIN AND I'LL FUCKING DO YOU.
YOU DOSS CUNT.
FSSSSSSSS
AW, BLEEDING HELL.
WHAT NOW?
THAT MUST HAVE GIVEN YOU A MOMENT'S UNWORTHY AMUSEMENT, CONSTANTINE.
BUT I IMAGINE THE DREAD CAME BACK QUICKLY. THE FEELING THAT THE GAME WAS ALREADY HALF OVER--

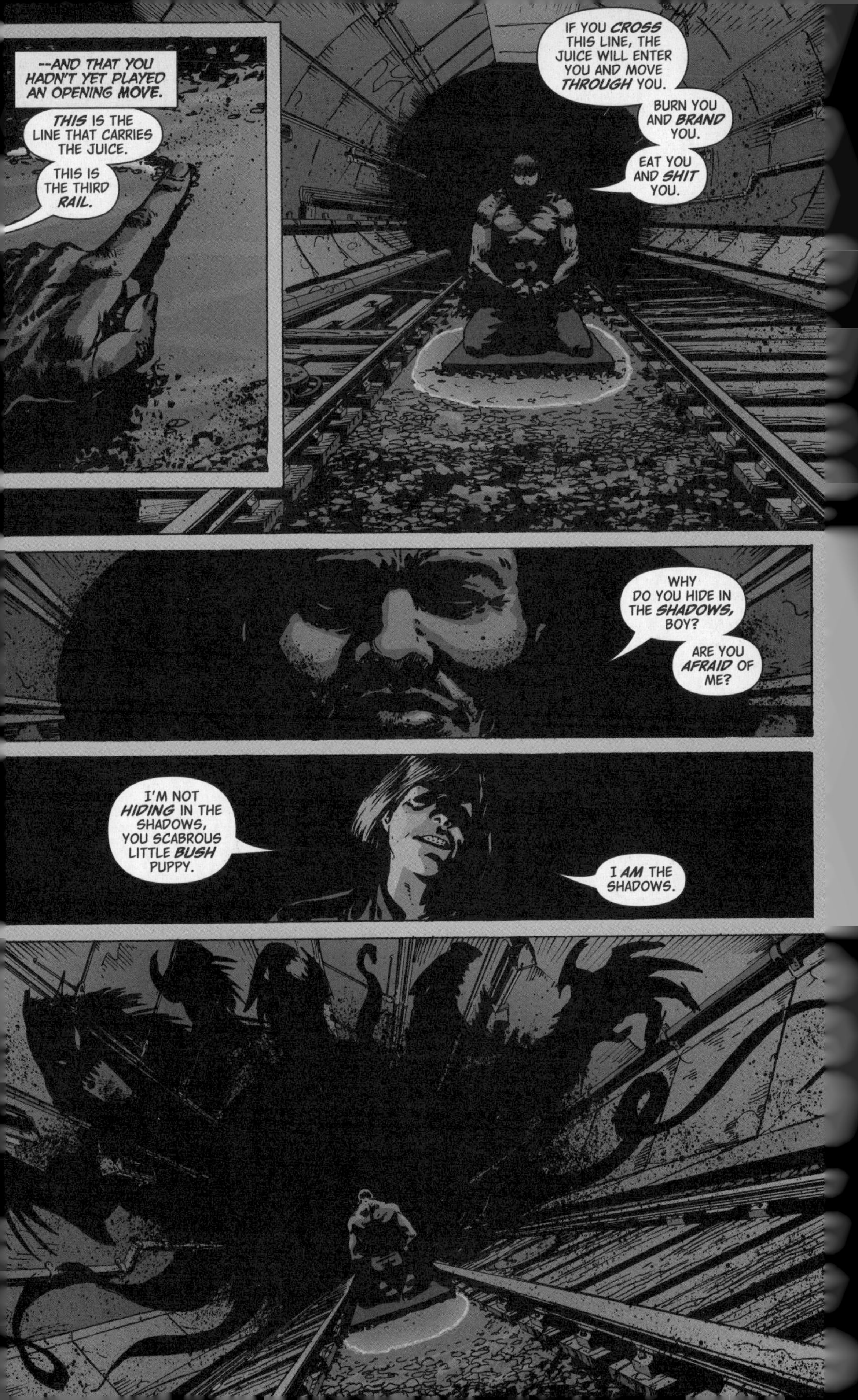
--AND THAT YOU HADN'T YET PLAYED AN OPENING MOVE.
THIS IS THE LINE THAT CARRIES THE JUICE.
THIS IS THE THIRD RAIL.
IF YOU CROSS THIS LINE, THE JUICE WILL ENTER YOU AND MOVE THROUGH YOU.
BURN YOU AND BRAND YOU.
EAT YOU AND SHIT YOU.
WHY DO YOU HIDE IN THE SHADOWS, BOY?
ARE YOU AFRAID OF ME?
I'M NOT HIDING IN THE SHADOWS, YOU SCABROUS LITTLE BUSH PUPPY.
I AM THE SHADOWS.

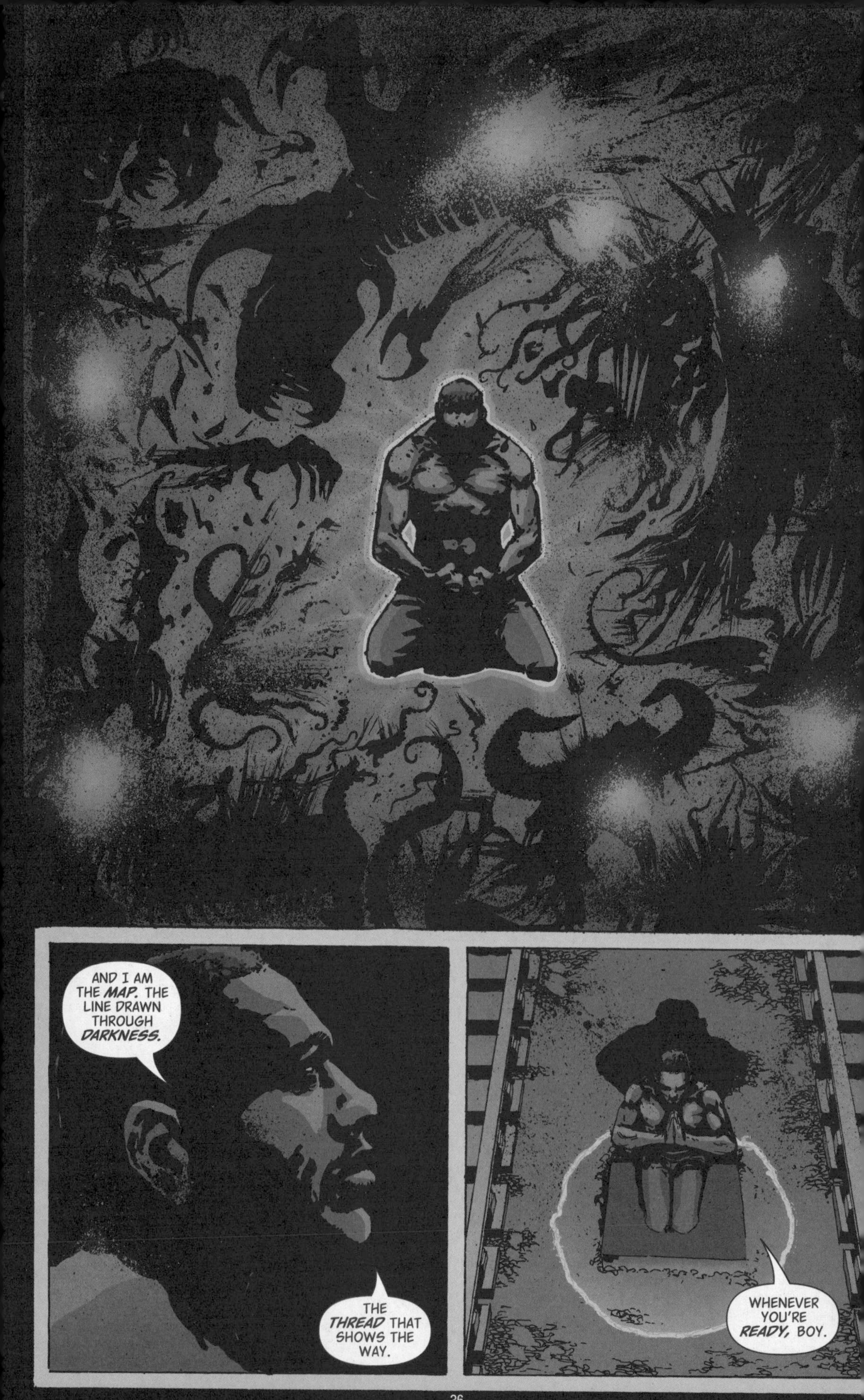
AND I AM THE MAP. THE LINE DRAWN THROUGH DARKNESS.
THE THREAD THAT SHOWS THE WAY.
WHENEVER YOU'RE READY, BOY.

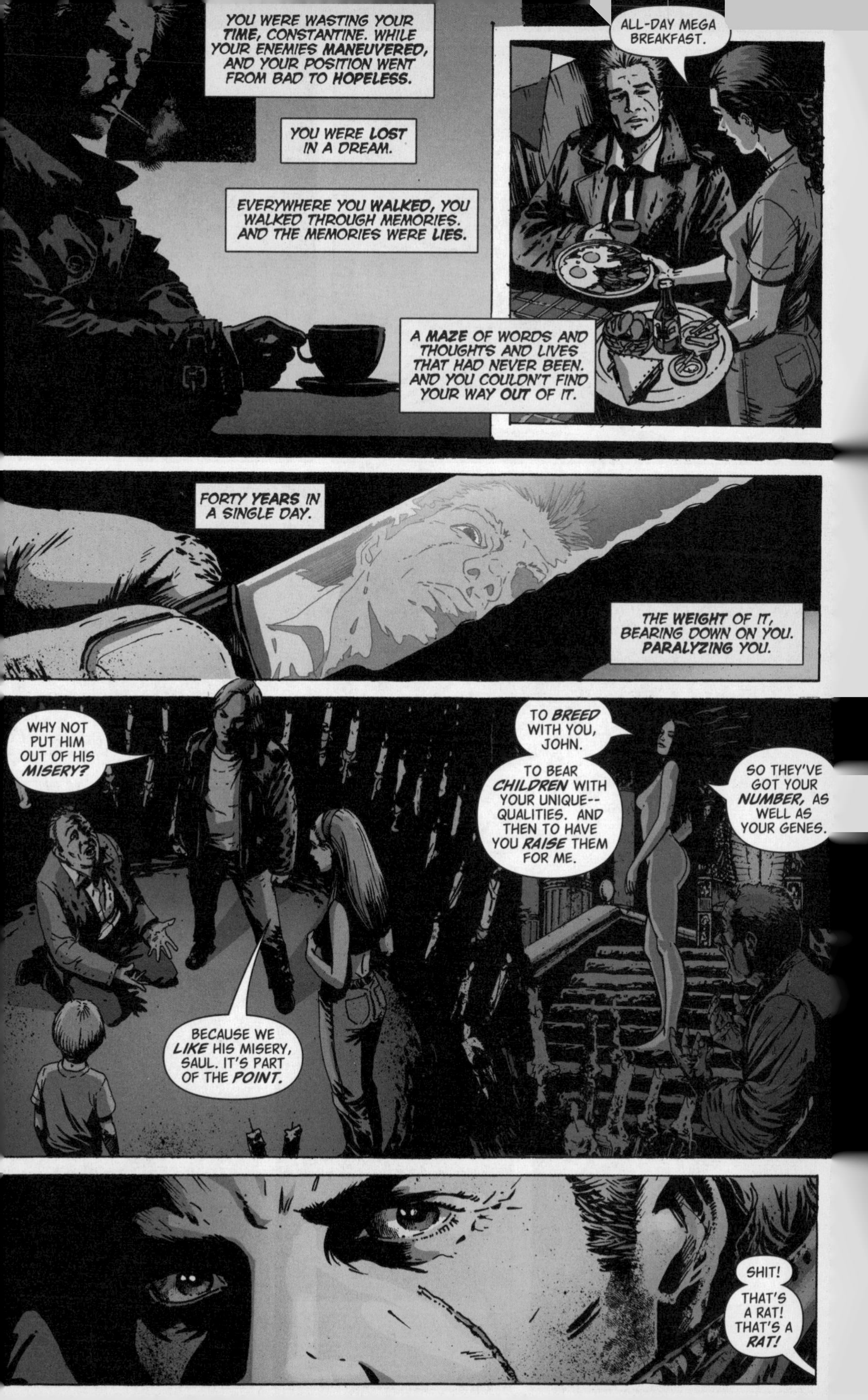
YOU WERE WASTING YOUR TIME, CONSTANTINE. WHILE YOUR ENEMIES MANEUVERED, AND YOUR POSITION WENT FROM BAD TO HOPELESS.
YOU WERE LOST IN A DREAM.
EVERYWHERE YOU WALKED, YOU WALKED THROUGH MEMORIES. AND THE MEMORIES WERE LIES.
ALL-DAY MEGA BREAKFAST.
A MAZE OF WORDS AND THOUGHTS AND LIVES THAT HAD NEVER BEEN. AND YOU COULDN'T FIND YOUR WAY OUT OF IT.
FORTY YEARS IN A SINGLE DAY.
THE WEIGHT OF IT, BEARING DOWN ON YOU. PARALYZING YOU.
WHY NOT PUT HIM OUT OF HIS MISERY?
BECAUSE WE LIKE HIS MISERY, SAUL. IT'S PART OF THE POINT.
TO BREED WITH YOU, JOHN.
TO BEAR CHILDREN WITH YOUR UNIQUE-- QUALITIES. AND THEN TO HAVE YOU RAISE THEM FOR ME.
SO THEY'VE GOT YOUR NUMBER, AS WELL AS YOUR GENES.
SHIT!
THAT'S A RAT! THAT'S A RAT!

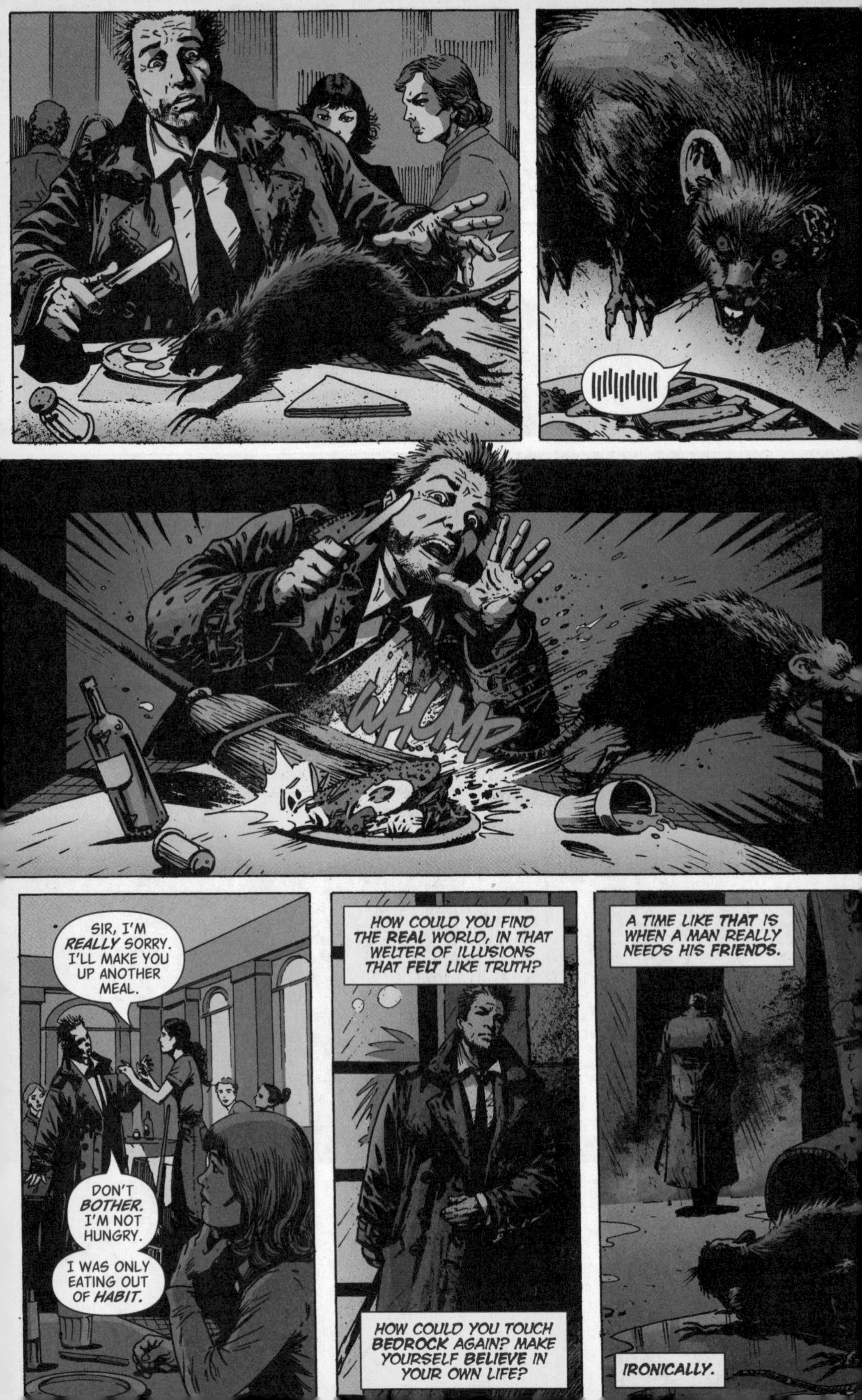
WHUMP
SIR, I'M REALLY SORRY. I'LL MAKE YOU UP ANOTHER MEAL.
DON'T BOTHER. I'M NOT HUNGRY.
I WAS ONLY EATING OUT OF HABIT.
HOW COULD YOU FIND THE REAL WORLD, IN THAT WELTER OF ILLUSIONS THAT FELT LIKE TRUTH?
HOW COULD YOU TOUCH BEDROCK AGAIN? MAKE YOURSELF BELIEVE IN YOUR OWN LIFE?
A TIME LIKE THAT IS WHEN A MAN REALLY NEEDS HIS FRIENDS.
IRONICALLY.

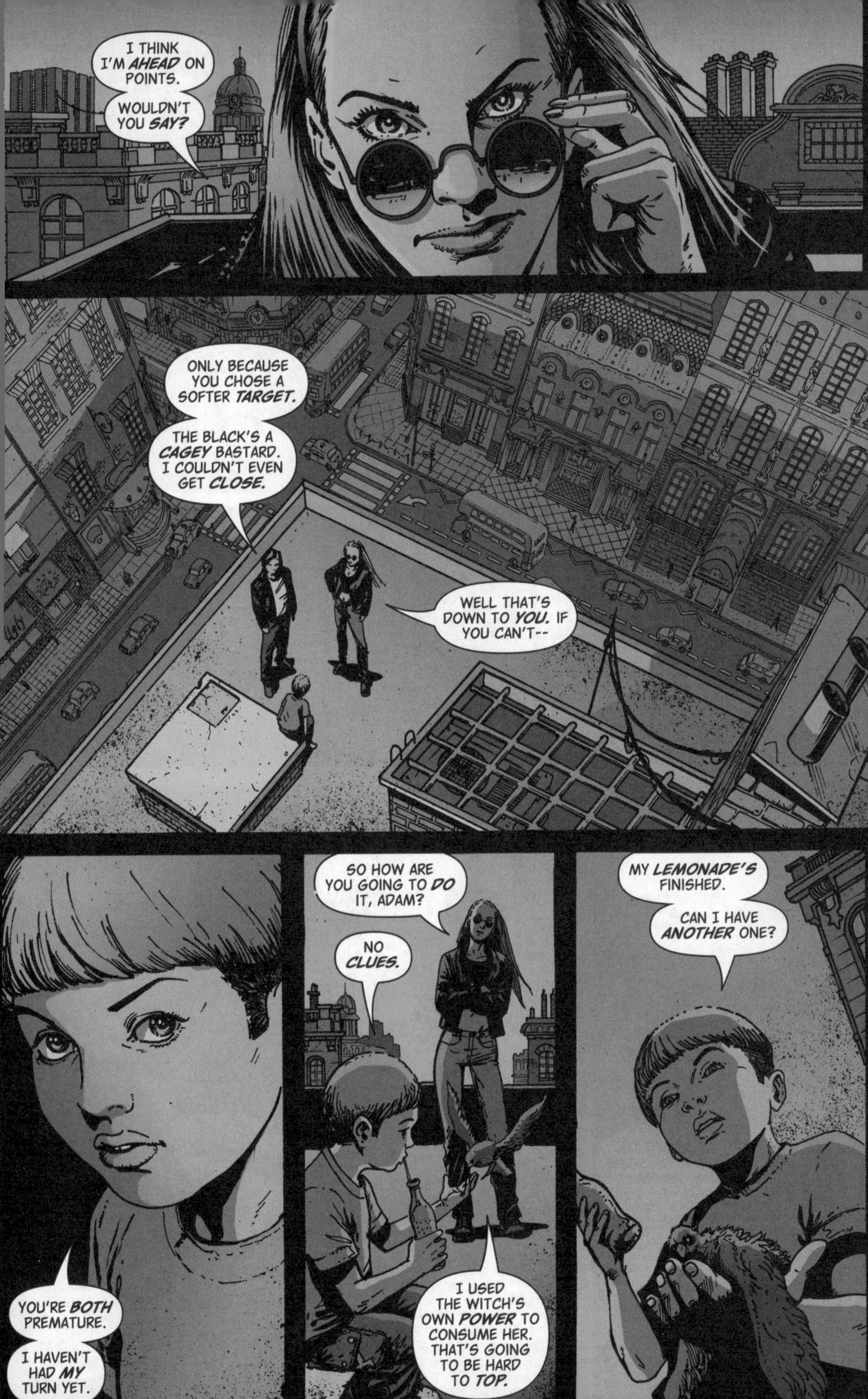
I THINK I'M AHEAD ON POINTS.
WOULDN'T YOU SAY?
ONLY BECAUSE YOU CHOSE A SOFTER TARGET.
THE BLACK'S A CAGEY BASTARD. I COULDN'T EVEN GET CLOSE.
WELL THAT'S DOWN TO YOU. IF YOU CAN'T--
YOU'RE BOTH PREMATURE.
I HAVEN'T HAD MY TURN YET.
SO HOW ARE YOU GOING TO DO IT, ADAM?
NO CLUES.
I USED THE WITCH'S OWN POWER TO CONSUME HER. THAT'S GOING TO BE HARD TO TOP.
MY LEMONADE'S FINISHED.
CAN I HAVE ANOTHER ONE?

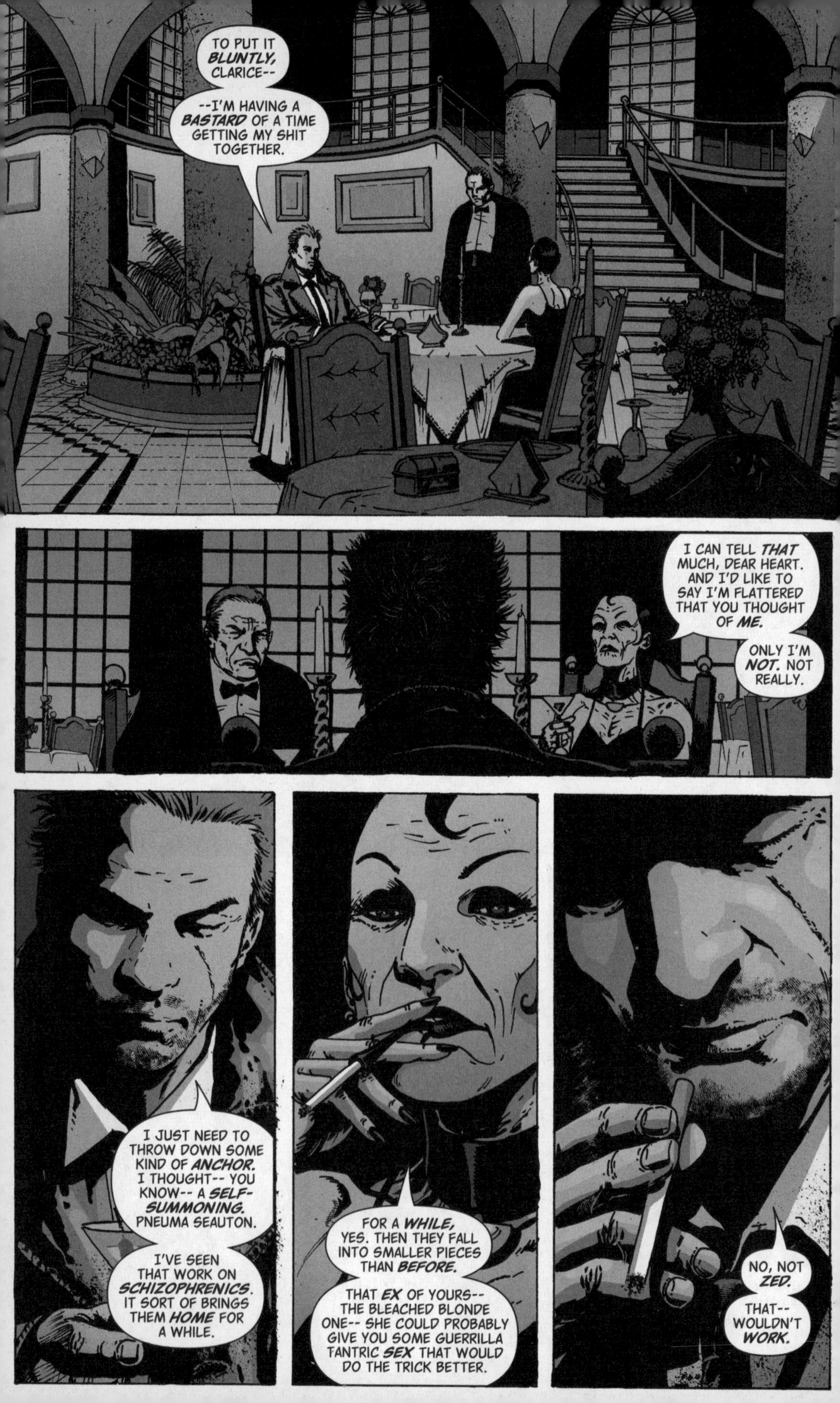

TO PUT IT BLUNTLY, CLARICE--
--I'M HAVING A BASTARD OF A TIME GETTING MY SHIT TOGETHER.
I CAN TELL THAT MUCH, DEAR HEART. AND I'D LIKE TO SAY I'M FLATTERED THAT YOU THOUGHT OF ME.
ONLY I'M NOT. NOT REALLY.
I JUST NEED TO THROW DOWN SOME KIND OF ANCHOR. I THOUGHT-- YOU KNOW-- A SELF-SUMMONING. PNEUMA SEAUTON.
I'VE SEEN THAT WORK ON SCHIZOPHRENICS. IT SORT OF BRINGS THEM HOME FOR A WHILE.
FOR A WHILE, YES. THEN THEY FALL INTO SMALLER PIECES THAN BEFORE.
THAT EX OF YOURS-- THE BLEACHED BLONDE ONE-- SHE COULD PROBABLY GIVE YOU SOME GUERRILLA TANTRIC SEX THAT WOULD DO THE TRICK BETTER.
NO, NOT ZED.
THAT-- WOULDN'T WORK.

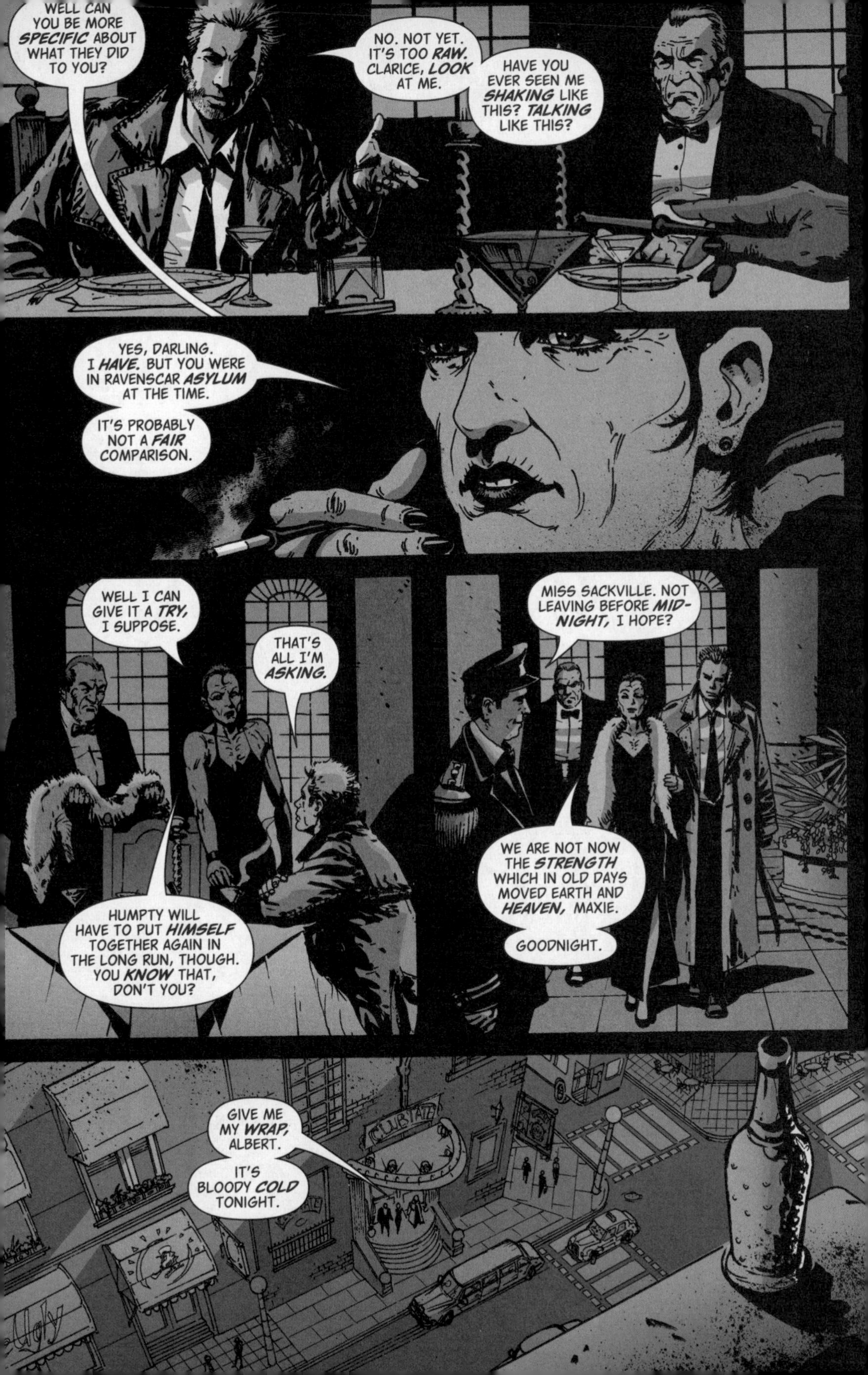
WELL CAN YOU BE MORE SPECIFIC ABOUT WHAT THEY DID TO YOU?
NO. NOT YET. IT'S TOO RAW. CLARICE, LOOK AT ME.
HAVE YOU EVER SEEN ME SHAKING LIKE THIS? TALKING LIKE THIS?
YES, DARLING. I HAVE. BUT YOU WERE IN RAVENSCAR ASYLUM AT THE TIME.
IT'S PROBABLY NOT A FAIR COMPARISON.
WELL I CAN GIVE IT A TRY, I SUPPOSE.
THAT'S ALL I'M ASKING.
HUMPTY WILL HAVE TO PUT HIMSELF TOGETHER AGAIN IN THE LONG RUN, THOUGH. YOU KNOW THAT, DON'T YOU?
MISS SACKVILLE. NOT LEAVING BEFORE MID-NIGHT, I HOPE?
WE ARE NOT NOW THE STRENGTH WHICH IN OLD DAYS MOVED EARTH AND HEAVEN, MAXIE.
GOODNIGHT.
GIVE ME MY WRAP, ALBERT.
IT'S BLOODY COLD TONIGHT.

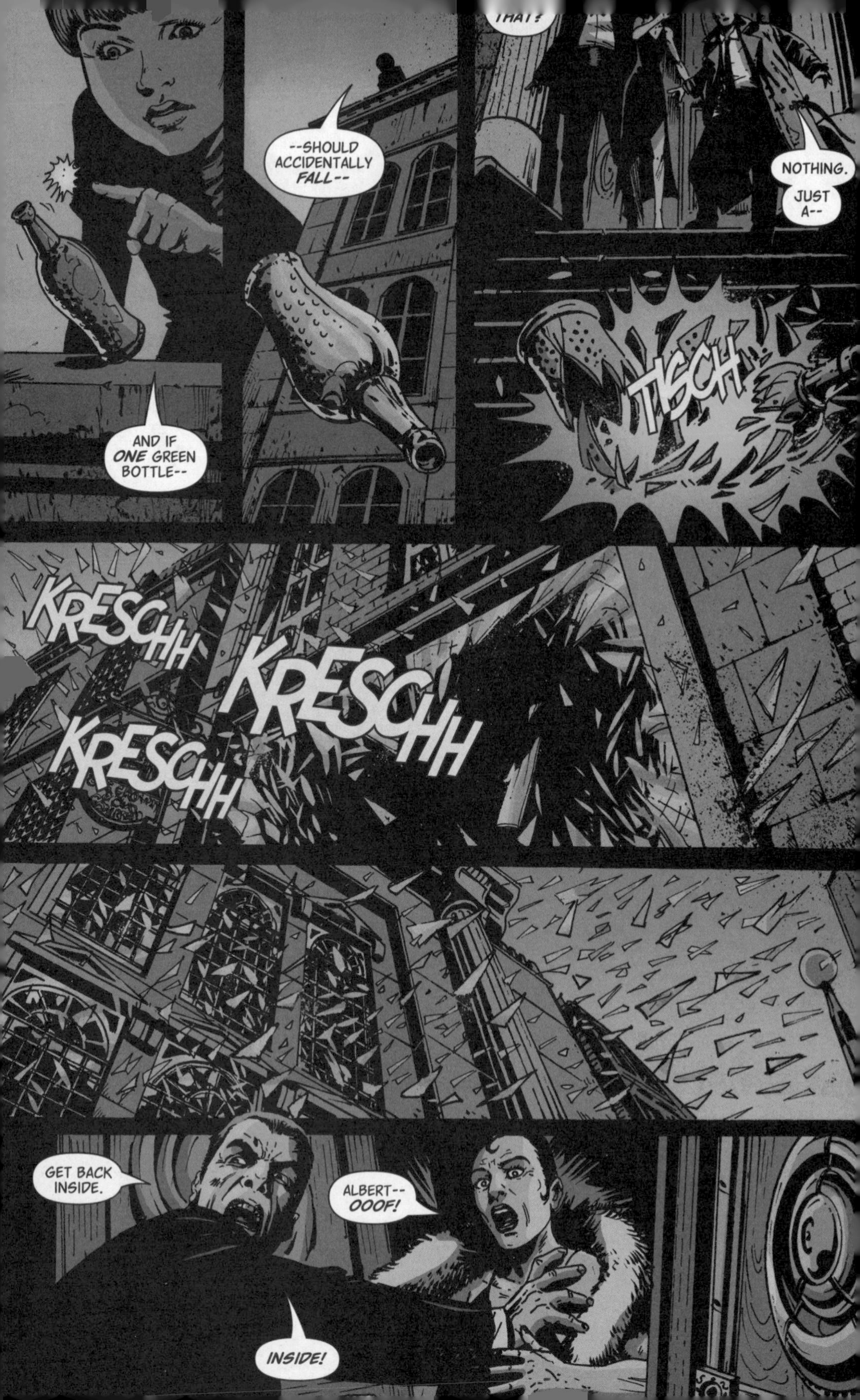
AND IF *ONE* GREEN BOTTLE--
--SHOULD ACCIDENTALLY *FALL*--
THAT?
NOTHING. JUST A--
TISCH
KRESCHH
KRESCHH
KRESCHH
GET BACK INSIDE.
ALBERT-- *OOOF!*
INSIDE!

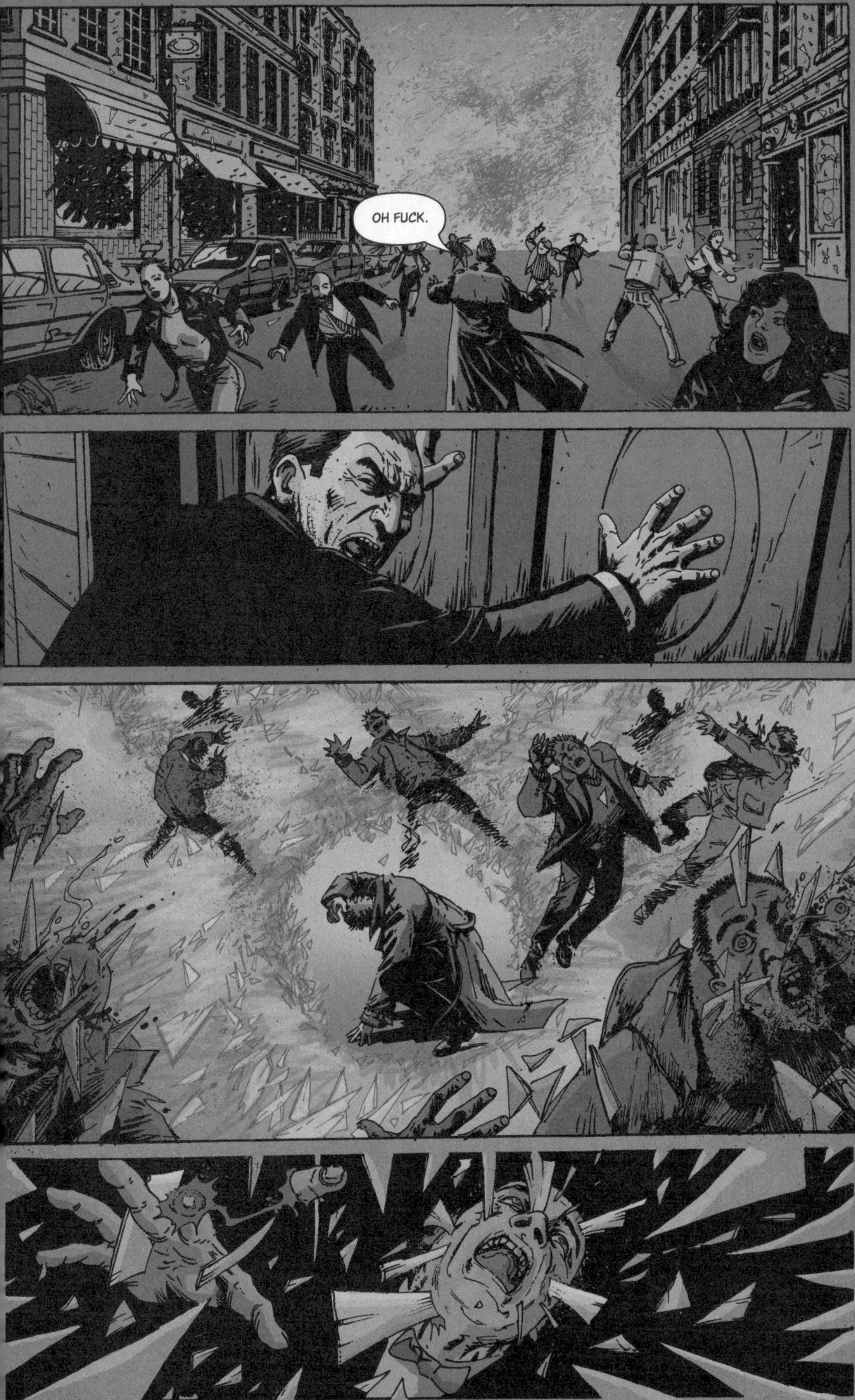
OH FUCK.

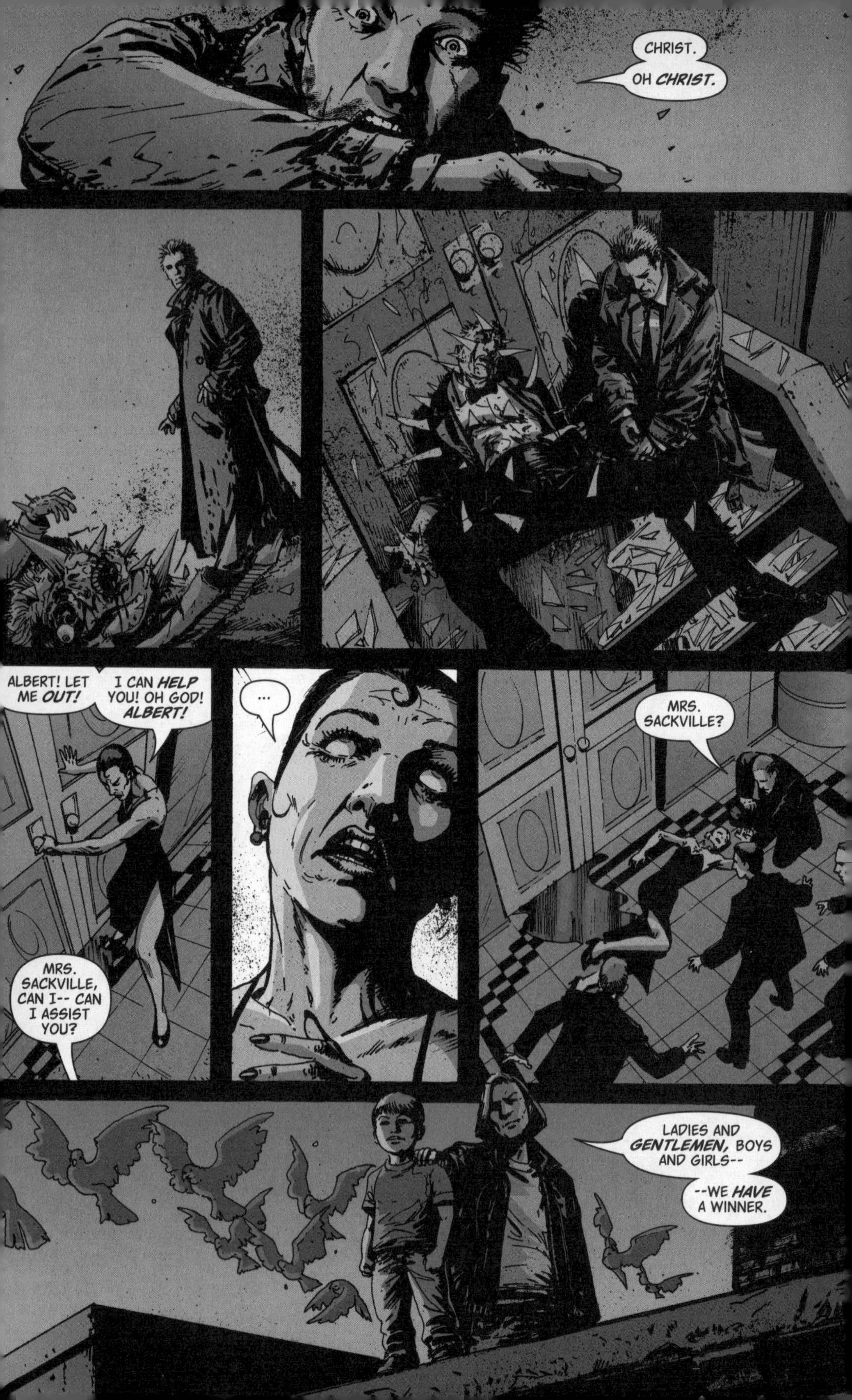
CHRIST.
OH CHRIST.
ALBERT! LET ME OUT!
I CAN HELP YOU! OH GOD! ALBERT!
MRS. SACKVILLE, CAN I-- CAN I ASSIST YOU?
...
MRS. SACKVILLE?
LADIES AND GENTLEMEN, BOYS AND GIRLS--
--WE HAVE A WINNER.

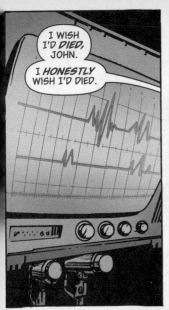

I WISH I'D *DIED,* JOHN. I *HONESTLY* WISH I'D DIED.

HOW CAN I GO *ON* WITHOUT ALBERT? HE DID *EVERYTHING* FOR ME.

IT'S LIKE HAVING MY *HEART* RIPPED OUT.

YEAH, I KNOW, CLARICE. BUT LOOK AT IT *THIS* WAY.

IT'S NOT LIKE IT WAS SOME KIND OF POINTLESS *ACCIDENT.* HE KNEW HE WAS TAKING THE *BULLET* FOR YOU.

HE WANTED YOU TO *LIVE.* SO LIVE WELL, AND YOU MAKE THAT *MEAN* SOMETHING.

THE PLATITUDES ARE A LITTLE HARD TO *TAKE,* JOHN. I NOTICED YOU MANAGED TO KEEP *YOURSELF* IN ONE PIECE.

IT-- IT DIDN'T GO *AFTER* ME. I WASN'T THE *TARGET.*

OF COURSE. HOW *SILLY* OF ME. IT WAS AFTER THE *TICKET* TOUTS ON SHAFTESBURY AVENUE.

JOHN *CONSTANTINE.*

COF! COF! COF!

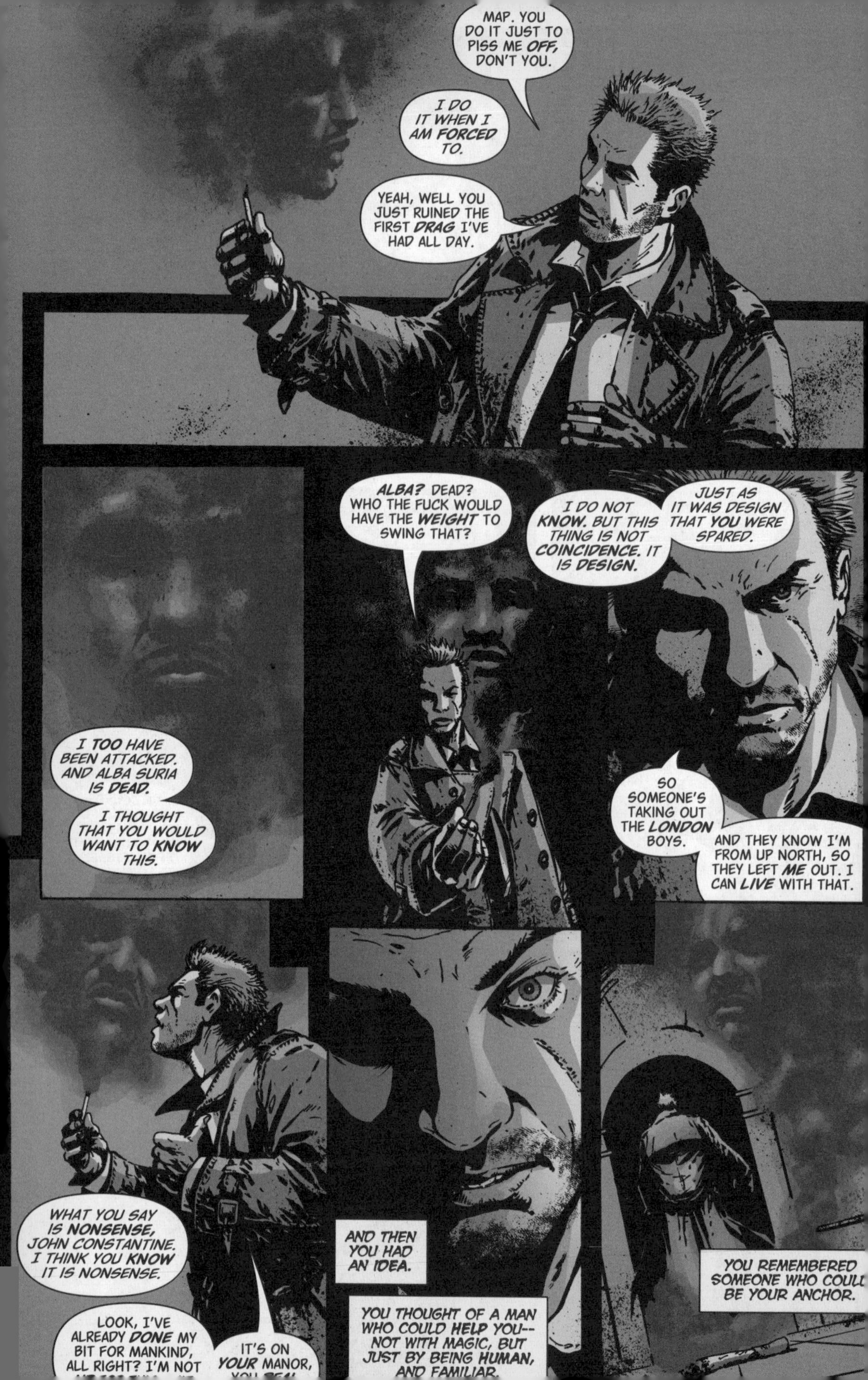
MAP. YOU DO IT JUST TO PISS ME *OFF*, DON'T YOU.
*I DO IT WHEN I AM **FORCED** TO.*
YEAH, WELL YOU JUST RUINED THE FIRST ***DRAG*** I'VE HAD ALL DAY.
*I **TOO** HAVE BEEN ATTACKED. AND ALBA SURIA IS **DEAD**.*
*I THOUGHT THAT YOU WOULD WANT TO **KNOW** THIS.*
ALBA? DEAD? WHO THE FUCK WOULD HAVE THE ***WEIGHT*** TO SWING THAT?
*I DO NOT **KNOW**. BUT THIS THING IS NOT **COINCIDENCE**. IT IS **DESIGN**.*
*JUST AS IT WAS DESIGN THAT **YOU** WERE SPARED.*
SO SOMEONE'S TAKING OUT THE ***LONDON*** BOYS.
AND THEY KNOW I'M FROM UP NORTH, SO THEY LEFT ***ME*** OUT. I CAN ***LIVE*** WITH THAT.
*WHAT YOU SAY IS **NONSENSE**, JOHN CONSTANTINE. I THINK YOU **KNOW** IT IS NONSENSE.*
LOOK, I'VE ALREADY ***DONE*** MY BIT FOR MANKIND, ALL RIGHT? I'M NOT
IT'S ON ***YOUR*** MANOR,
AND THEN YOU HAD AN IDEA.
*YOU THOUGHT OF A MAN WHO COULD **HELP** YOU-- NOT WITH MAGIC, BUT JUST BY BEING **HUMAN**, AND FAMILIAR.*
YOU REMEMBERED SOMEONE WHO COUL BE YOUR ANCHOR.

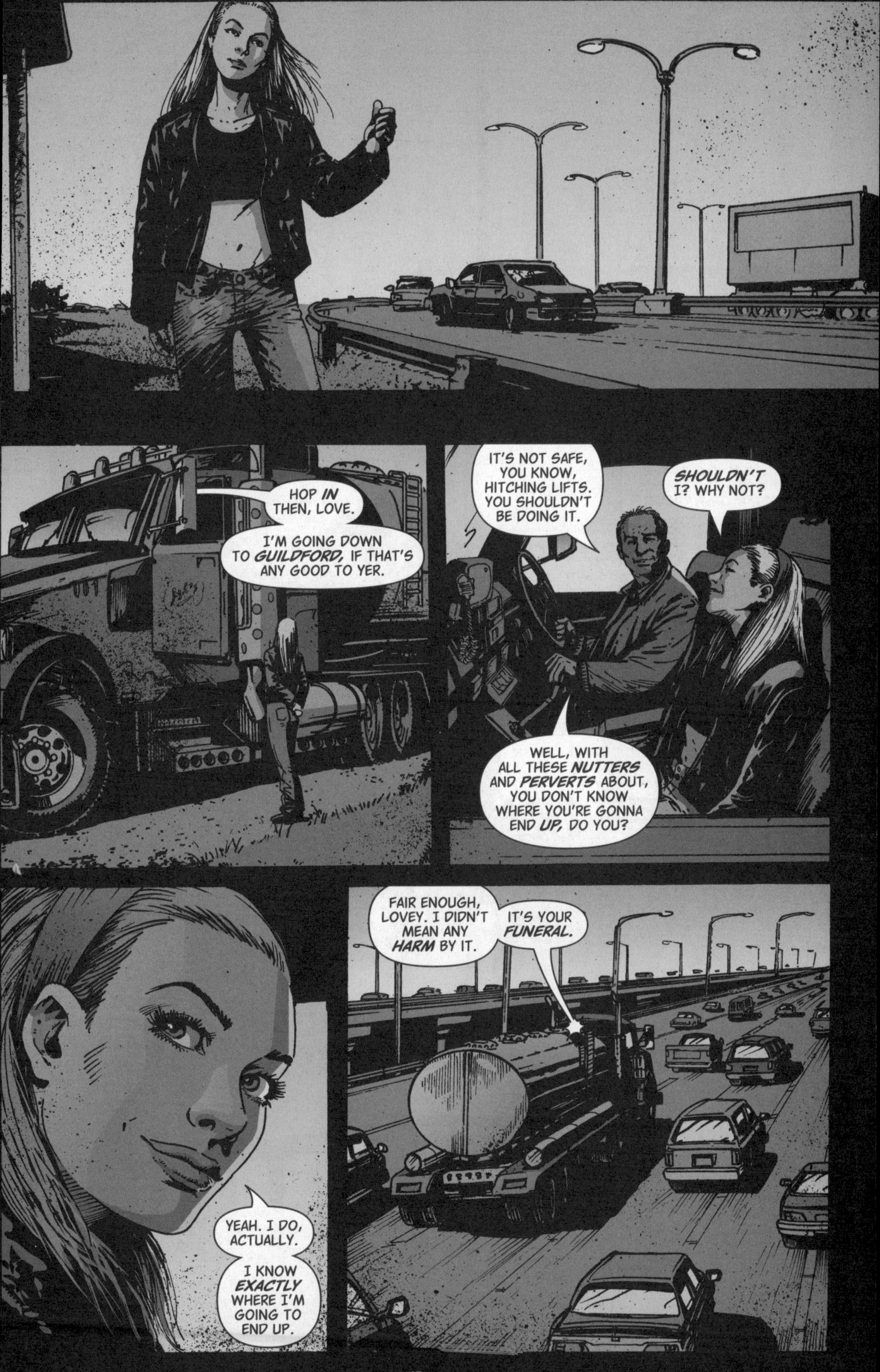
HOP *IN* THEN, LOVE.
I'M GOING DOWN TO *GUILDFORD,* IF THAT'S ANY GOOD TO YER.
IT'S NOT SAFE, YOU KNOW, HITCHING LIFTS. YOU SHOULDN'T BE DOING IT.
SHOULDN'T I? WHY NOT?
WELL, WITH ALL THESE *NUTTERS* AND *PERVERTS* ABOUT, YOU DON'T KNOW WHERE YOU'RE GONNA END *UP,* DO YOU?
YEAH. I DO, ACTUALLY.
I KNOW *EXACTLY* WHERE I'M GOING TO END UP.
FAIR ENOUGH, LOVEY. I DIDN'T MEAN ANY *HARM* BY IT.
IT'S YOUR *FUNERAL.*

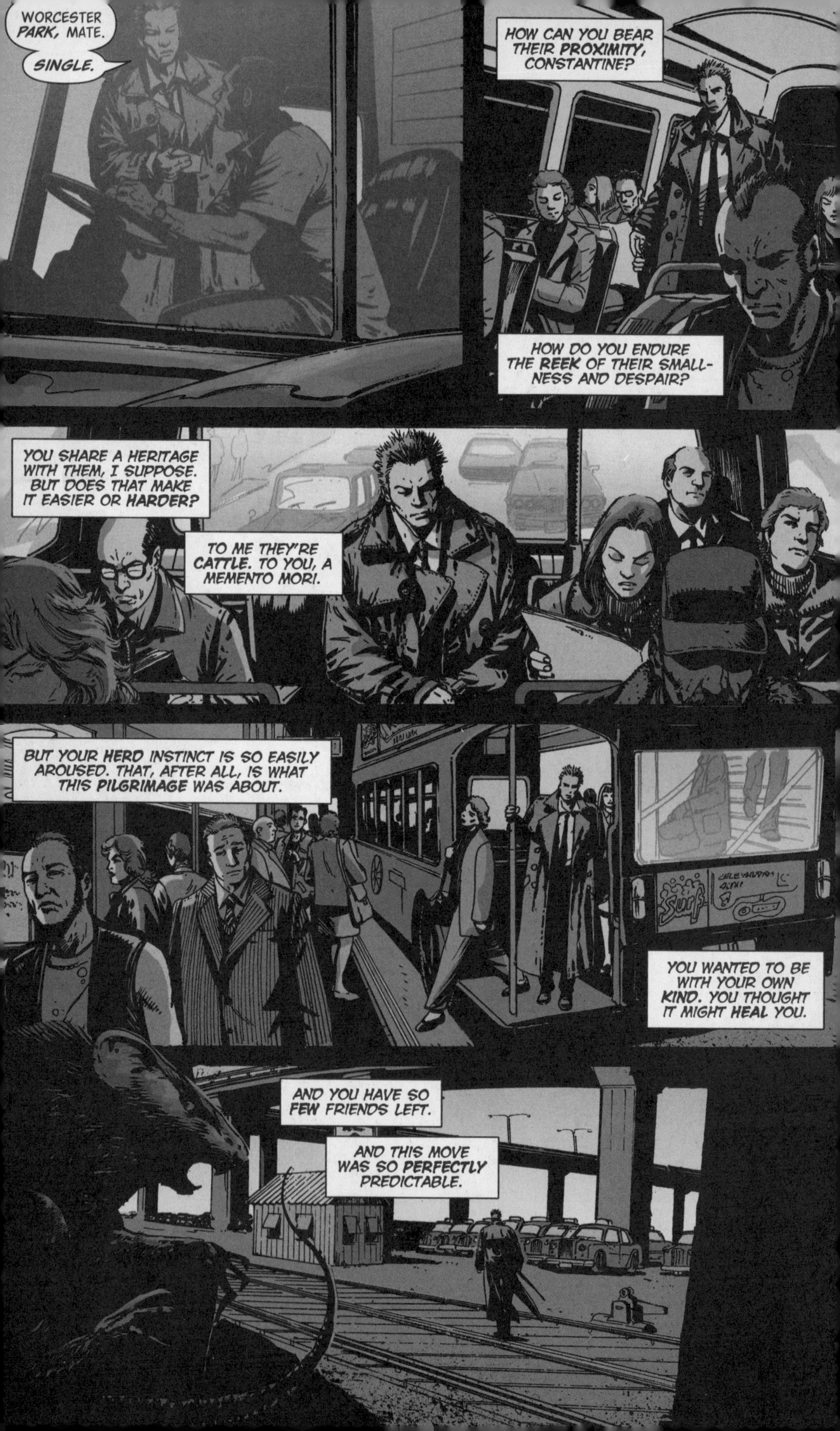
WORCESTER PARK, MATE.
SINGLE.
HOW CAN YOU BEAR THEIR PROXIMITY, CONSTANTINE?
HOW DO YOU ENDURE THE REEK OF THEIR SMALLNESS AND DESPAIR?
YOU SHARE A HERITAGE WITH THEM, I SUPPOSE. BUT DOES THAT MAKE IT EASIER OR HARDER?
TO ME THEY'RE CATTLE. TO YOU, A MEMENTO MORI.
BUT YOUR HERO INSTINCT IS SO EASILY AROUSED. THAT, AFTER ALL, IS WHAT THIS PILGRIMAGE WAS ABOUT.
YOU WANTED TO BE WITH YOUR OWN KIND. YOU THOUGHT IT MIGHT HEAL YOU.
AND YOU HAVE SO FEW FRIENDS LEFT.
AND THIS MOVE WAS SO PERFECTLY PREDICTABLE.

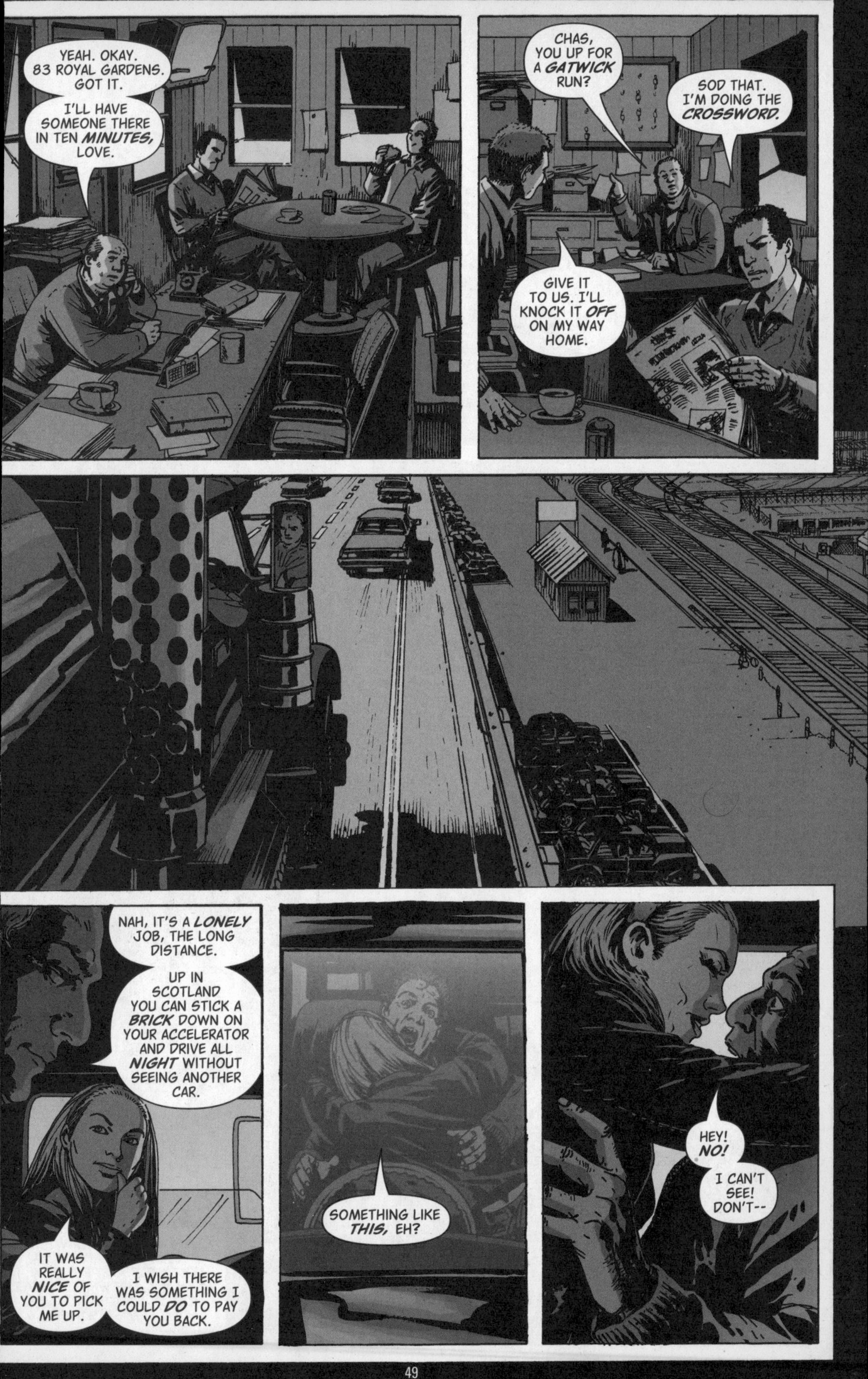
YEAH. OKAY. 83 ROYAL GARDENS. GOT IT.
I'LL HAVE SOMEONE THERE IN TEN *MINUTES,* LOVE.
CHAS, YOU UP FOR A *GATWICK* RUN?
SOD THAT. I'M DOING THE *CROSSWORD.*
GIVE IT TO US. I'LL KNOCK IT *OFF* ON MY WAY HOME.
NAH, IT'S A *LONELY* JOB, THE LONG DISTANCE.
UP IN SCOTLAND YOU CAN STICK A *BRICK* DOWN ON YOUR ACCELERATOR AND DRIVE ALL *NIGHT* WITHOUT SEEING ANOTHER CAR.
IT WAS REALLY *NICE* OF YOU TO PICK ME UP.
I WISH THERE WAS SOMETHING I COULD *DO* TO PAY YOU BACK.
SOMETHING LIKE *THIS,* EH?
HEY! *NO!*
I CAN'T SEE! DON'T--

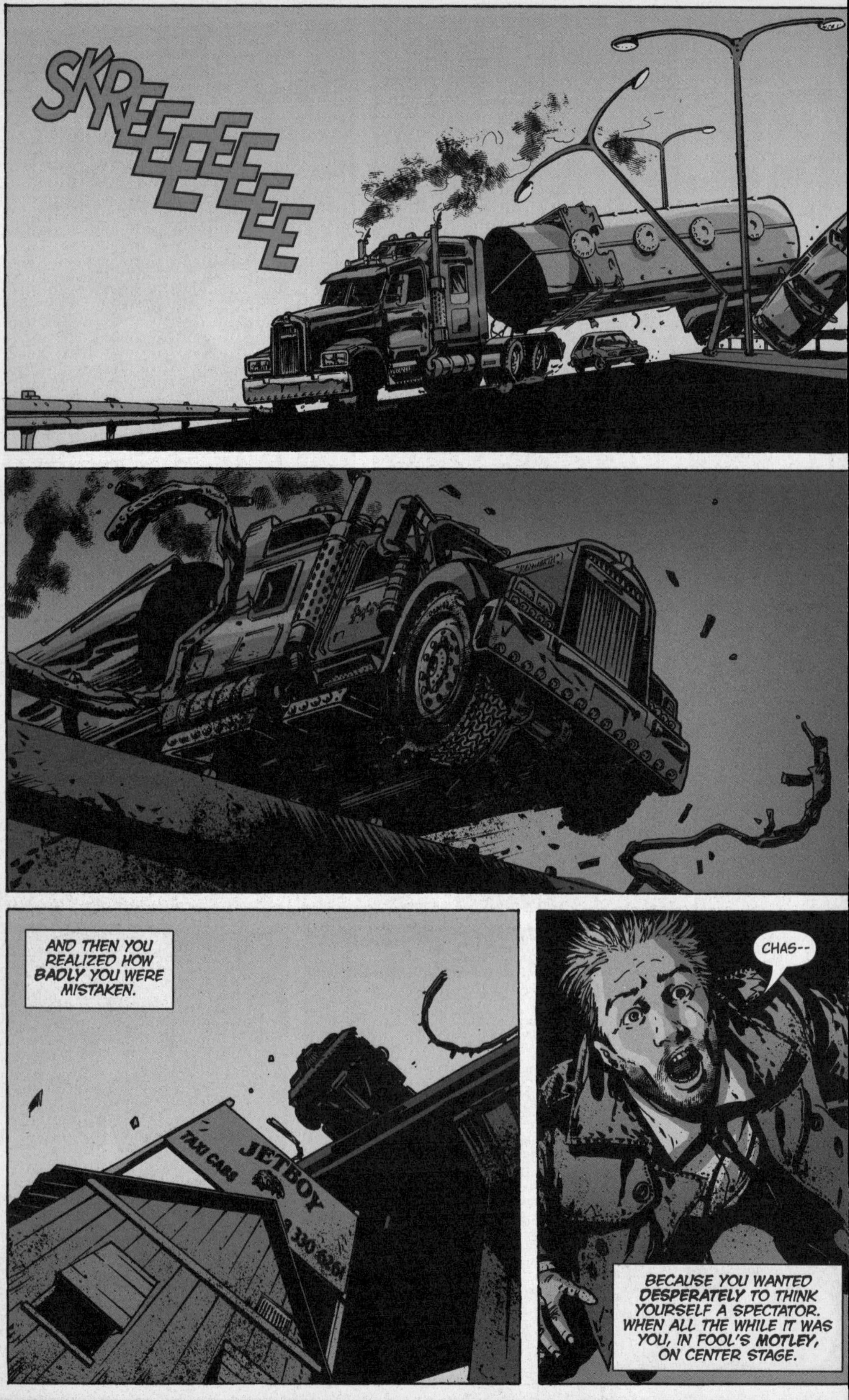
SKREEEEEEEEE
AND THEN YOU REALIZED HOW BADLY YOU WERE MISTAKEN.
JETBOY
TAXI CABS
CHAS--
BECAUSE YOU WANTED DESPERATELY TO THINK YOURSELF A SPECTATOR. WHEN ALL THE WHILE IT WAS YOU, IN FOOL'S MOTLEY, ON CENTER STAGE.

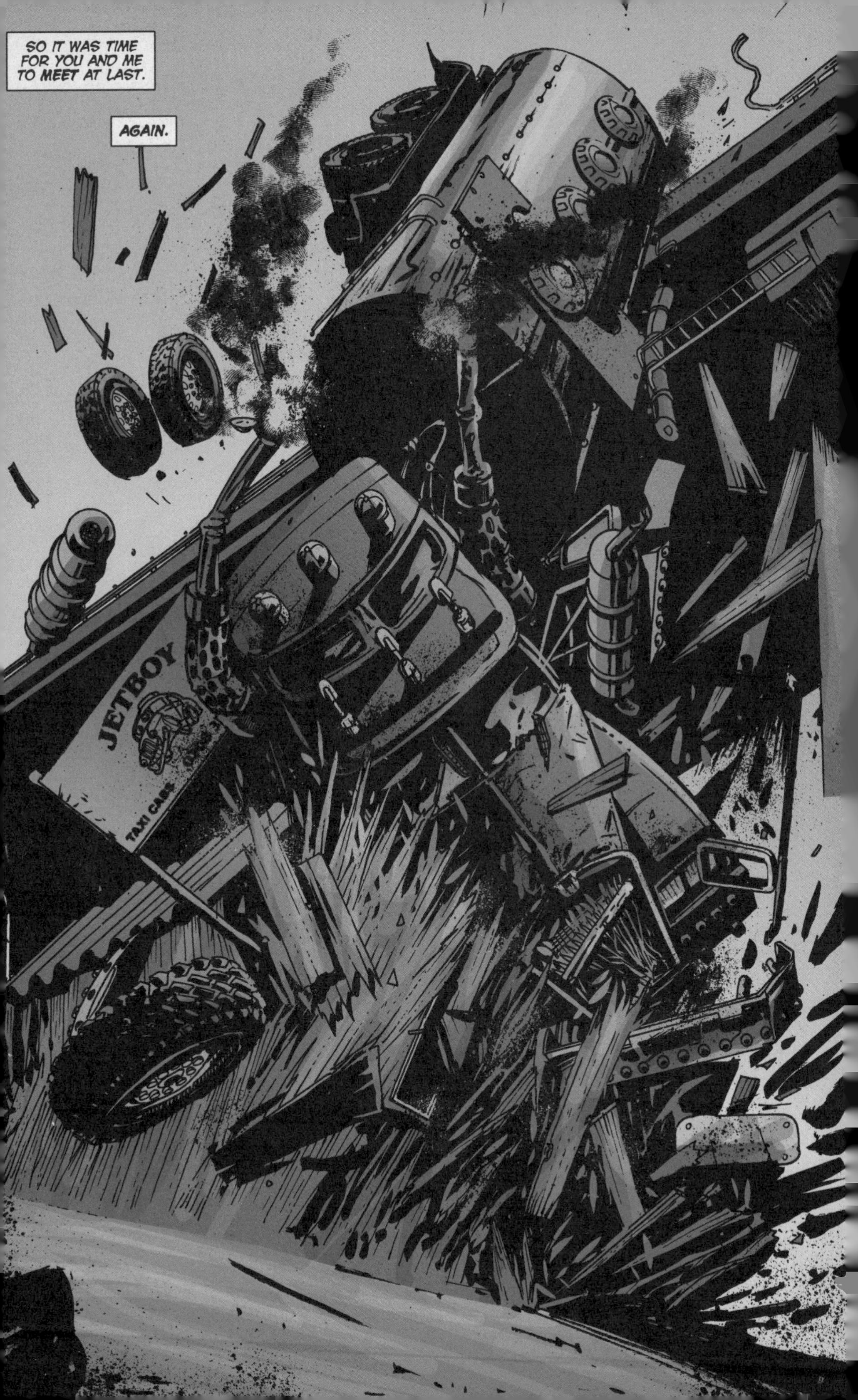
SO IT WAS TIME FOR YOU AND ME TO MEET AT LAST.
AGAIN.
JETBOY
TAXI CABS

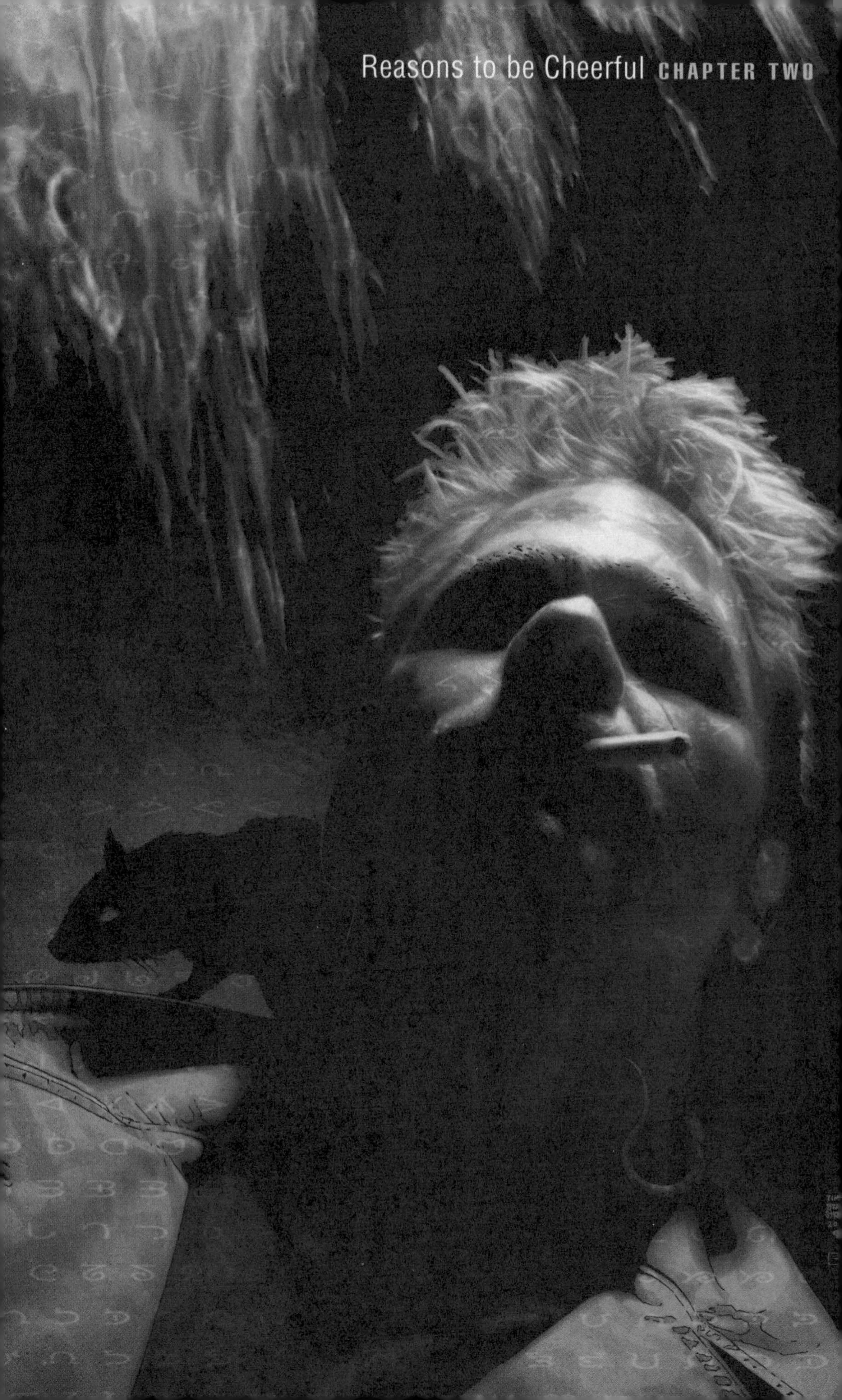

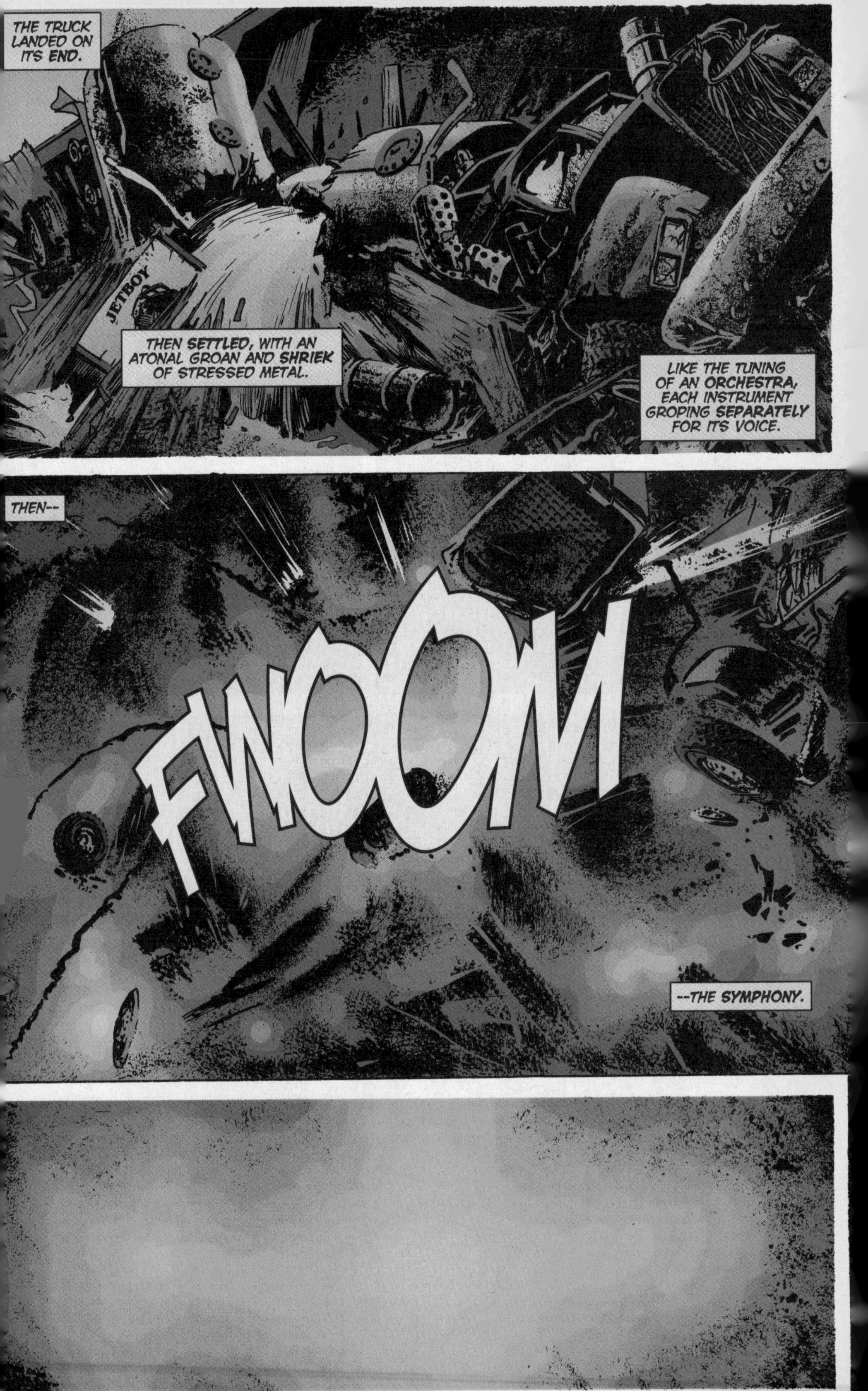
THE TRUCK LANDED ON ITS END.
JETBOY
THEN SETTLED, WITH AN ATONAL GROAN AND SHRIEK OF STRESSED METAL.
LIKE THE TUNING OF AN ORCHESTRA, EACH INSTRUMENT GROPING SEPARATELY FOR ITS VOICE.
THEN--
FWOOM
--THE SYMPHONY.

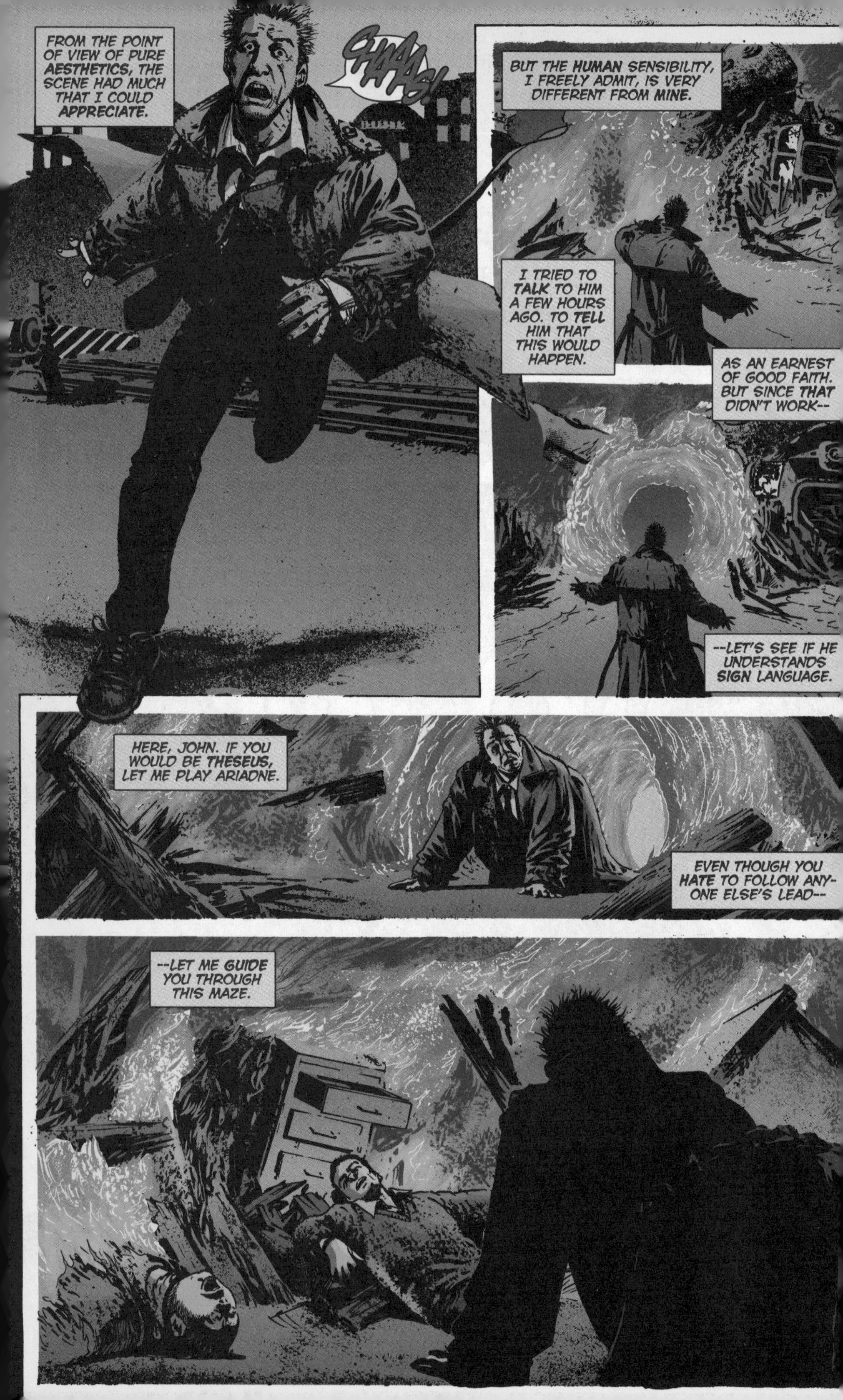
FROM THE POINT OF VIEW OF PURE AESTHETICS, THE SCENE HAD MUCH THAT I COULD APPRECIATE.
CHAAAS!
BUT THE HUMAN SENSIBILITY, I FREELY ADMIT, IS VERY DIFFERENT FROM MINE.
I TRIED TO TALK TO HIM A FEW HOURS AGO. TO TELL HIM THAT THIS WOULD HAPPEN.
AS AN EARNEST OF GOOD FAITH. BUT SINCE THAT DIDN'T WORK--
--LET'S SEE IF HE UNDERSTANDS SIGN LANGUAGE.
HERE, JOHN. IF YOU WOULD BE THESEUS, LET ME PLAY ARIADNE.
EVEN THOUGH YOU HATE TO FOLLOW ANY-ONE ELSE'S LEAD--
--LET ME GUIDE YOU THROUGH THIS MAZE.

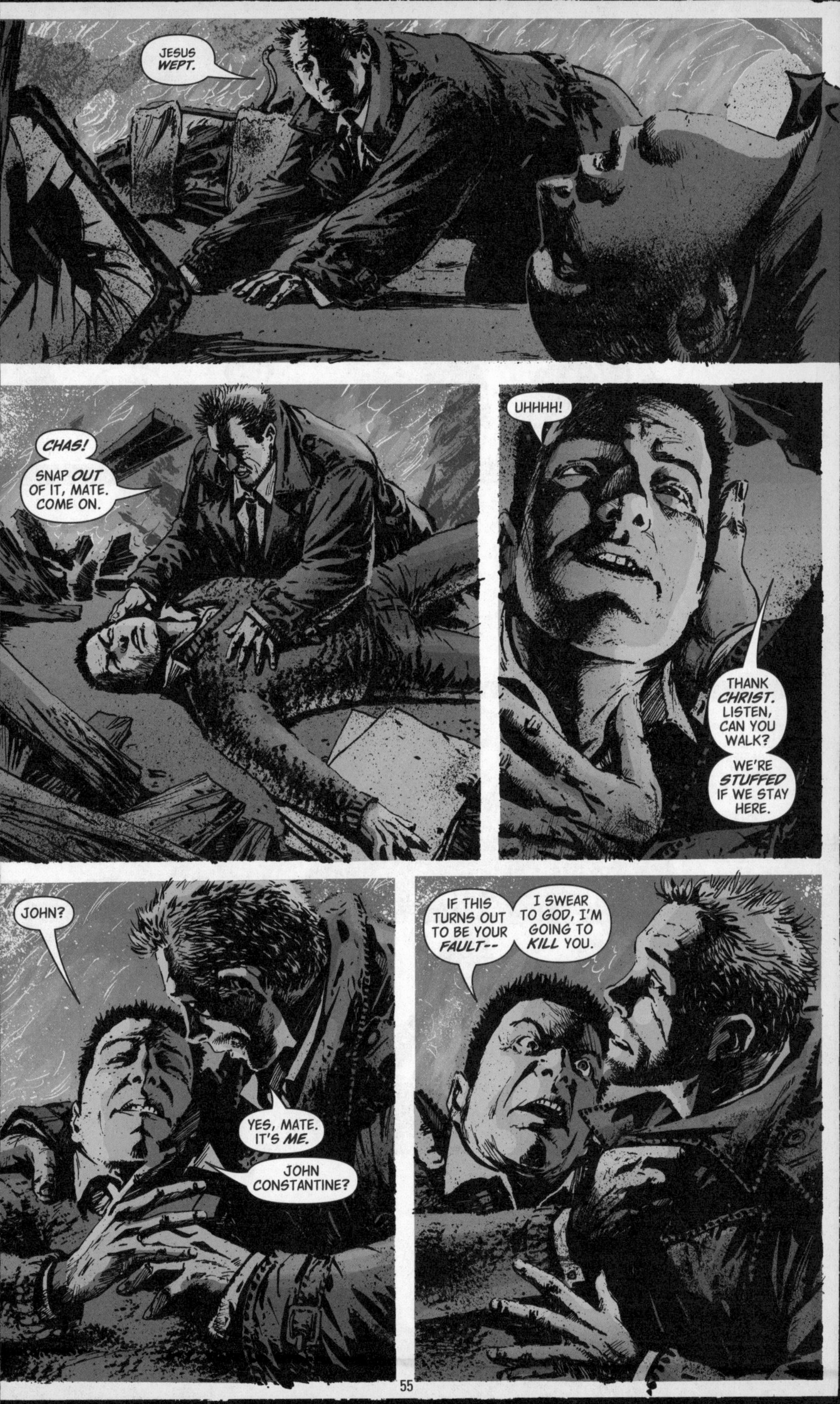
JESUS WEPT.
CHAS!
SNAP OUT OF IT, MATE. COME ON.
UHHHH!
THANK CHRIST. LISTEN, CAN YOU WALK?
WE'RE STUFFED IF WE STAY HERE.
JOHN?
YES, MATE. IT'S ME.
JOHN CONSTANTINE?
IF THIS TURNS OUT TO BE YOUR FAULT--
I SWEAR TO GOD, I'M GOING TO KILL YOU.

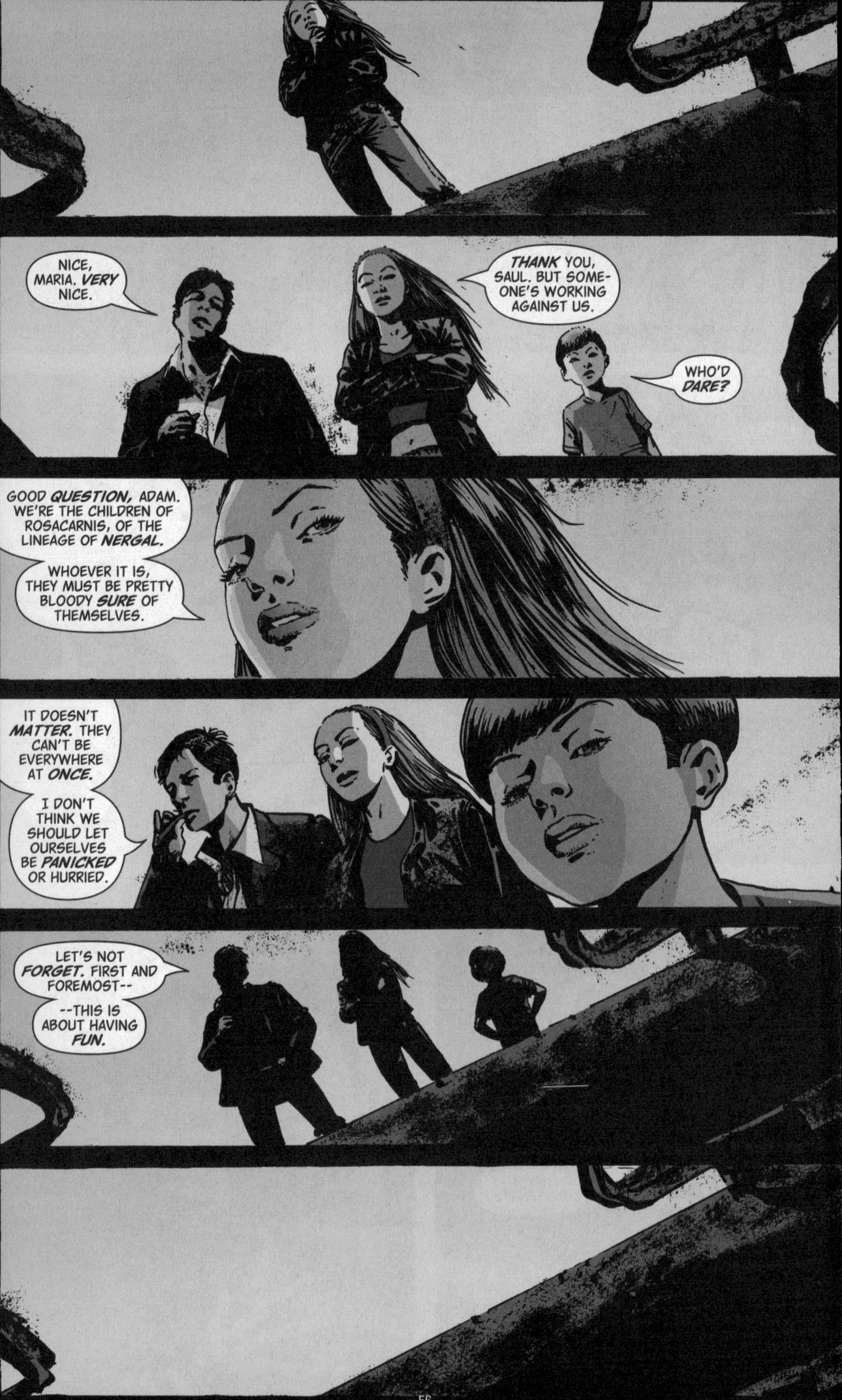

NICE, MARIA. VERY NICE.
THANK YOU, SAUL. BUT SOME-ONE'S WORKING AGAINST US.
WHO'D DARE?
GOOD QUESTION, ADAM. WE'RE THE CHILDREN OF ROSACARNIS, OF THE LINEAGE OF NERGAL.
WHOEVER IT IS, THEY MUST BE PRETTY BLOODY SURE OF THEMSELVES.
IT DOESN'T MATTER. THEY CAN'T BE EVERYWHERE AT ONCE.
I DON'T THINK WE SHOULD LET OURSELVES BE PANICKED OR HURRIED.
LET'S NOT FORGET. FIRST AND FOREMOST--
--THIS IS ABOUT HAVING FUN.

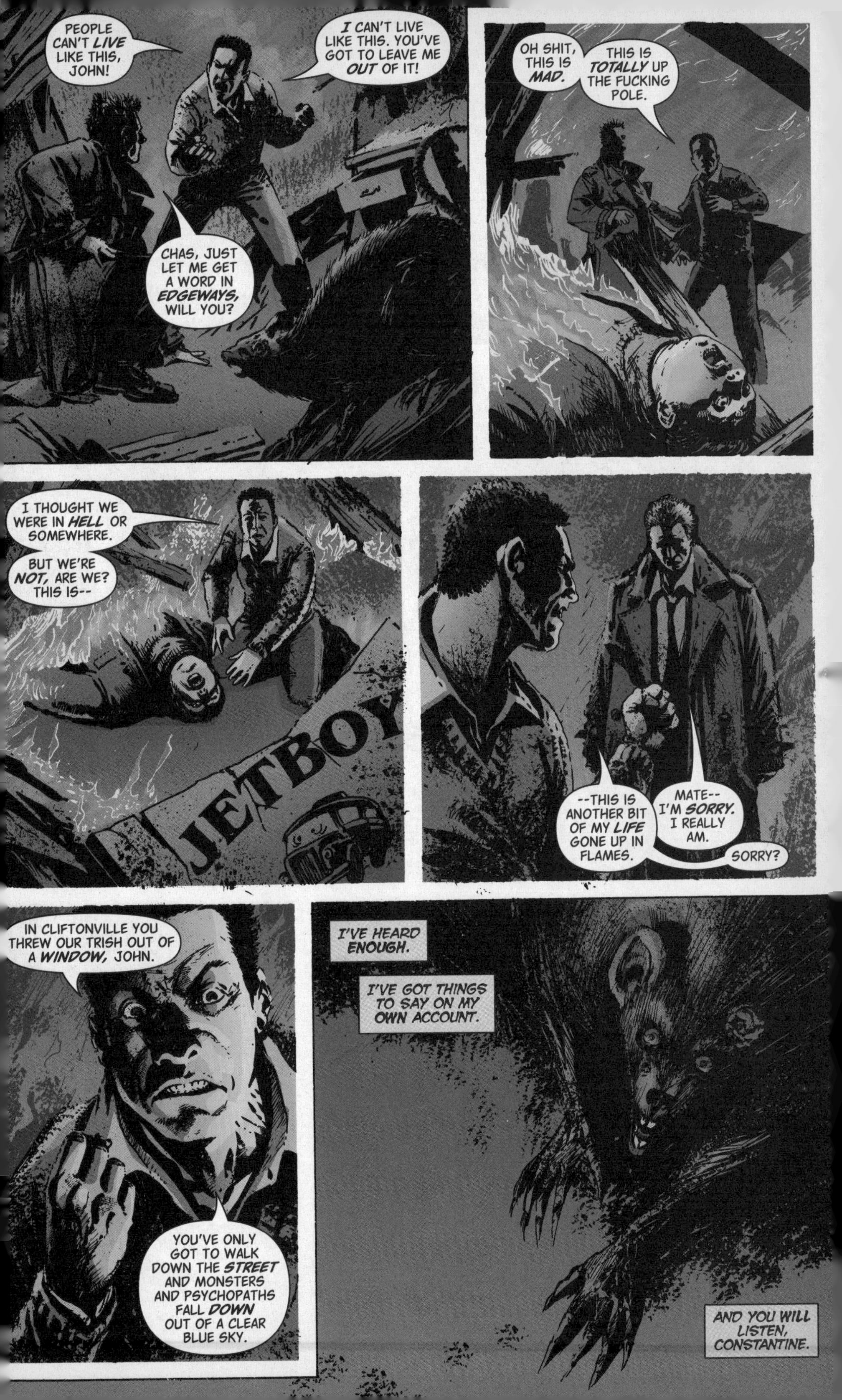
PEOPLE CAN'T LIVE LIKE THIS, JOHN!
I CAN'T LIVE LIKE THIS. YOU'VE GOT TO LEAVE ME OUT OF IT!
CHAS, JUST LET ME GET A WORD IN EDGEWAYS, WILL YOU?
OH SHIT, THIS IS MAD.
THIS IS TOTALLY UP THE FUCKING POLE.
I THOUGHT WE WERE IN HELL OR SOMEWHERE.
BUT WE'RE NOT, ARE WE? THIS IS--
JETBOY
--THIS IS ANOTHER BIT OF MY LIFE GONE UP IN FLAMES.
MATE-- I'M SORRY. I REALLY AM.
SORRY?
IN CLIFTONVILLE YOU THREW OUR TRISH OUT OF A WINDOW, JOHN.
YOU'VE ONLY GOT TO WALK DOWN THE STREET AND MONSTERS AND PSYCHOPATHS FALL DOWN OUT OF A CLEAR BLUE SKY.
I'VE HEARD ENOUGH.
I'VE GOT THINGS TO SAY ON MY OWN ACCOUNT.
AND YOU WILL LISTEN, CONSTANTINE.

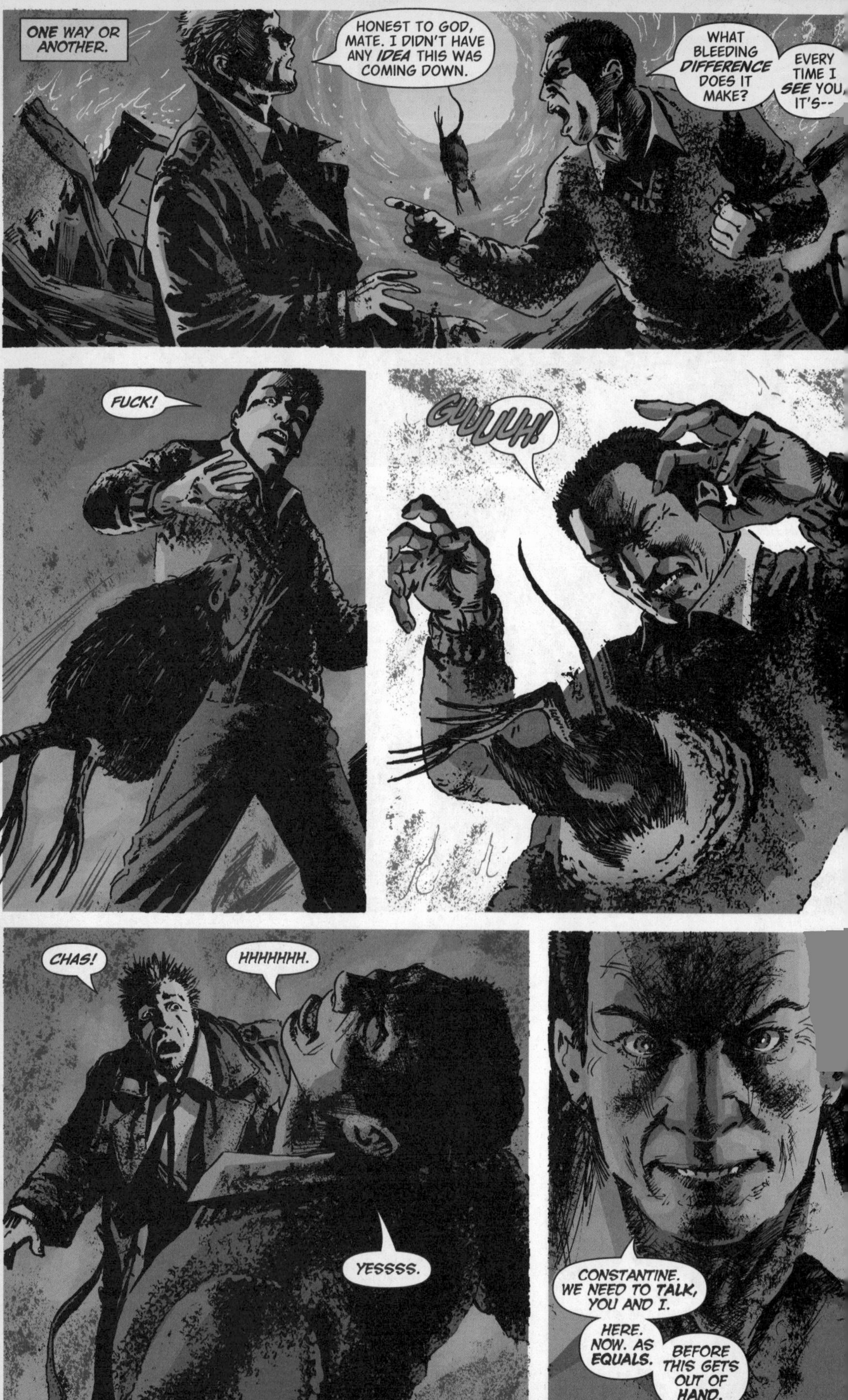
ONE WAY OR ANOTHER.
HONEST TO GOD, MATE. I DIDN'T HAVE ANY IDEA THIS WAS COMING DOWN.
WHAT BLEEDING DIFFERENCE DOES IT MAKE?
EVERY TIME I SEE YOU, IT'S--
FUCK!
GUUUUH!
CHAS!
HHHHHHH.
YESSSS.
CONSTANTINE. WE NEED TO TALK, YOU AND I.
HERE. NOW. AS EQUALS.
BEFORE THIS GETS OUT OF HAND.

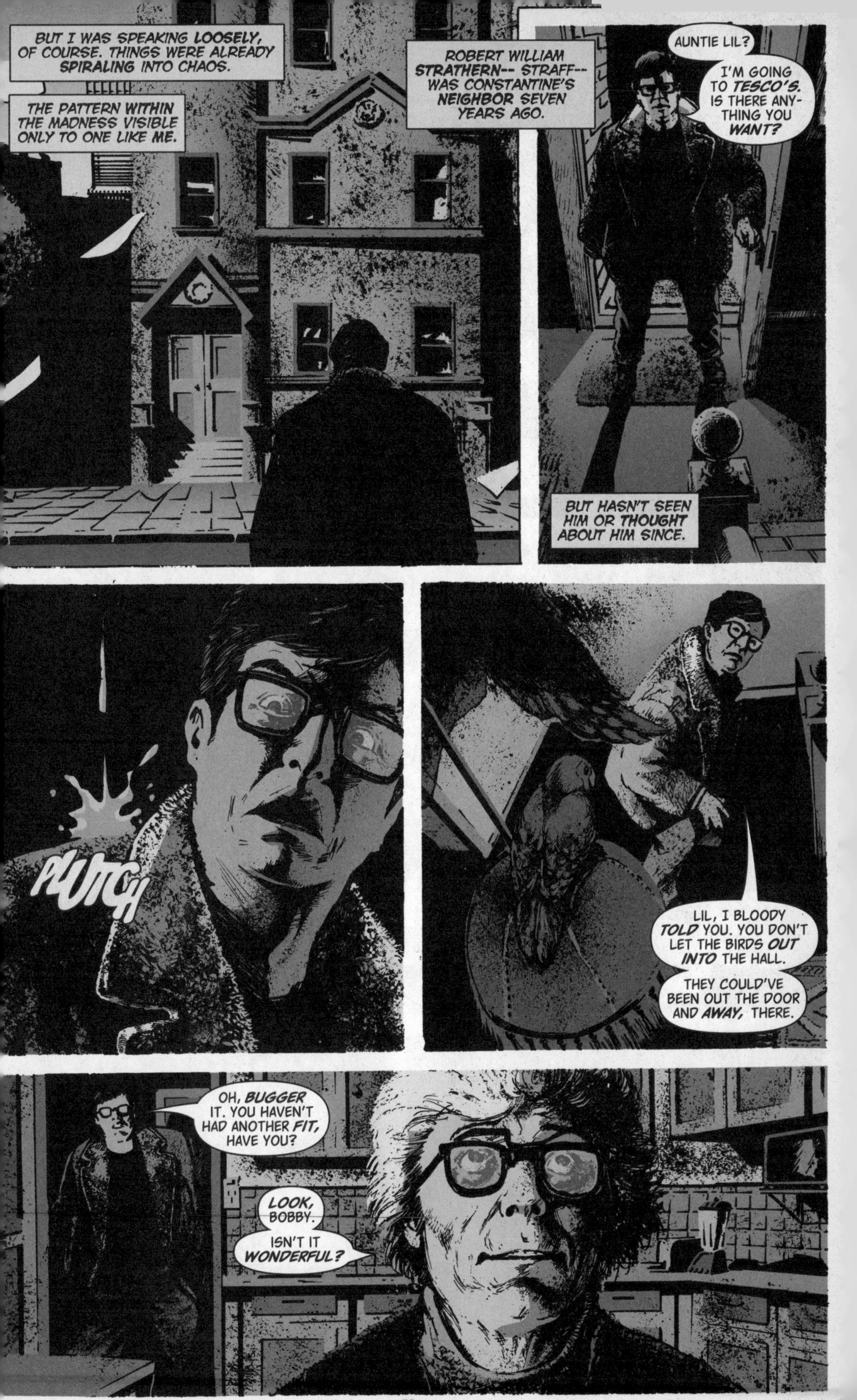
BUT I WAS SPEAKING LOOSELY, OF COURSE. THINGS WERE ALREADY SPIRALING INTO CHAOS.
THE PATTERN WITHIN THE MADNESS VISIBLE ONLY TO ONE LIKE ME.
ROBERT WILLIAM STRATHERN-- STRAFF-- WAS CONSTANTINE'S NEIGHBOR SEVEN YEARS AGO.
AUNTIE LIL?
I'M GOING TO TESCO'S. IS THERE ANYTHING YOU WANT?
BUT HASN'T SEEN HIM OR THOUGHT ABOUT HIM SINCE.
PLUTCH
LIL, I BLOODY TOLD YOU. YOU DON'T LET THE BIRDS OUT INTO THE HALL.
THEY COULD'VE BEEN OUT THE DOOR AND AWAY, THERE.
OH, BUGGER IT. YOU HAVEN'T HAD ANOTHER FIT, HAVE YOU?
LOOK, BOBBY.
ISN'T IT WONDERFUL?

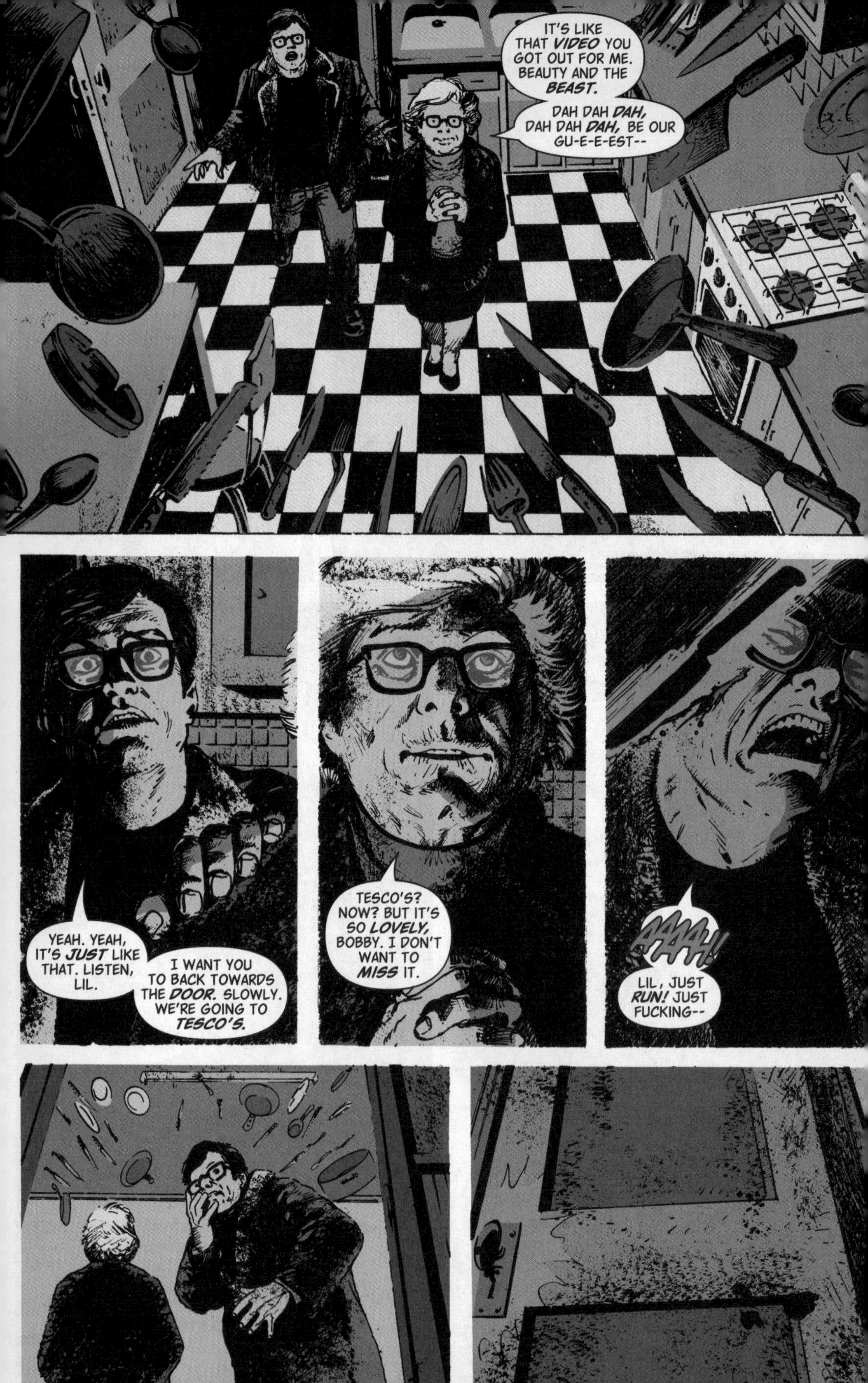

IT'S LIKE THAT VIDEO YOU GOT OUT FOR ME. BEAUTY AND THE BEAST.
DAH DAH DAH, DAH DAH DAH, BE OUR GU-E-E-EST--
YEAH. YEAH, IT'S JUST LIKE THAT. LISTEN, LIL.
I WANT YOU TO BACK TOWARDS THE DOOR. SLOWLY. WE'RE GOING TO TESCO'S.
TESCO'S? NOW? BUT IT'S SO LOVELY, BOBBY. I DON'T WANT TO MISS IT.
AAAAH!
LIL, JUST RUN! JUST FUCKING--

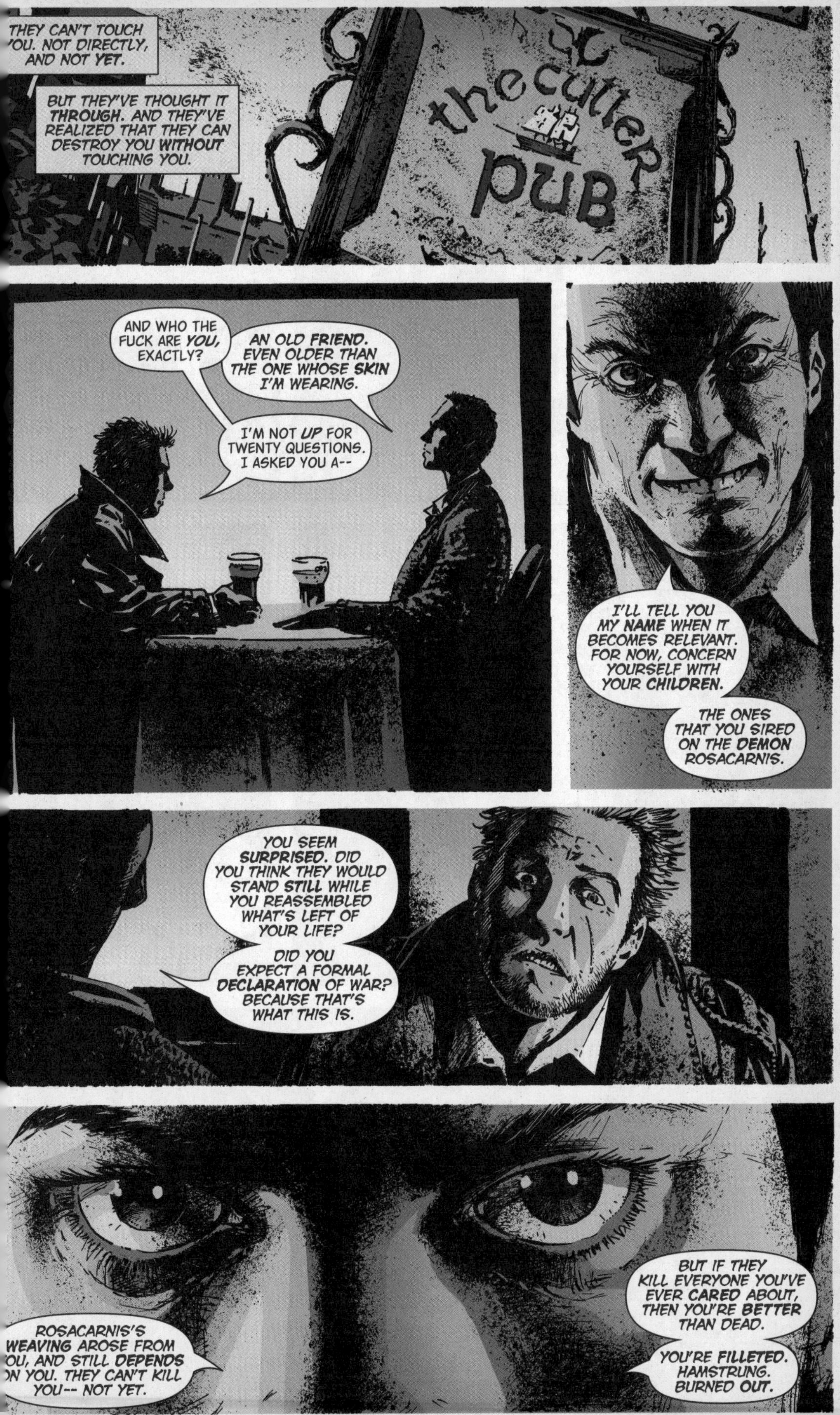
THEY CAN'T TOUCH YOU. NOT DIRECTLY, AND NOT YET.
BUT THEY'VE THOUGHT IT THROUGH. AND THEY'VE REALIZED THAT THEY CAN DESTROY YOU WITHOUT TOUCHING YOU.
the cutter PUB
AND WHO THE FUCK ARE YOU, EXACTLY?
AN OLD FRIEND. EVEN OLDER THAN THE ONE WHOSE SKIN I'M WEARING.
I'M NOT UP FOR TWENTY QUESTIONS. I ASKED YOU A--
I'LL TELL YOU MY NAME WHEN IT BECOMES RELEVANT. FOR NOW, CONCERN YOURSELF WITH YOUR CHILDREN.
THE ONES THAT YOU SIRED ON THE DEMON ROSACARNIS.
YOU SEEM SURPRISED. DID YOU THINK THEY WOULD STAND STILL WHILE YOU REASSEMBLED WHAT'S LEFT OF YOUR LIFE?
DID YOU EXPECT A FORMAL DECLARATION OF WAR? BECAUSE THAT'S WHAT THIS IS.
ROSACARNIS'S WEAVING AROSE FROM YOU, AND STILL DEPENDS ON YOU. THEY CAN'T KILL YOU-- NOT YET.
BUT IF THEY KILL EVERYONE YOU'VE EVER CARED ABOUT, THEN YOU'RE BETTER THAN DEAD.
YOU'RE FILLETED. HAMSTRUNG. BURNED OUT.

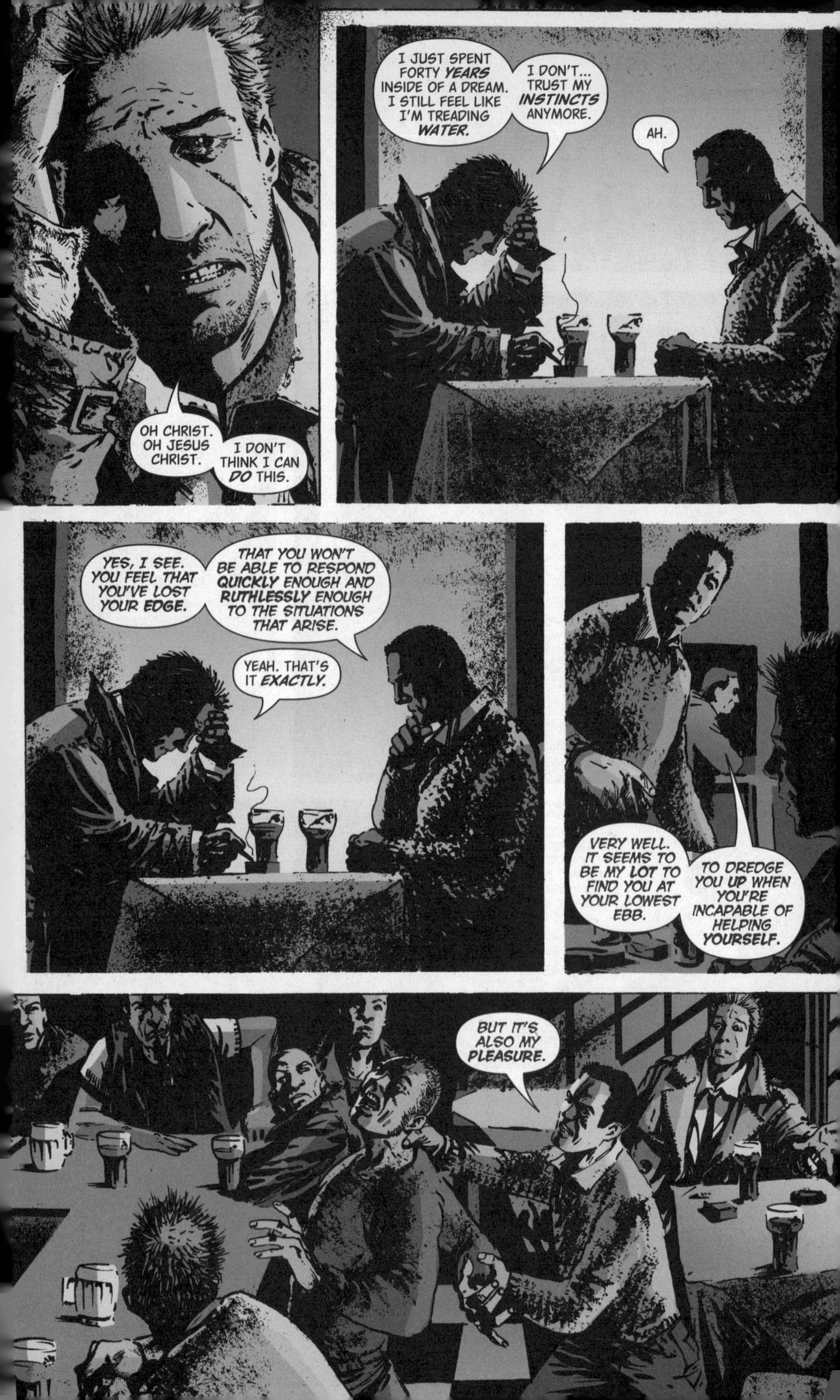
OH CHRIST. OH JESUS CHRIST.
I DON'T THINK I CAN DO THIS.
I JUST SPENT FORTY YEARS INSIDE OF A DREAM. I STILL FEEL LIKE I'M TREADING WATER.
I DON'T... TRUST MY INSTINCTS ANYMORE.
AH.
YES, I SEE. YOU FEEL THAT YOU'VE LOST YOUR EDGE.
THAT YOU WON'T BE ABLE TO RESPOND QUICKLY ENOUGH AND RUTHLESSLY ENOUGH TO THE SITUATIONS THAT ARISE.
YEAH. THAT'S IT EXACTLY.
VERY WELL. IT SEEMS TO BE MY LOT TO FIND YOU AT YOUR LOWEST EBB.
TO DREDGE YOU UP WHEN YOU'RE INCAPABLE OF HELPING YOURSELF.
BUT IT'S ALSO MY PLEASURE.

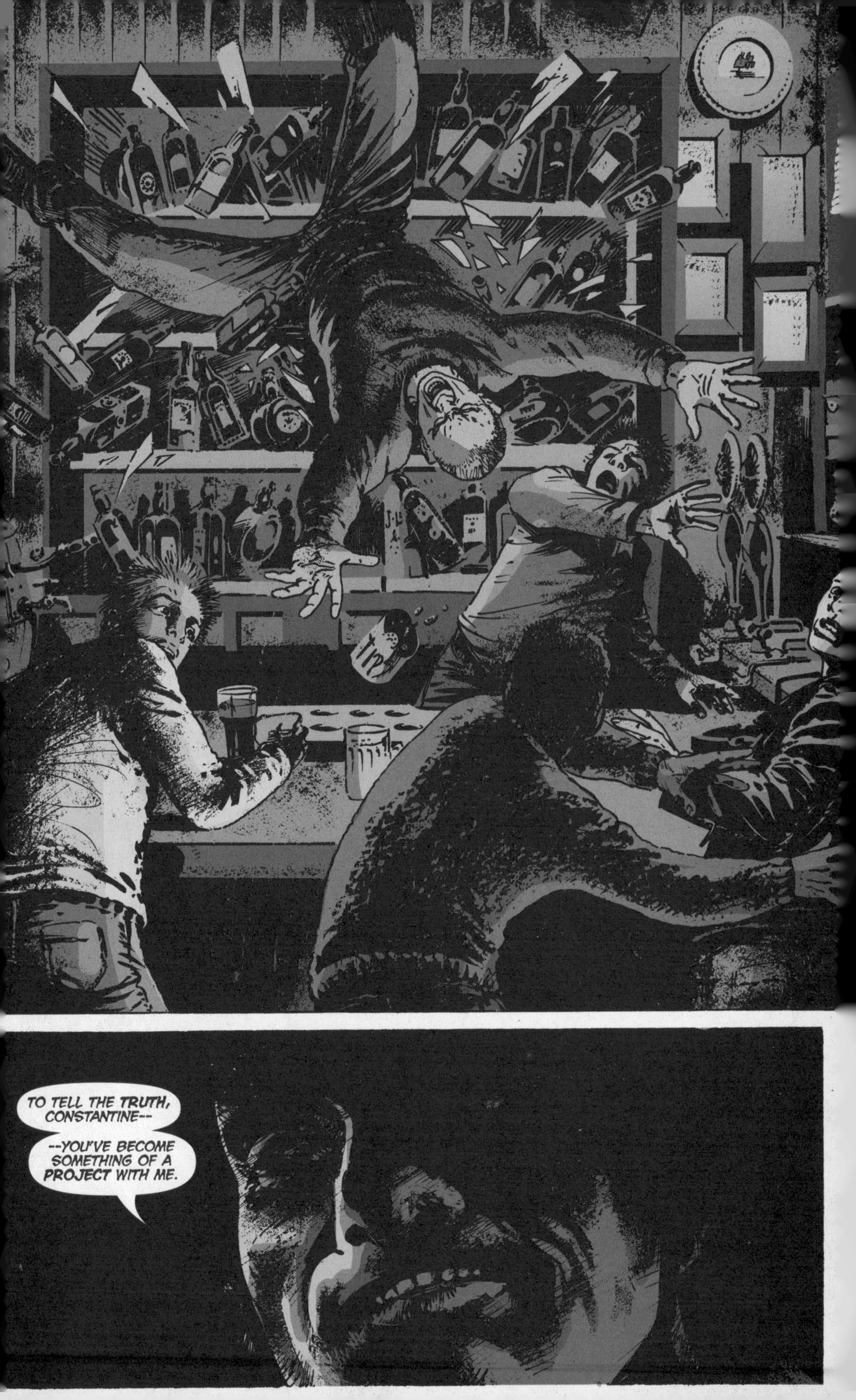
TO TELL THE TRUTH, CONSTANTINE--
--YOU'VE BECOME SOMETHING OF A PROJECT WITH ME.

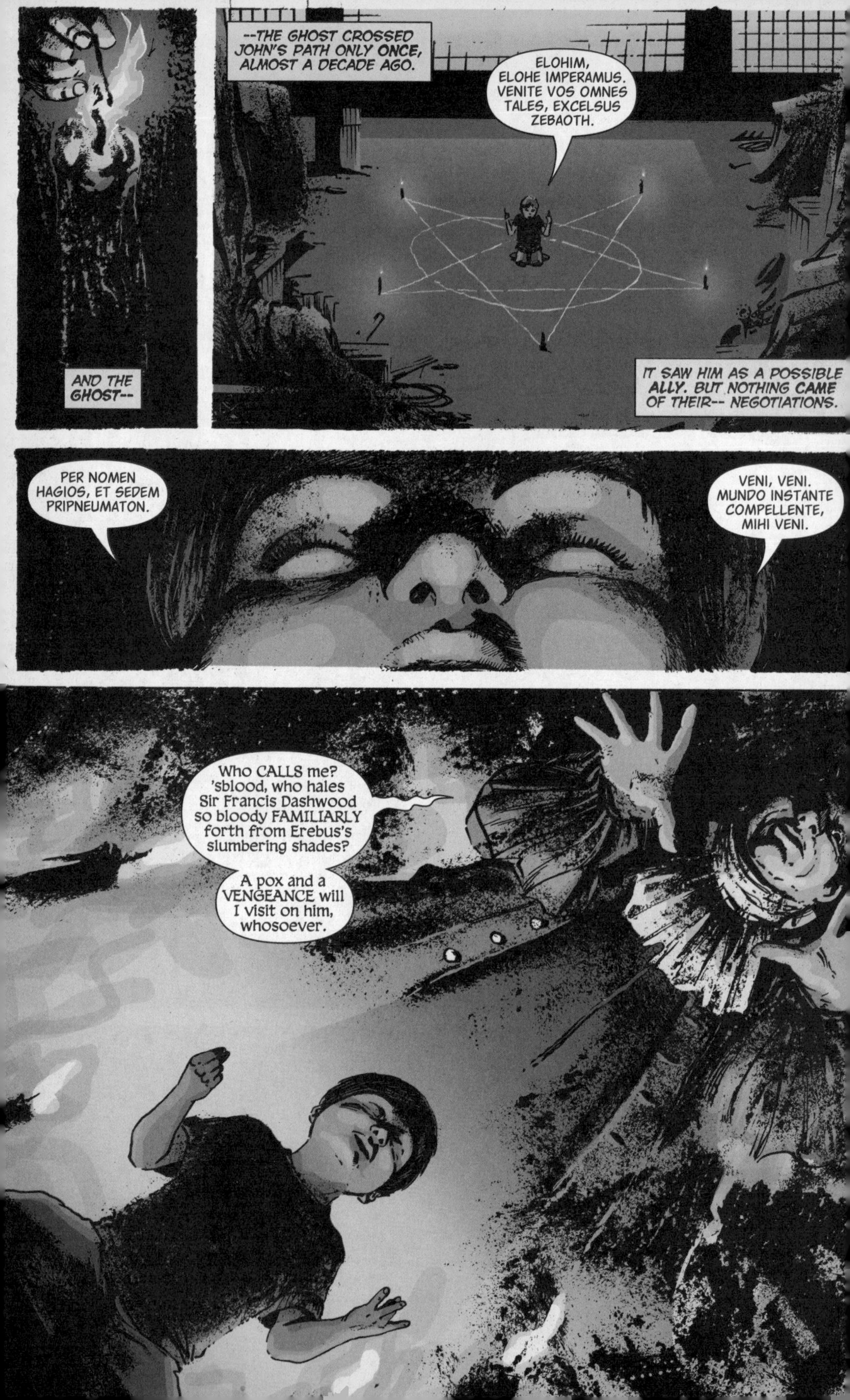
AND THE GHOST--
--THE GHOST CROSSED JOHN'S PATH ONLY ONCE, ALMOST A DECADE AGO.
ELOHIM, ELOHE IMPERAMUS. VENITE VOS OMNES TALES, EXCELSUS ZEBAOTH.
IT SAW HIM AS A POSSIBLE ALLY. BUT NOTHING CAME OF THEIR-- NEGOTIATIONS.
PER NOMEN HAGIOS, ET SEDEM PRIPNEUMATON.
VENI, VENI. MUNDO INSTANTE COMPELLENTE, MIHI VENI.
Who CALLS me? 'sblood, who hales Sir Francis Dashwood so bloody FAMILIARLY forth from Erebus's slumbering shades?
A pox and a VENGEANCE will I visit on him, whosoever.

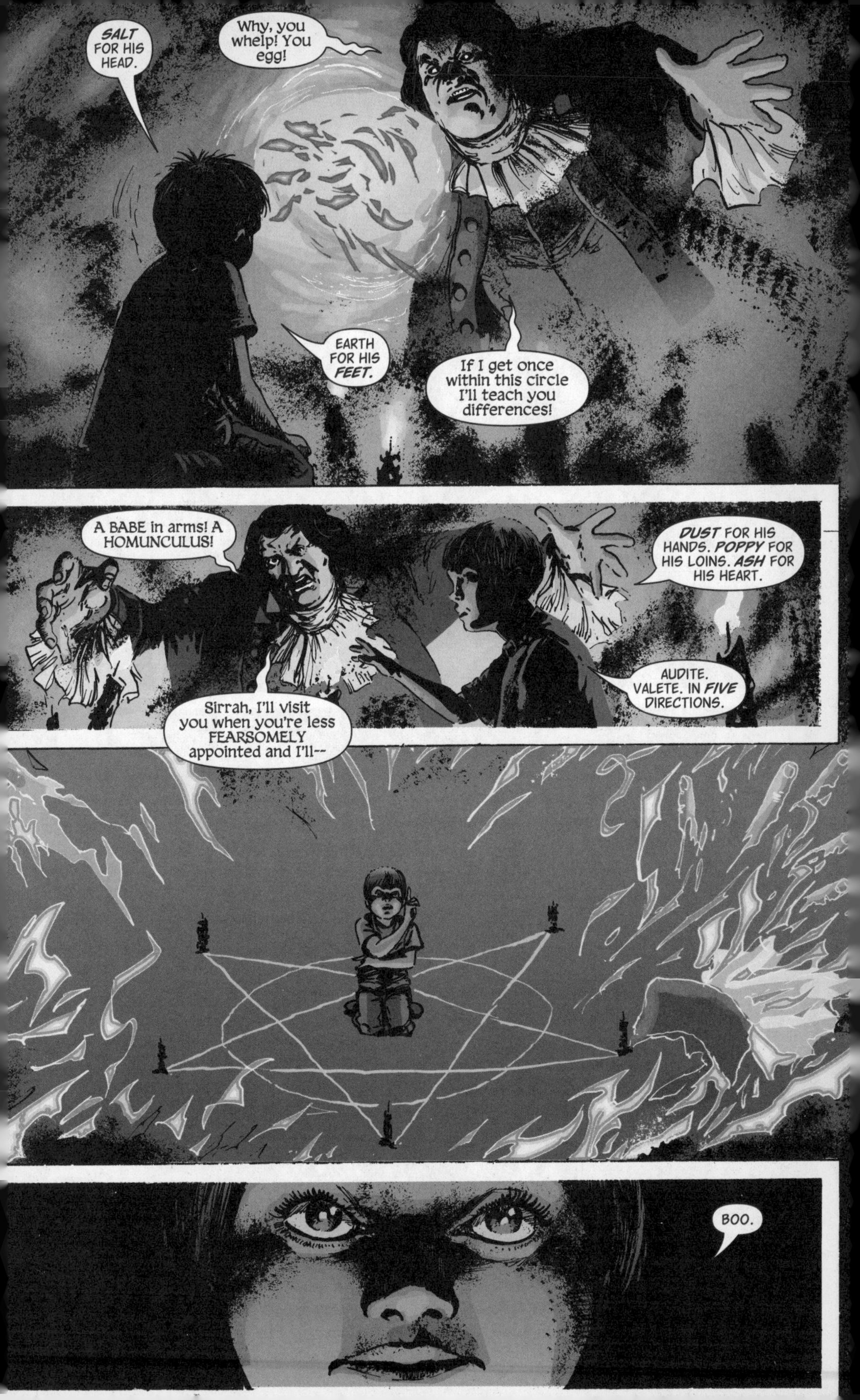
SALT FOR HIS HEAD.
Why, you whelp! You egg!
EARTH FOR HIS FEET.
If I get once within this circle I'll teach you differences!
A BABE in arms! A HOMUNCULUS!
DUST FOR HIS HANDS. POPPY FOR HIS LOINS. ASH FOR HIS HEART.
Sirrah, I'll visit you when you're less FEARSOMELY appointed and I'll--
AUDITE. VALETE. IN FIVE DIRECTIONS.
BOO.

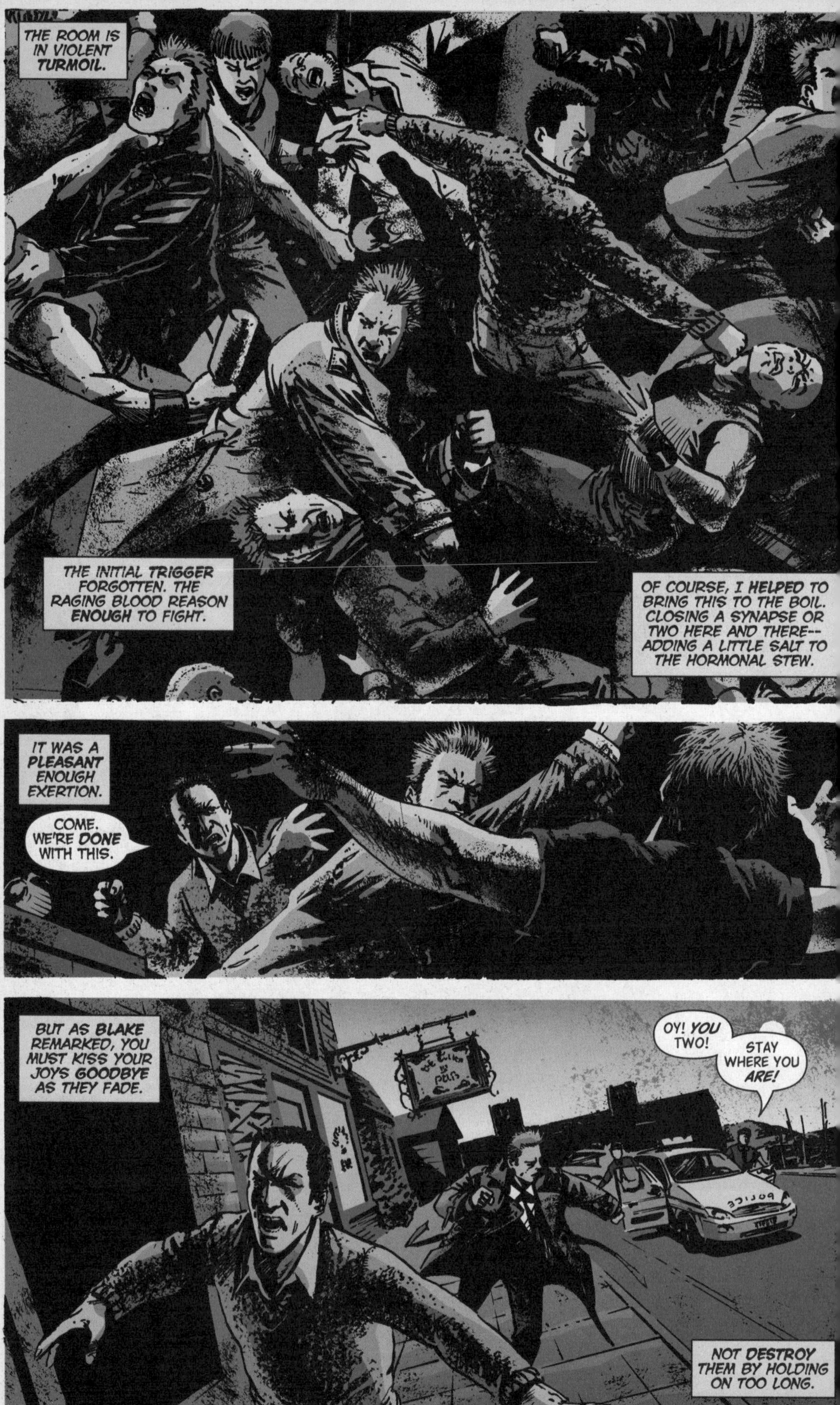
THE ROOM IS IN VIOLENT TURMOIL.
THE INITIAL TRIGGER FORGOTTEN. THE RAGING BLOOD REASON ENOUGH TO FIGHT.
OF COURSE, I HELPED TO BRING THIS TO THE BOIL. CLOSING A SYNAPSE OR TWO HERE AND THERE-- ADDING A LITTLE SALT TO THE HORMONAL STEW.
IT WAS A PLEASANT ENOUGH EXERTION.
COME. WE'RE DONE WITH THIS.
BUT AS BLAKE REMARKED, YOU MUST KISS YOUR JOYS GOODBYE AS THEY FADE.
OY! YOU TWO!
STAY WHERE YOU ARE!
POLICE
NOT DESTROY THEM BY HOLDING ON TOO LONG.

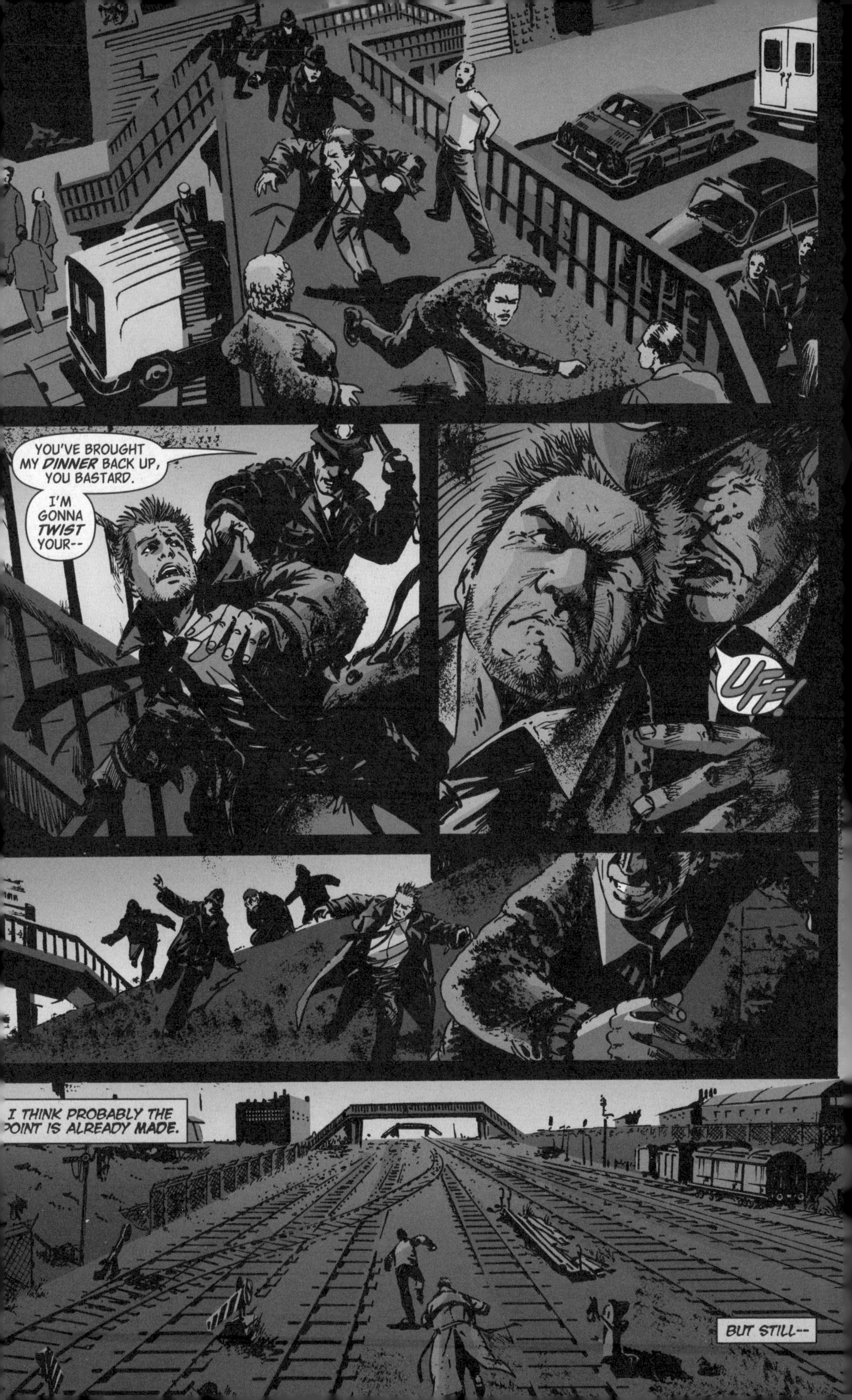
YOU'VE BROUGHT MY DINNER BACK UP, YOU BASTARD.
I'M GONNA TWIST YOUR--
UFF!
I THINK PROBABLY THE POINT IS ALREADY MADE.
BUT STILL--

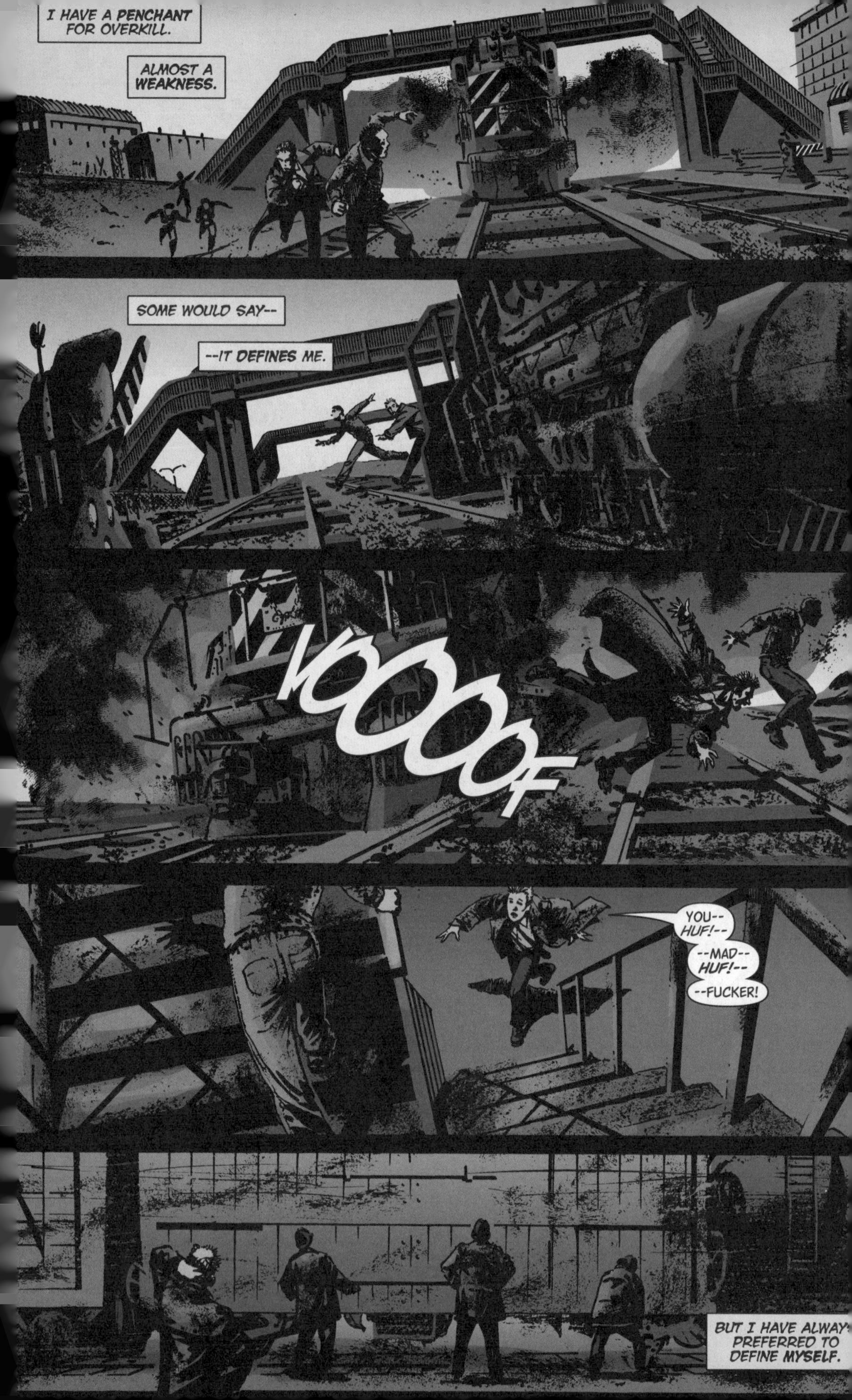
I HAVE A PENCHANT FOR OVERKILL.
ALMOST A WEAKNESS.
SOME WOULD SAY--
--IT DEFINES ME.
VOOOOF
YOU--
HUF!--
--MAD--
HUF!--
--FUCKER!
BUT I HAVE ALWAY PREFERRED TO DEFINE MYSELF.

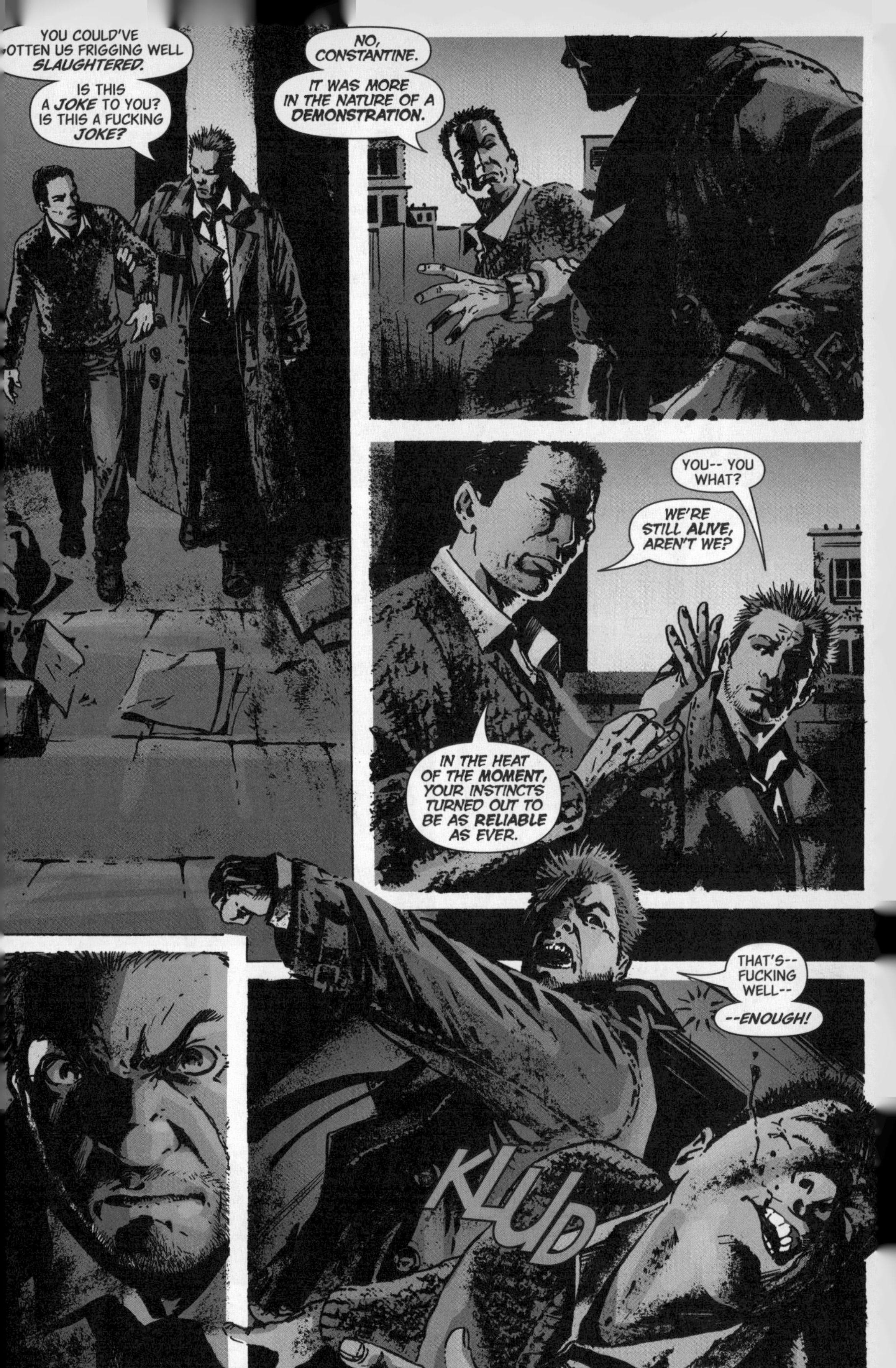

YOU COULD'VE GOTTEN US FRIGGING WELL SLAUGHTERED.
IS THIS A JOKE TO YOU? IS THIS A FUCKING JOKE?
NO, CONSTANTINE.
IT WAS MORE IN THE NATURE OF A DEMONSTRATION.
YOU-- YOU WHAT?
WE'RE STILL ALIVE, AREN'T WE?
IN THE HEAT OF THE MOMENT, YOUR INSTINCTS TURNED OUT TO BE AS RELIABLE AS EVER.
THAT'S-- FUCKING WELL--
--ENOUGH!
KLUD

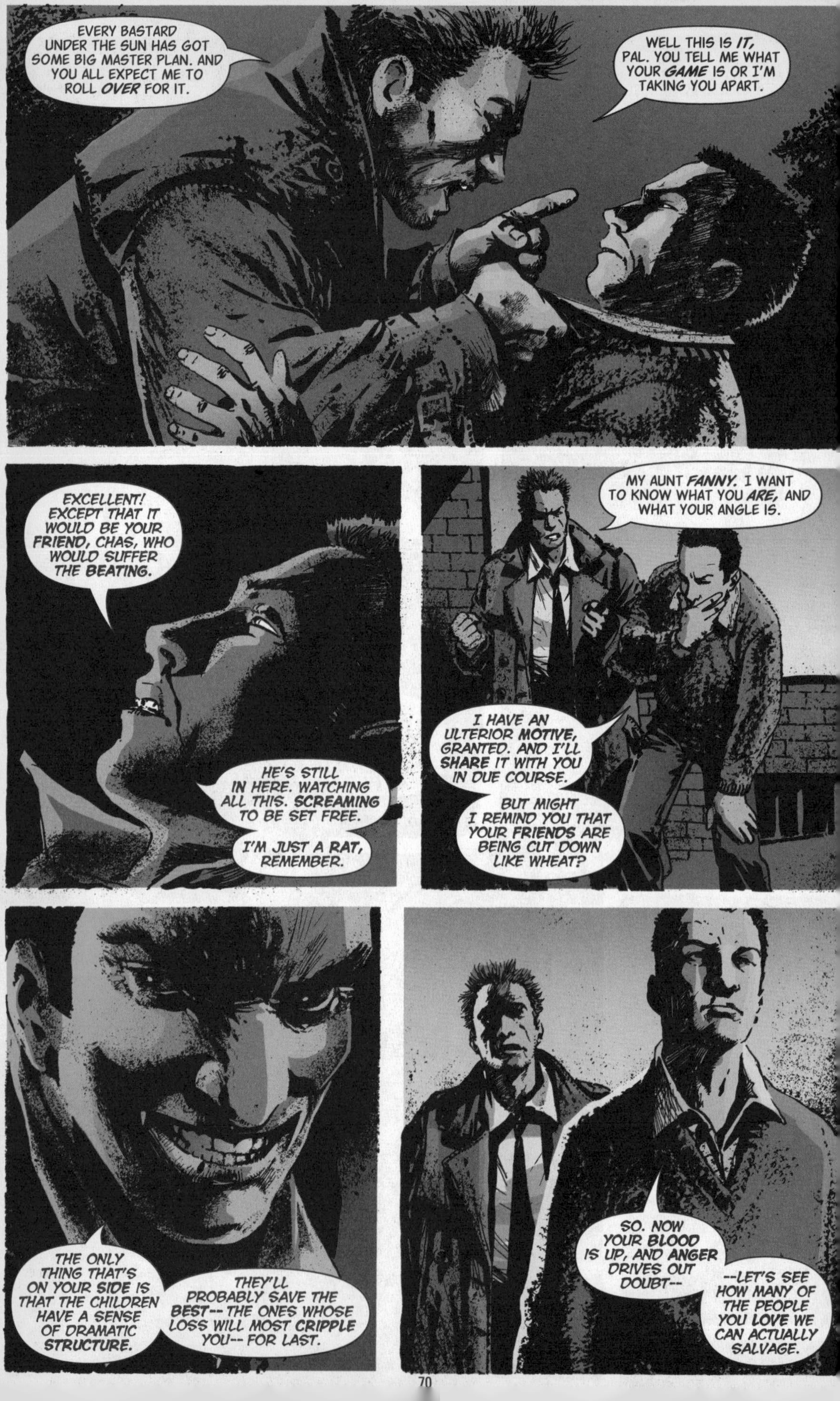
EVERY BASTARD UNDER THE SUN HAS GOT SOME BIG MASTER PLAN. AND YOU ALL EXPECT ME TO ROLL *OVER* FOR IT.
WELL THIS IS *IT,* PAL. YOU TELL ME WHAT YOUR *GAME* IS OR I'M TAKING YOU APART.
EXCELLENT! EXCEPT THAT IT WOULD BE YOUR FRIEND, CHAS, WHO WOULD SUFFER THE BEATING.
HE'S STILL IN HERE. WATCHING ALL THIS. SCREAMING TO BE SET FREE.
I'M JUST A RAT, REMEMBER.
MY AUNT *FANNY.* I WANT TO KNOW WHAT YOU *ARE,* AND WHAT YOUR ANGLE IS.
I HAVE AN ULTERIOR MOTIVE, GRANTED. AND I'LL SHARE IT WITH YOU IN DUE COURSE.
BUT MIGHT I REMIND YOU THAT YOUR FRIENDS ARE BEING CUT DOWN LIKE WHEAT?
THE ONLY THING THAT'S ON YOUR SIDE IS THAT THE CHILDREN HAVE A SENSE OF DRAMATIC STRUCTURE.
THEY'LL PROBABLY SAVE THE BEST-- THE ONES WHOSE LOSS WILL MOST CRIPPLE YOU-- FOR LAST.
SO. NOW YOUR BLOOD IS UP, AND ANGER DRIVES OUT DOUBT--
--LET'S SEE HOW MANY OF THE PEOPLE YOU LOVE WE CAN ACTUALLY SALVAGE.

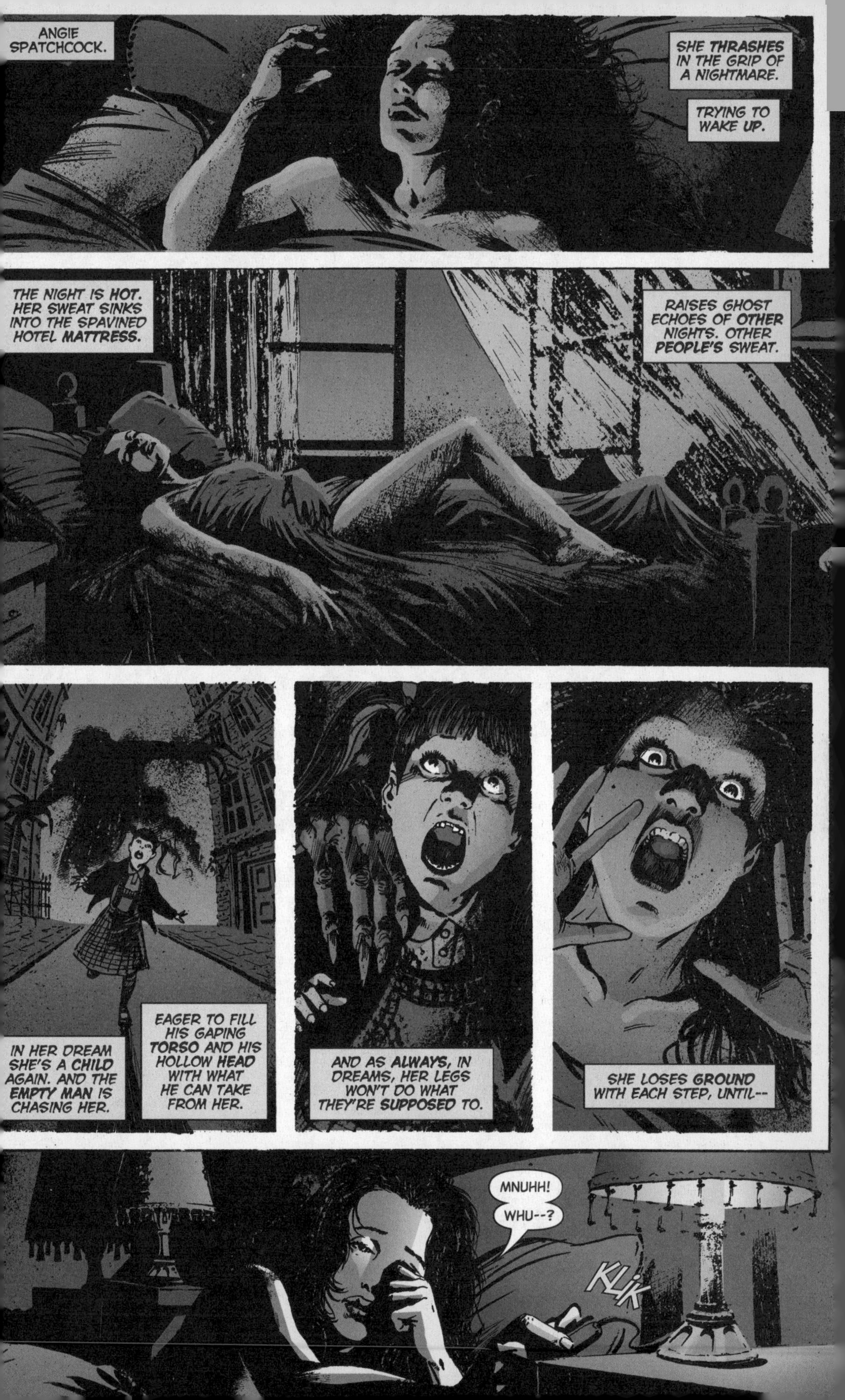

ANGIE SPATCHCOCK.
SHE THRASHES IN THE GRIP OF A NIGHTMARE.
TRYING TO WAKE UP.
THE NIGHT IS HOT. HER SWEAT SINKS INTO THE SPAVINED HOTEL MATTRESS.
RAISES GHOST ECHOES OF OTHER NIGHTS. OTHER PEOPLE'S SWEAT.
IN HER DREAM SHE'S A CHILD AGAIN. AND THE EMPTY MAN IS CHASING HER.
EAGER TO FILL HIS GAPING TORSO AND HIS HOLLOW HEAD WITH WHAT HE CAN TAKE FROM HER.
AND AS ALWAYS, IN DREAMS, HER LEGS WON'T DO WHAT THEY'RE SUPPOSED TO.
SHE LOSES GROUND WITH EACH STEP, UNTIL--
MNUHH!
WHU--?
KLIK

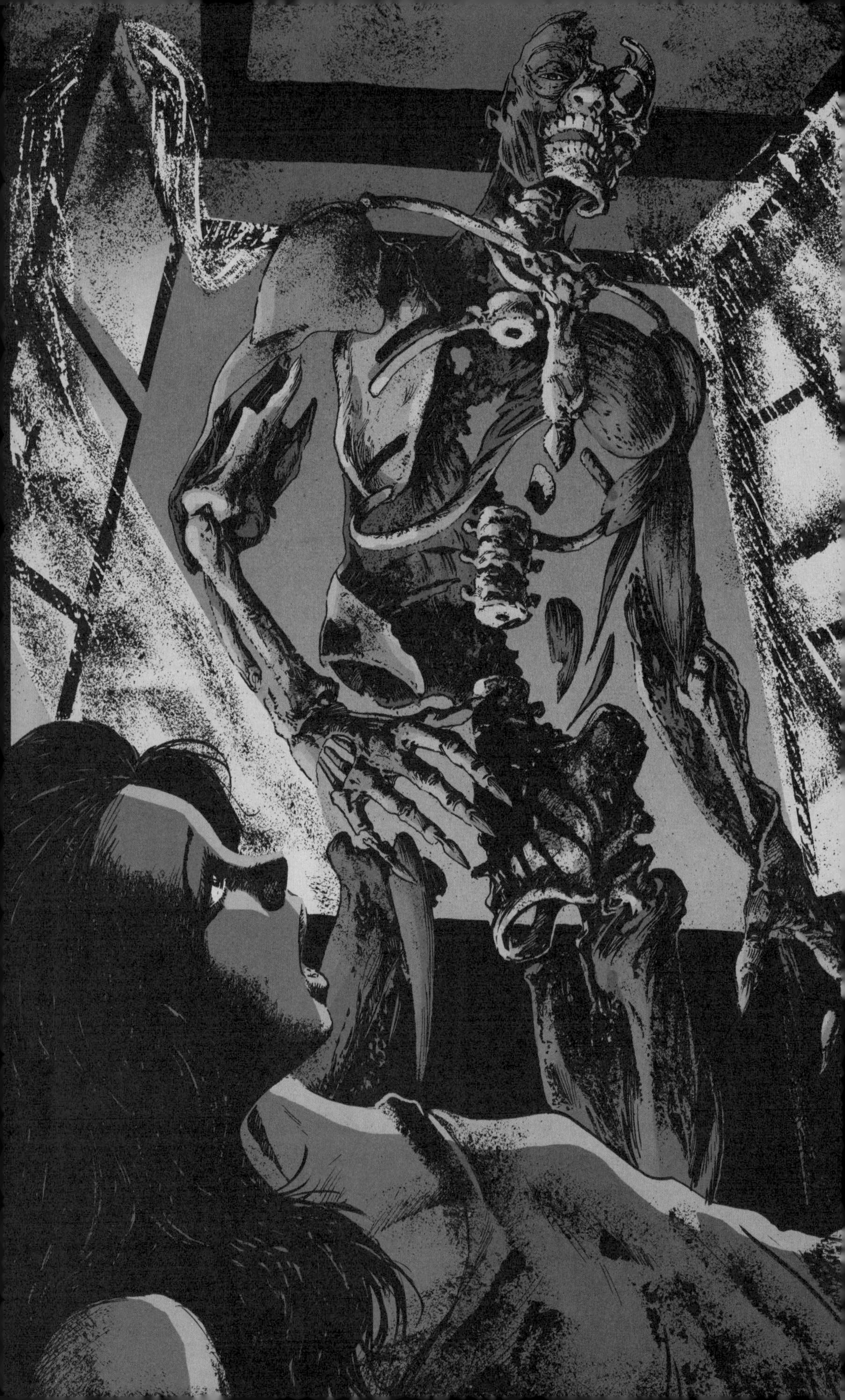

GEMMA MASTERS.

MOMMA WON'T MISS YOU, MOMMA WON'T MISS YOU, MOMMA WON'T FUCKING MISS YOU MUUUUUUUCH!

NNA THER IN, ?

YOU GEM. AM.

YEAH, OKAY, SIMON.

OKAY, LET'S DO IT.

NOT HERE.

IT'S OUT IN THE VAN.

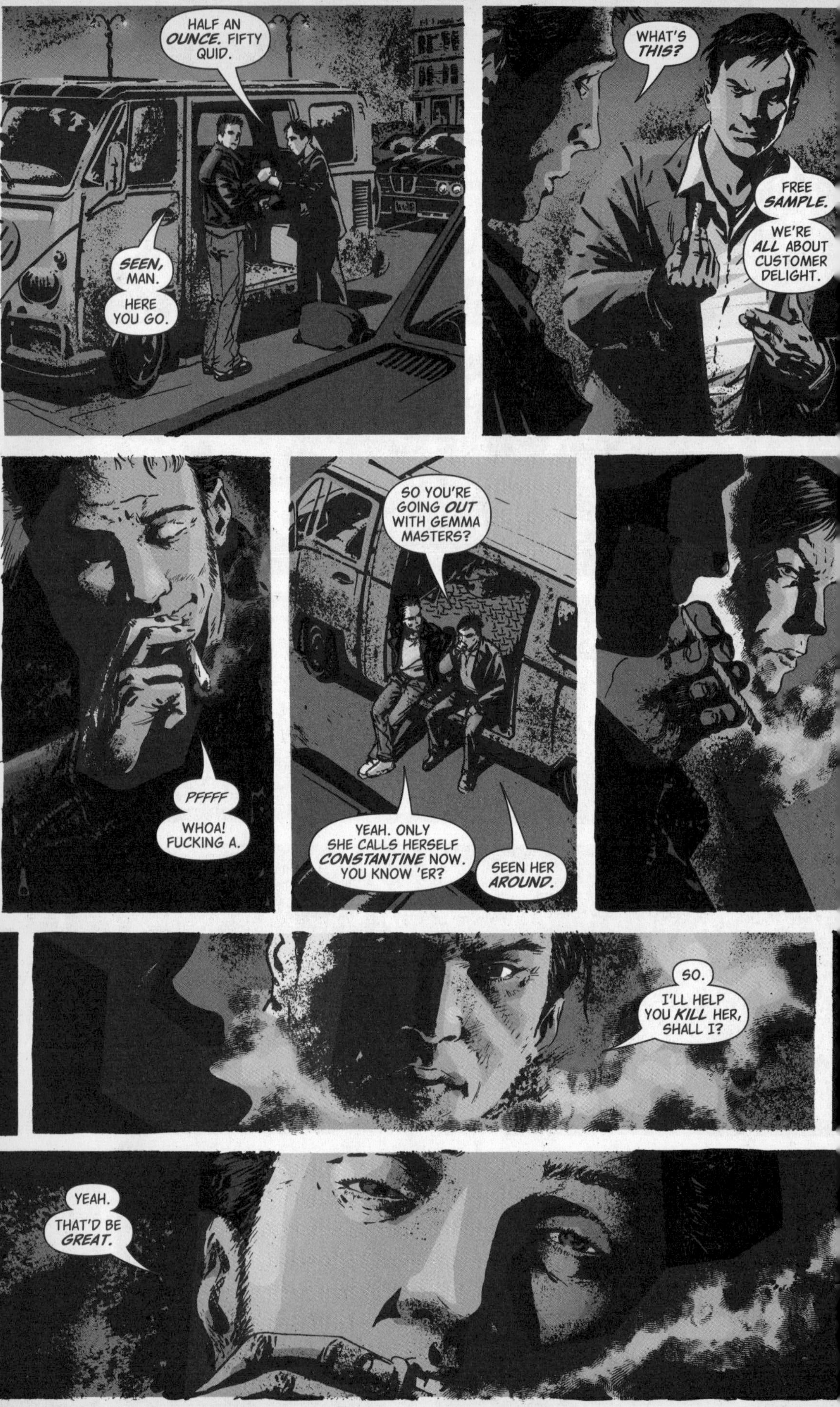
HALF AN OUNCE. FIFTY QUID.
SEEN, MAN.
HERE YOU GO.
WHAT'S THIS?
FREE SAMPLE.
WE'RE ALL ABOUT CUSTOMER DELIGHT.
PFFFF
WHOA! FUCKING A.
SO YOU'RE GOING OUT WITH GEMMA MASTERS?
YEAH. ONLY SHE CALLS HERSELF CONSTANTINE NOW. YOU KNOW 'ER?
SEEN HER AROUND.
SO.
I'LL HELP YOU KILL HER, SHALL I?
YEAH.
THAT'D BE GREAT.

Reasons to be Cheerful CHAPTER THREE

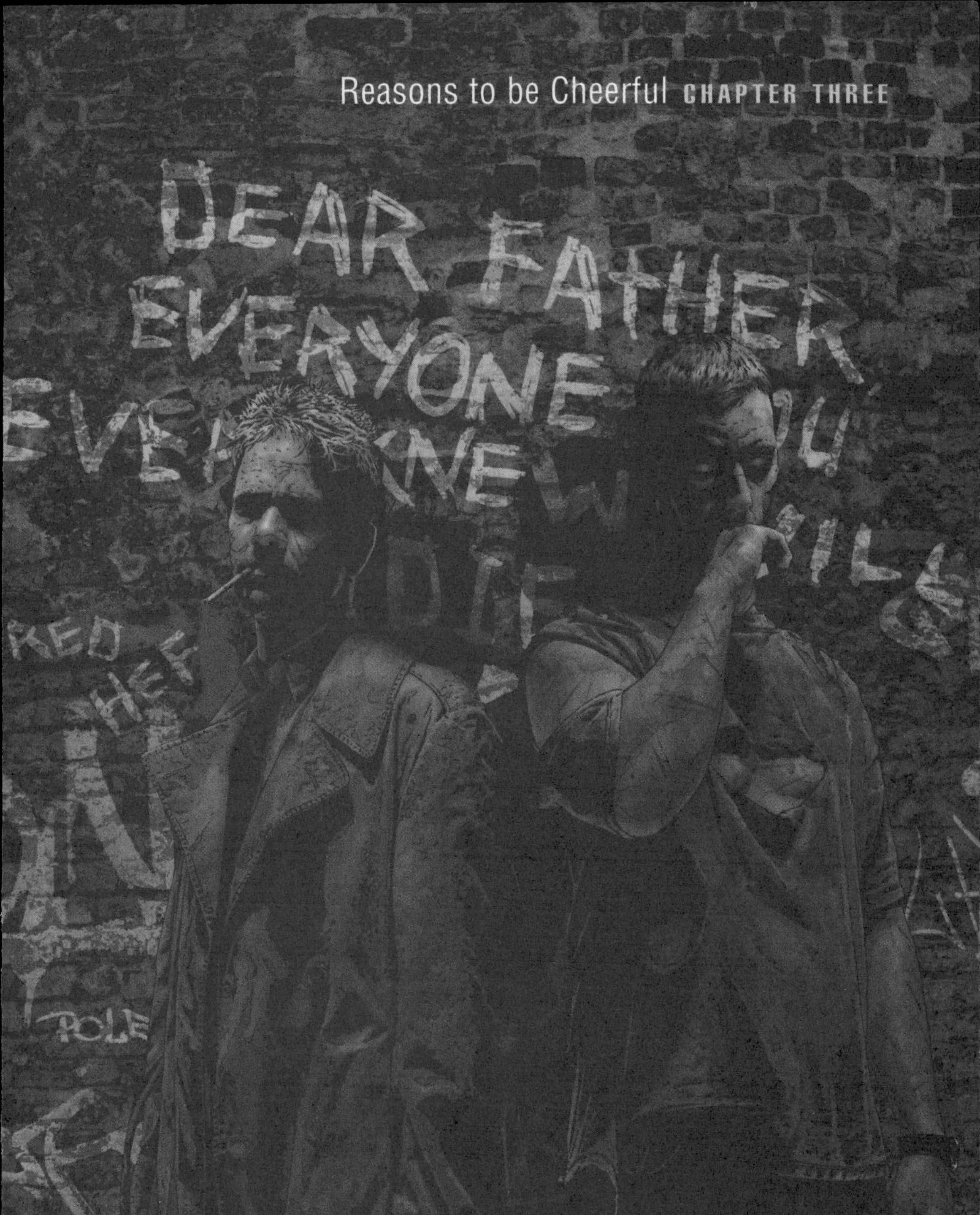
DEAR FATHER
EVERYONE
POLE

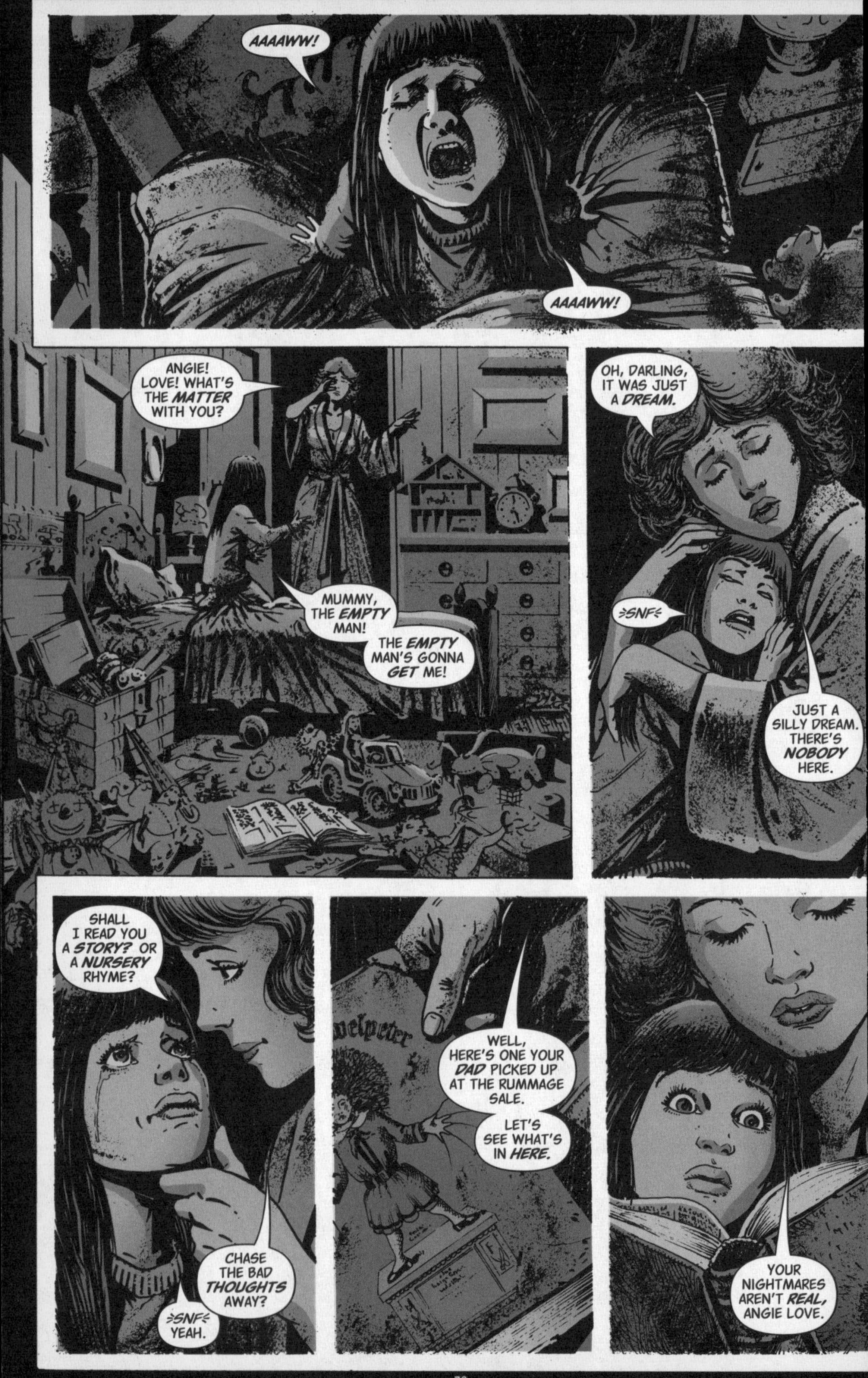
AAAAWW!
AAAAWW!
ANGIE! LOVE! WHAT'S THE MATTER WITH YOU?
MUMMY, THE EMPTY MAN!
THE EMPTY MAN'S GONNA GET ME!
OH, DARLING, IT WAS JUST A DREAM.
SNF
JUST A SILLY DREAM. THERE'S NOBODY HERE.
SHALL I READ YOU A STORY? OR A NURSERY RHYME?
CHASE THE BAD THOUGHTS AWAY?
SNF YEAH.
WELL, HERE'S ONE YOUR DAD PICKED UP AT THE RUMMAGE SALE.
LET'S SEE WHAT'S IN HERE.
YOUR NIGHTMARES AREN'T REAL, ANGIE LOVE.

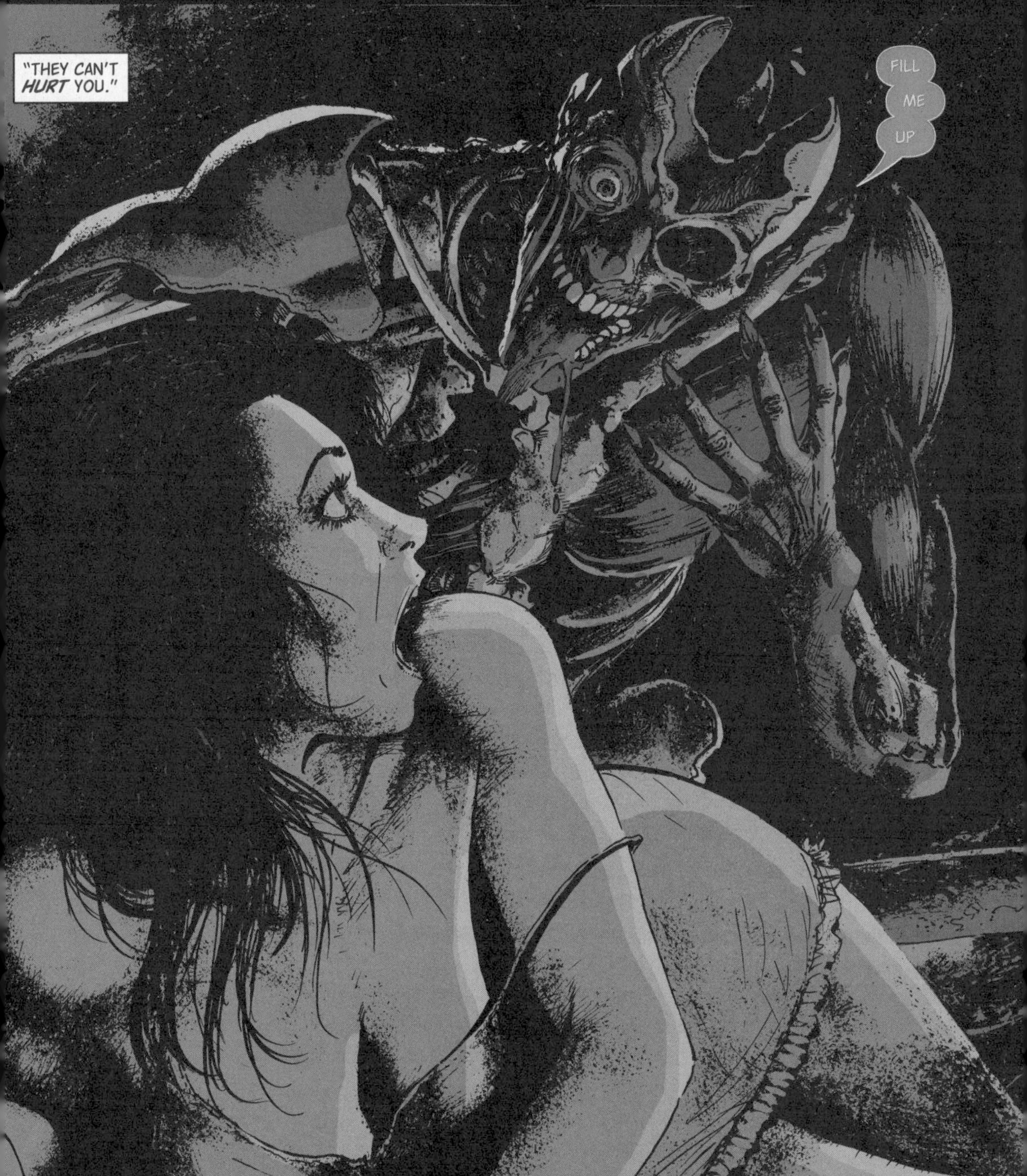
"THEY CAN'T *HURT* YOU."
FILL ME UP

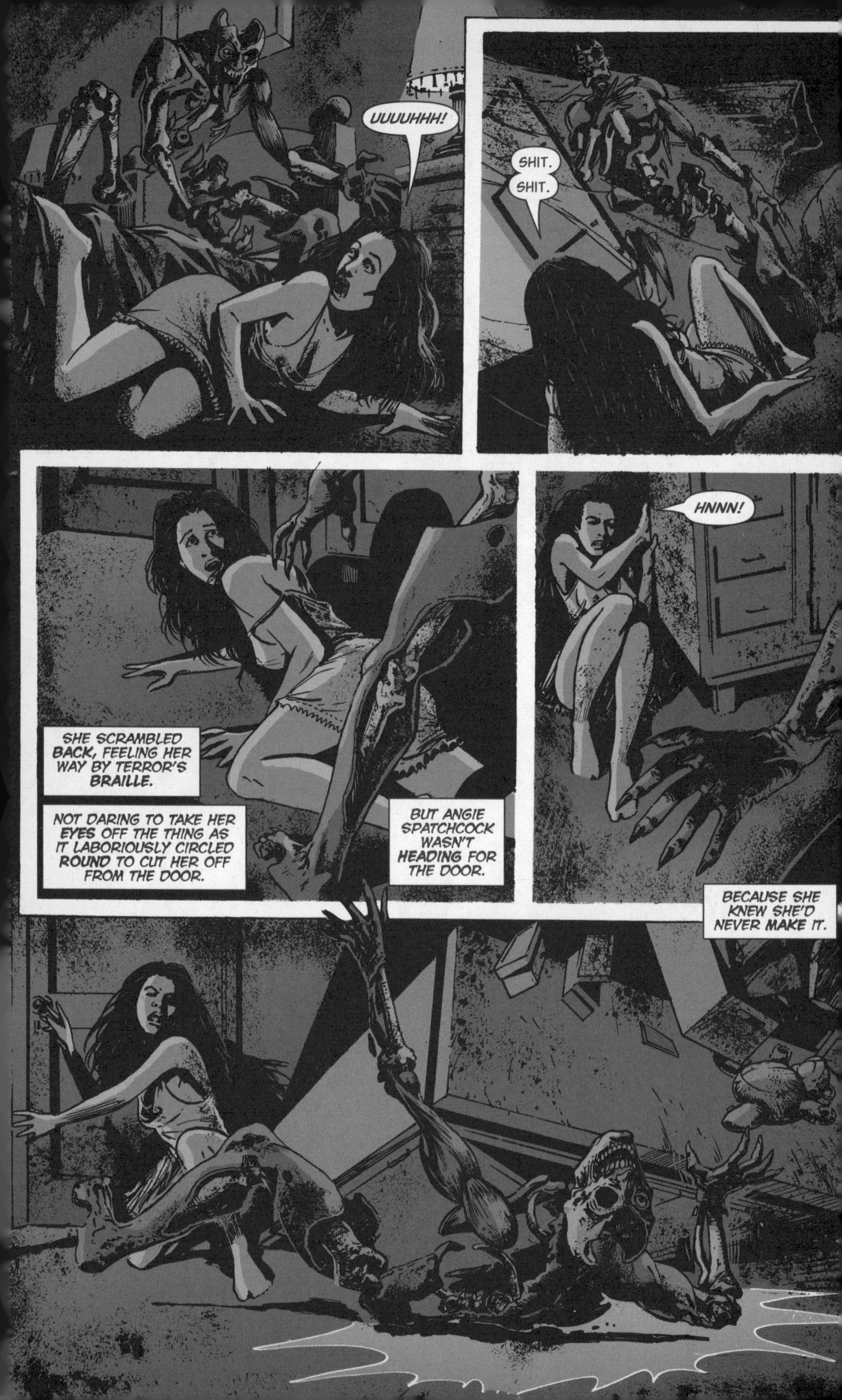

UUUUHHH!
SHIT.
SHIT.
SHE SCRAMBLED BACK, FEELING HER WAY BY TERROR'S BRAILLE.
NOT DARING TO TAKE HER EYES OFF THE THING AS IT LABORIOUSLY CIRCLED ROUND TO CUT HER OFF FROM THE DOOR.
BUT ANGIE SPATCHCOCK WASN'T HEADING FOR THE DOOR.
HNNN!
BECAUSE SHE KNEW SHE'D NEVER MAKE IT.

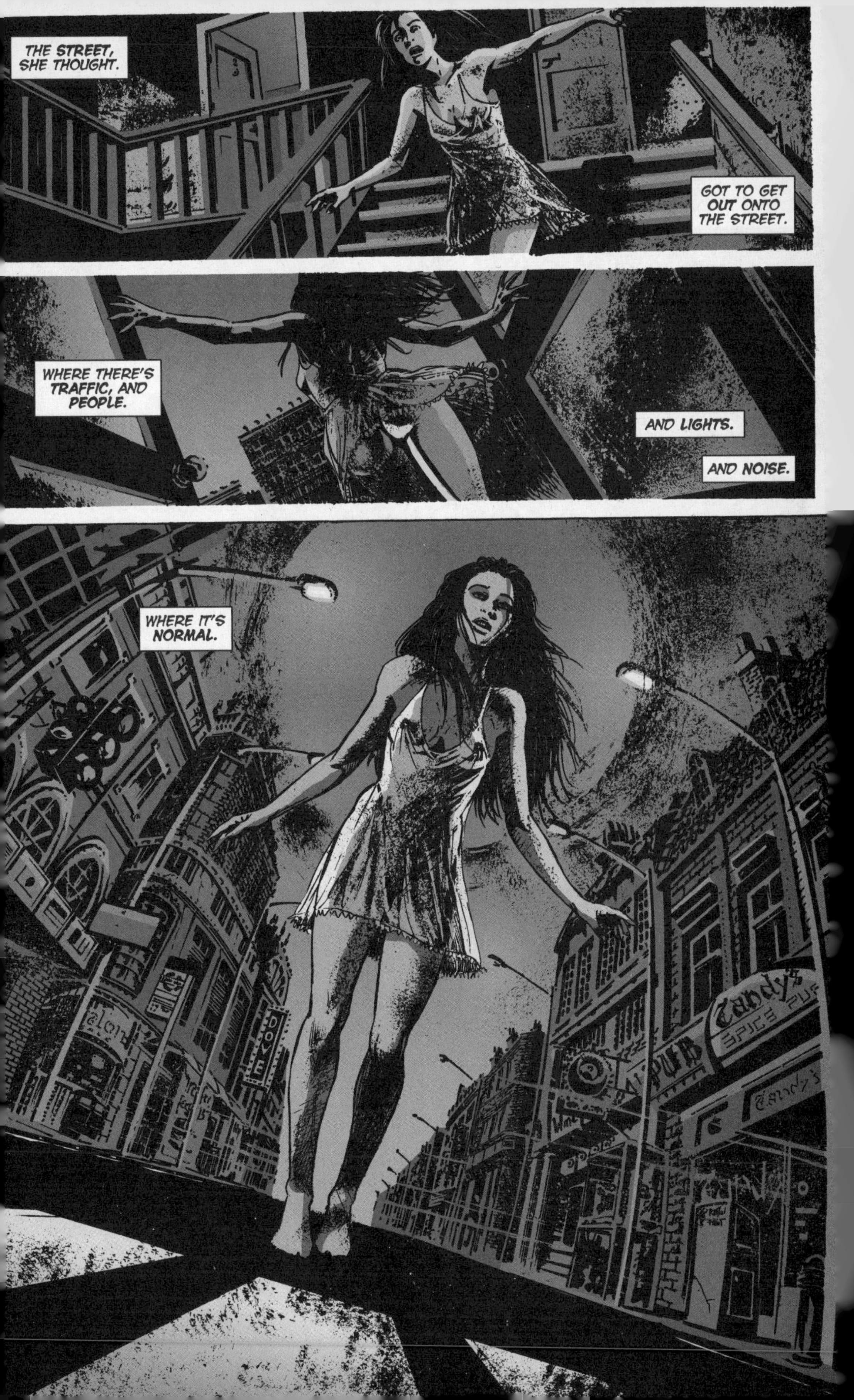
THE STREET, SHE THOUGHT.
GOT TO GET OUT ONTO THE STREET.
WHERE THERE'S TRAFFIC, AND PEOPLE.
AND LIGHTS.
AND NOISE.
WHERE IT'S NORMAL.
DOVE
PUB
Candy's
SPICE PUB

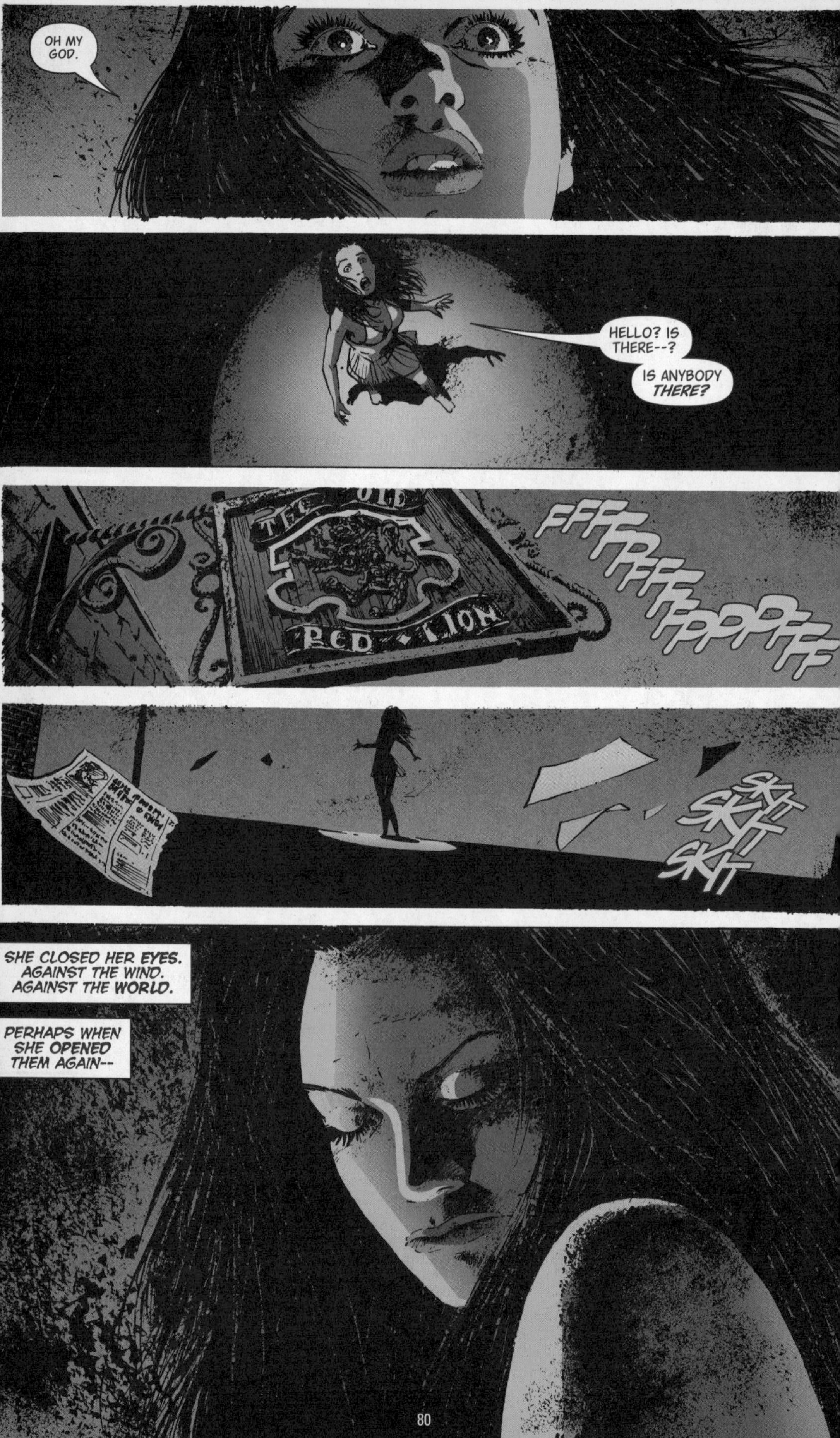
OH MY GOD.
HELLO? IS THERE--?
IS ANYBODY *THERE?*
FFFFFPFFFFFPPPPFFFF
SKIT SKIT SKIT
SHE CLOSED HER EYES. AGAINST THE WIND. AGAINST THE WORLD.
PERHAPS WHEN SHE OPENED THEM AGAIN--

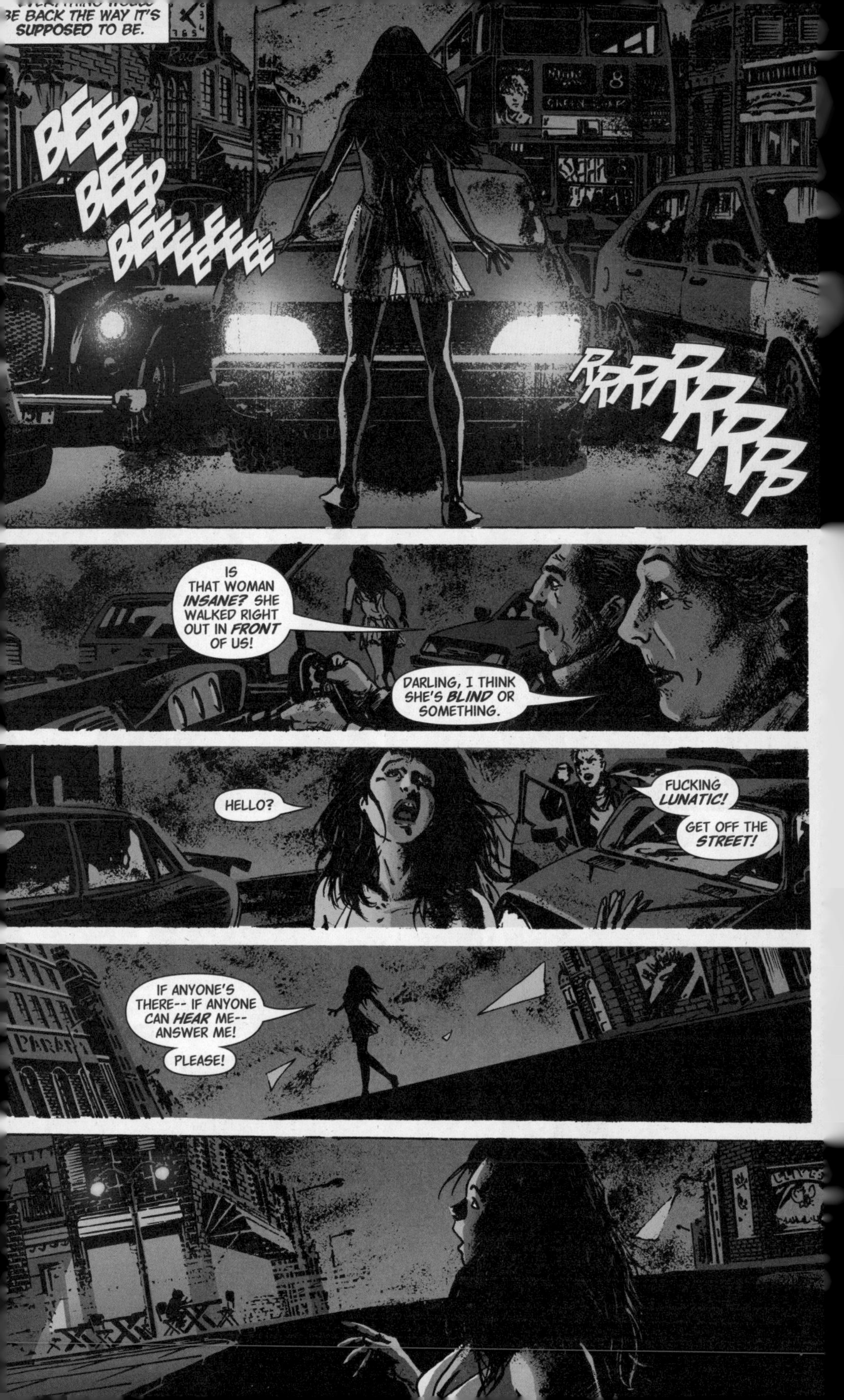
BE BACK THE WAY IT'S SUPPOSED TO BE.
BEEP
BEEP
IS THAT WOMAN *INSANE?* SHE WALKED RIGHT OUT IN *FRONT* OF US!
DARLING, I THINK SHE'S *BLIND* OR SOMETHING.
HELLO?
FUCKING *LUNATIC!*
GET OFF THE *STREET!*
IF ANYONE'S THERE-- IF ANYONE CAN *HEAR* ME-- ANSWER ME!
PLEASE!

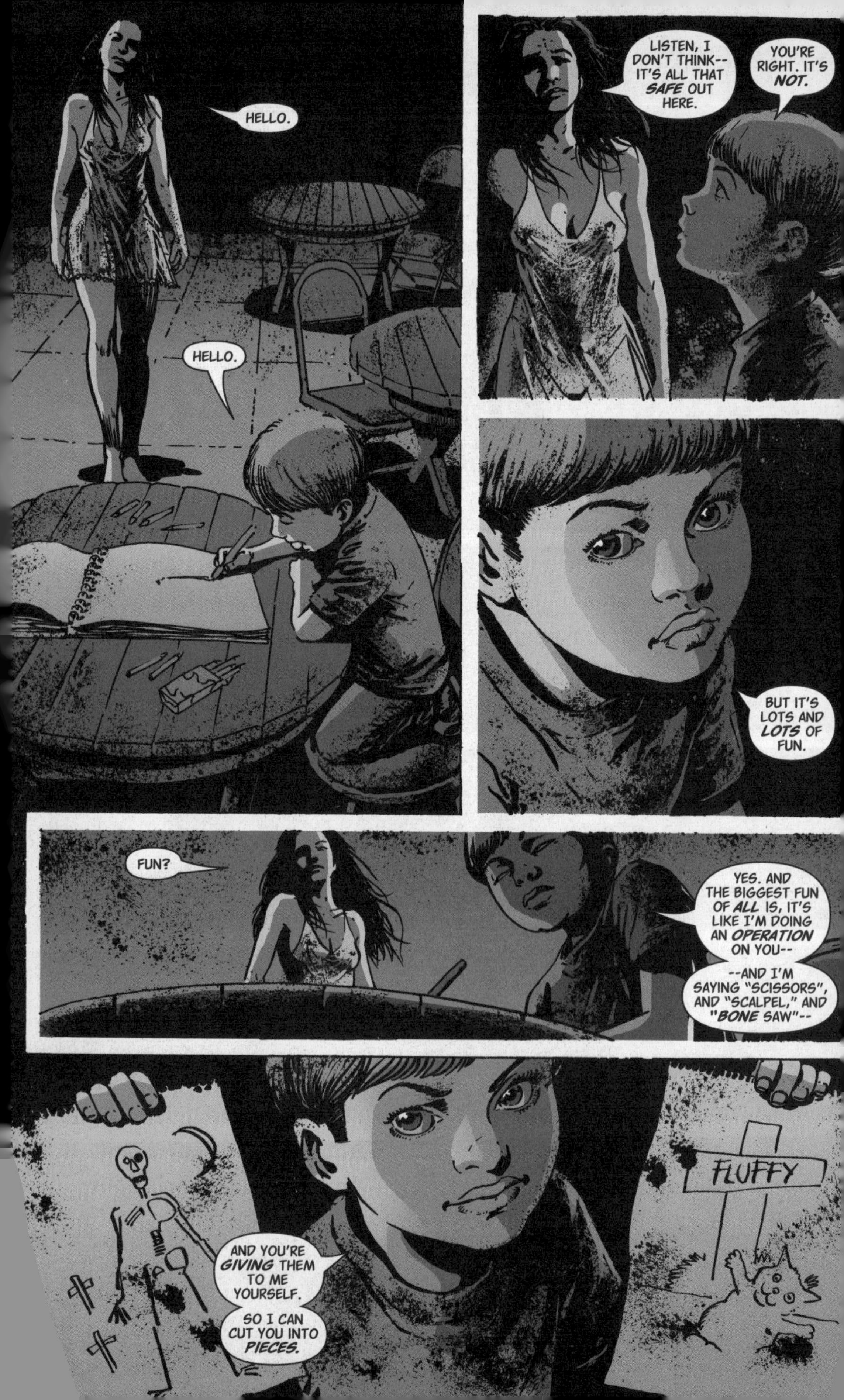
HELLO.
HELLO.
LISTEN, I DON'T THINK-- IT'S ALL THAT SAFE OUT HERE.
YOU'RE RIGHT. IT'S NOT.
BUT IT'S LOTS AND LOTS OF FUN.
FUN?
YES. AND THE BIGGEST FUN OF ALL IS, IT'S LIKE I'M DOING AN OPERATION ON YOU--
--AND I'M SAYING "SCISSORS", AND "SCALPEL," AND "BONE SAW"--
FLUFFY
AND YOU'RE GIVING THEM TO ME YOURSELF.
SO I CAN CUT YOU INTO PIECES.

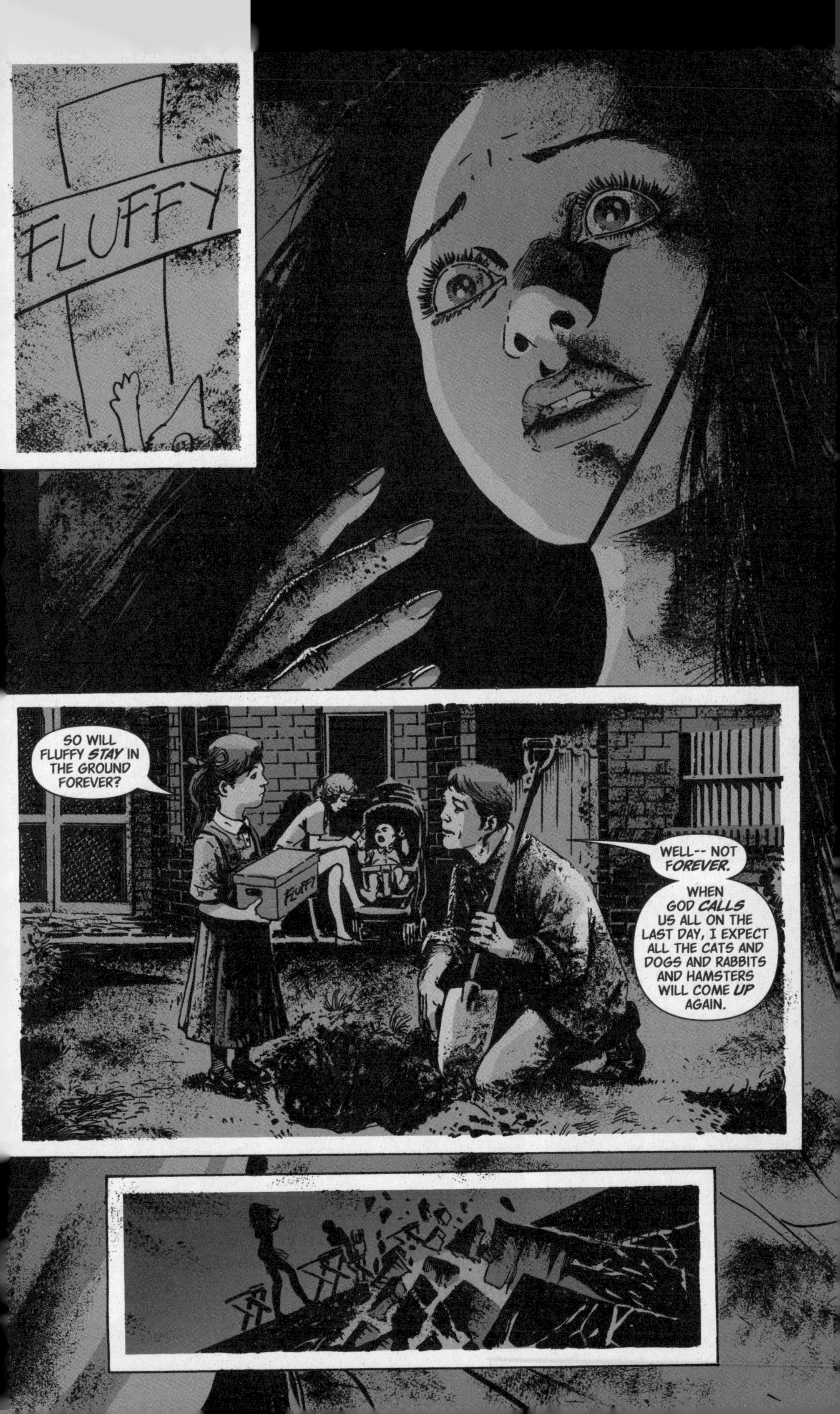
FLUFFY
SO WILL FLUFFY STAY IN THE GROUND FOREVER?
FLUFFY
WELL-- NOT FOREVER.
WHEN GOD CALLS US ALL ON THE LAST DAY, I EXPECT ALL THE CATS AND DOGS AND RABBITS AND HAMSTERS WILL COME UP AGAIN.

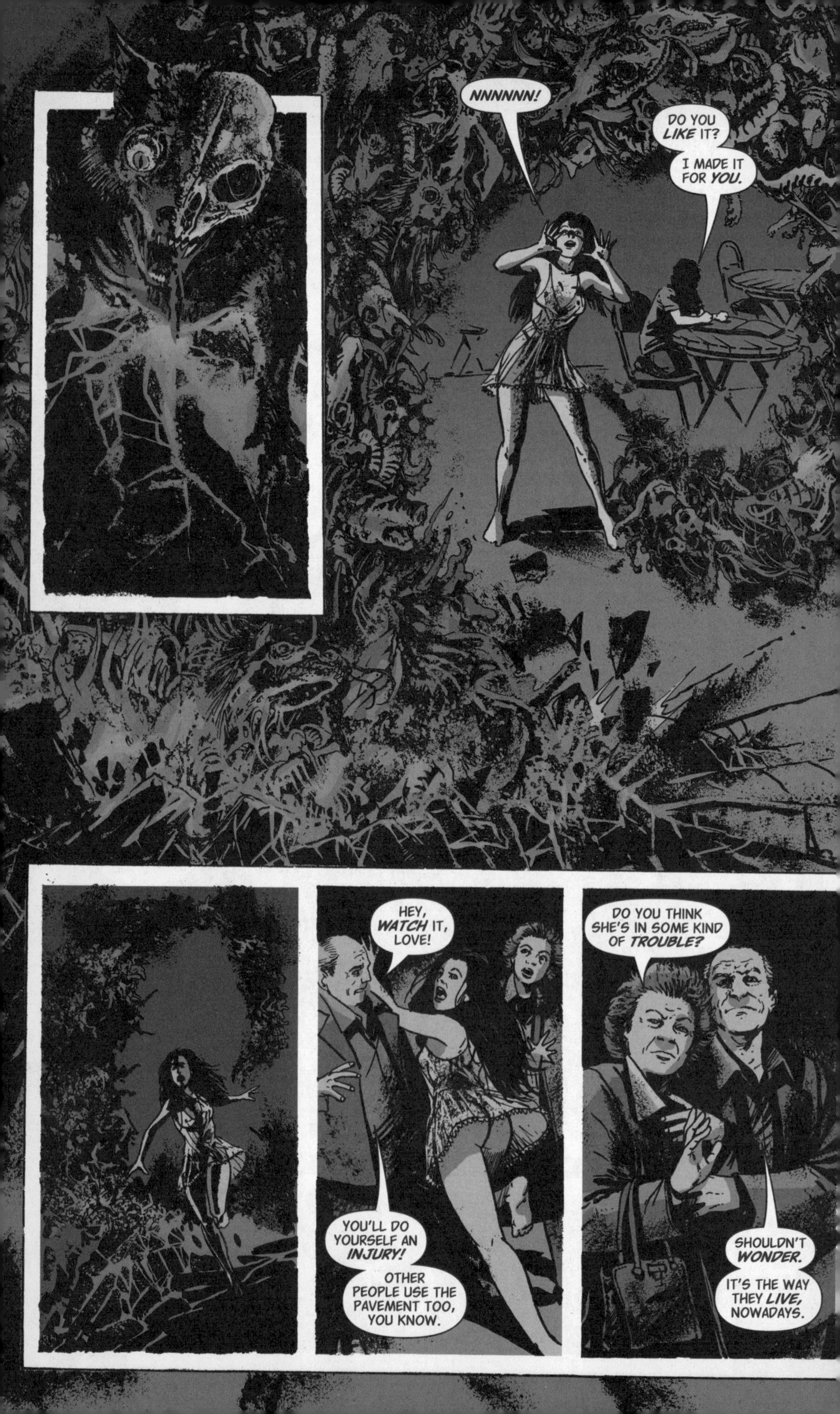
NNNNNN!
DO YOU LIKE IT?
I MADE IT FOR YOU.
HEY, WATCH IT, LOVE!
YOU'LL DO YOURSELF AN INJURY!
OTHER PEOPLE USE THE PAVEMENT TOO, YOU KNOW.
DO YOU THINK SHE'S IN SOME KIND OF TROUBLE?
SHOULDN'T WONDER.
IT'S THE WAY THEY LIVE, NOWADAYS.

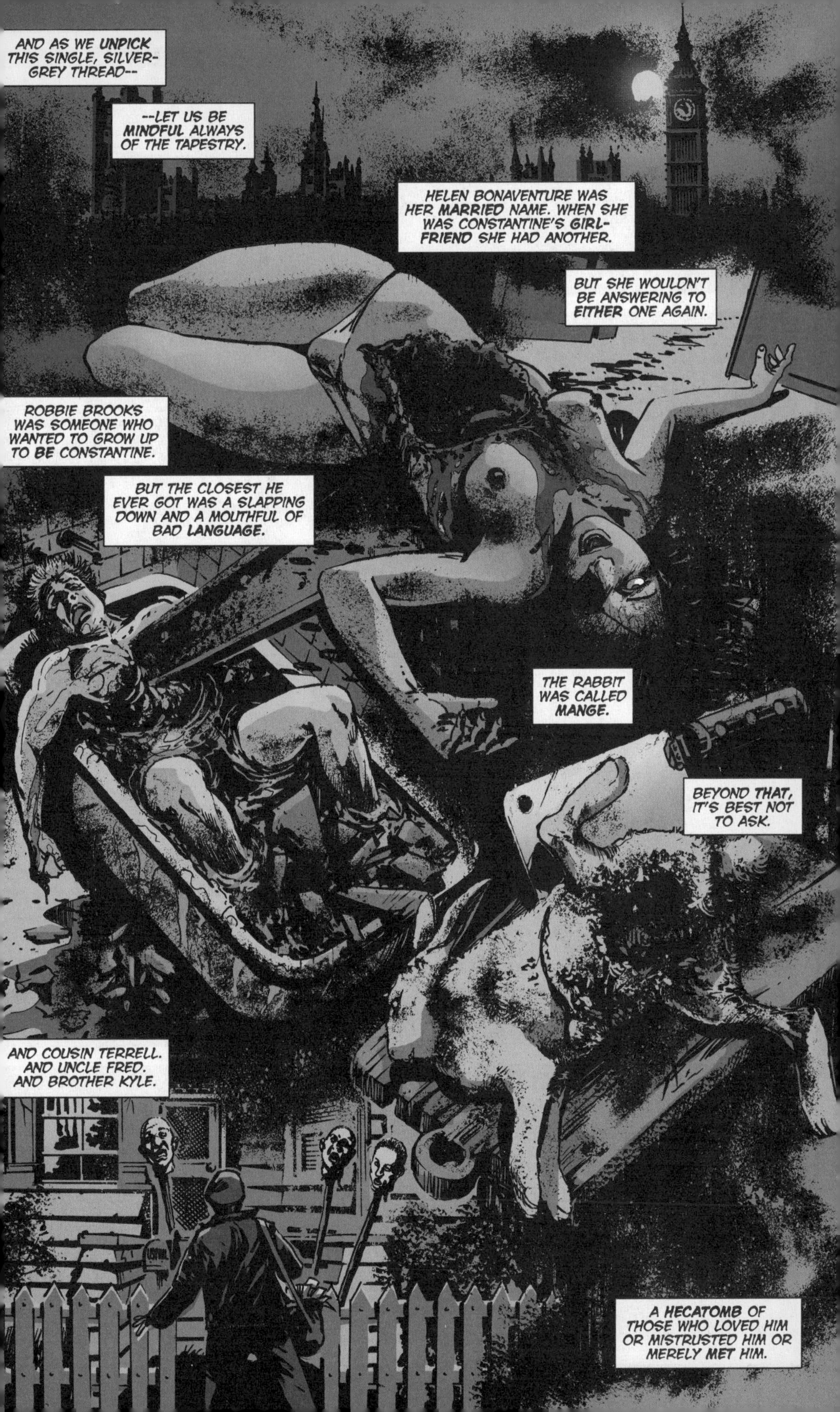
AND AS WE UNPICK THIS SINGLE, SILVER-GREY THREAD--
--LET US BE MINDFUL ALWAYS OF THE TAPESTRY.
HELEN BONAVENTURE WAS HER MARRIED NAME. WHEN SHE WAS CONSTANTINE'S GIRL-FRIEND SHE HAD ANOTHER.
BUT SHE WOULDN'T BE ANSWERING TO EITHER ONE AGAIN.
ROBBIE BROOKS WAS SOMEONE WHO WANTED TO GROW UP TO BE CONSTANTINE.
BUT THE CLOSEST HE EVER GOT WAS A SLAPPING DOWN AND A MOUTHFUL OF BAD LANGUAGE.
THE RABBIT WAS CALLED MANGE.
BEYOND THAT, IT'S BEST NOT TO ASK.
AND COUSIN TERRELL. AND UNCLE FRED. AND BROTHER KYLE.
A HECATOMB OF THOSE WHO LOVED HIM OR MISTRUSTED HIM OR MERELY MET HIM.

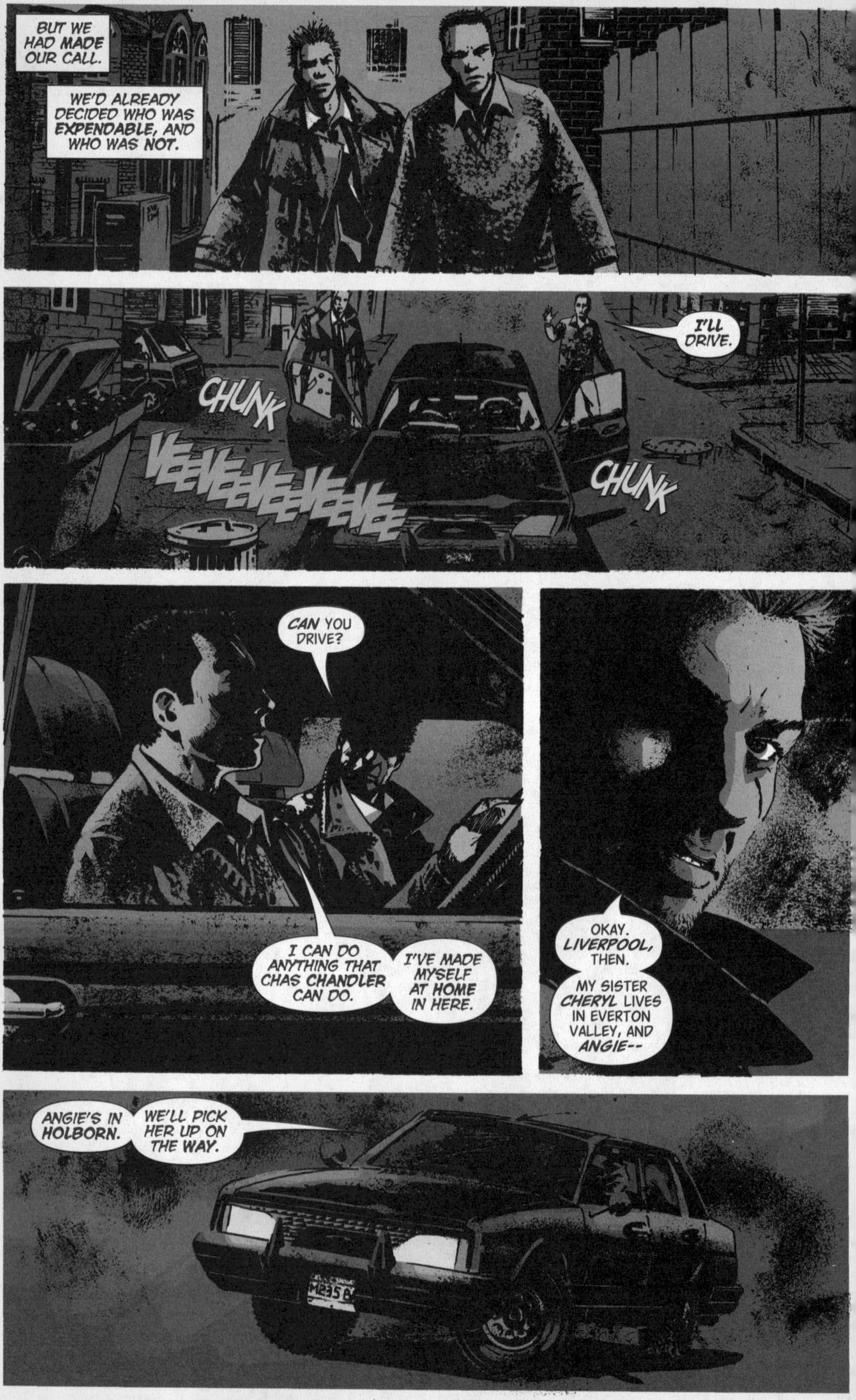

BUT WE HAD MADE OUR CALL.
WE'D ALREADY DECIDED WHO WAS EXPENDABLE, AND WHO WAS NOT.
I'LL DRIVE.
CHUNK
VEEEVEEEVEEEVEEEVEEE
CHUNK
CAN YOU DRIVE?
I CAN DO ANYTHING THAT CHAS CHANDLER CAN DO.
I'VE MADE MYSELF AT HOME IN HERE.
OKAY. LIVERPOOL, THEN.
MY SISTER CHERYL LIVES IN EVERTON VALLEY, AND ANGIE--
ANGIE'S IN HOLBORN.
WE'LL PICK HER UP ON THE WAY.

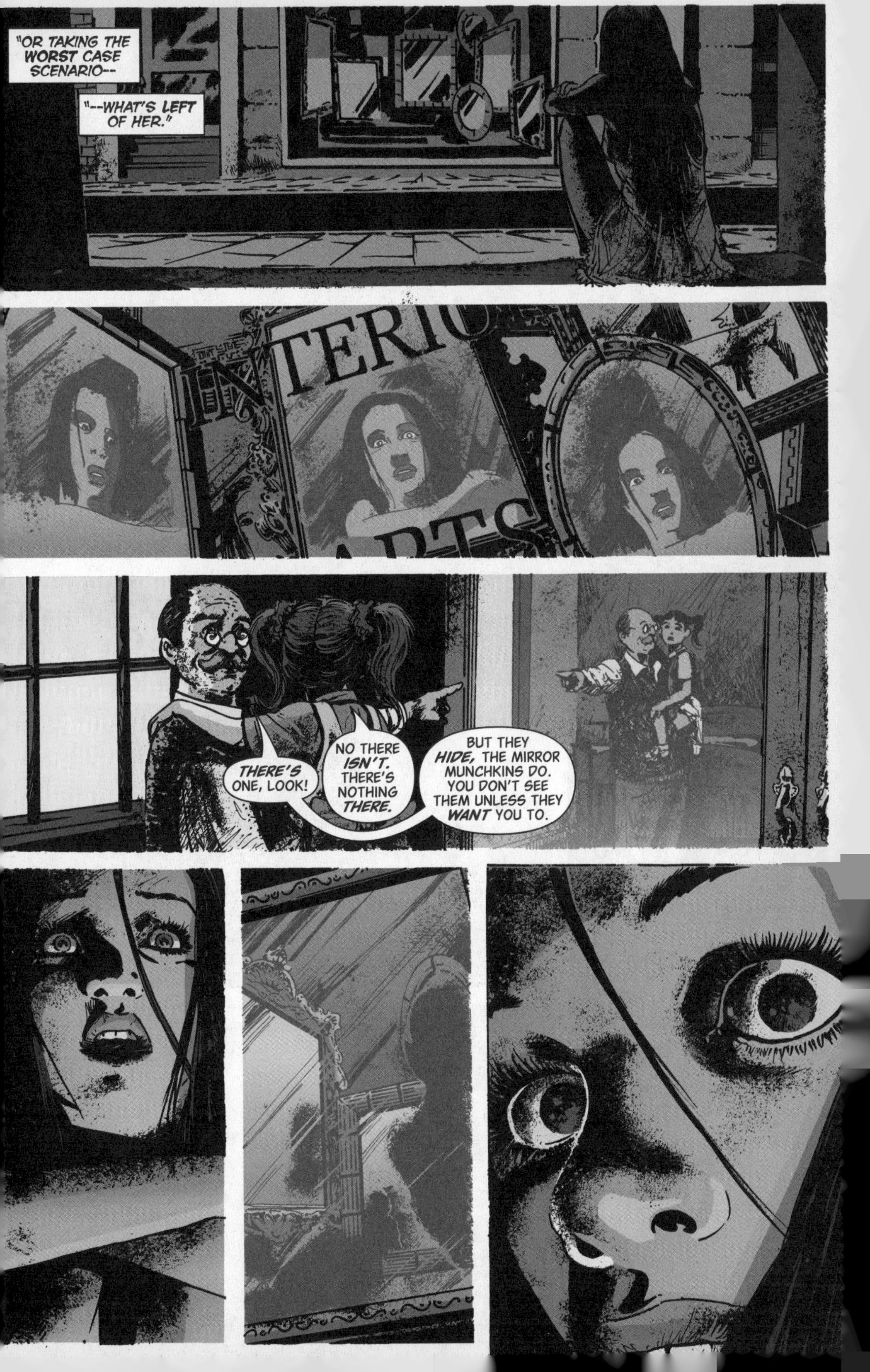
"OR TAKING THE WORST CASE SCENARIO--
"--WHAT'S LEFT OF HER."
INTERIO
ARTS
THERE'S ONE, LOOK!
NO THERE ISN'T. THERE'S NOTHING THERE.
BUT THEY HIDE, THE MIRROR MUNCHKINS DO. YOU DON'T SEE THEM UNLESS THEY WANT YOU TO.

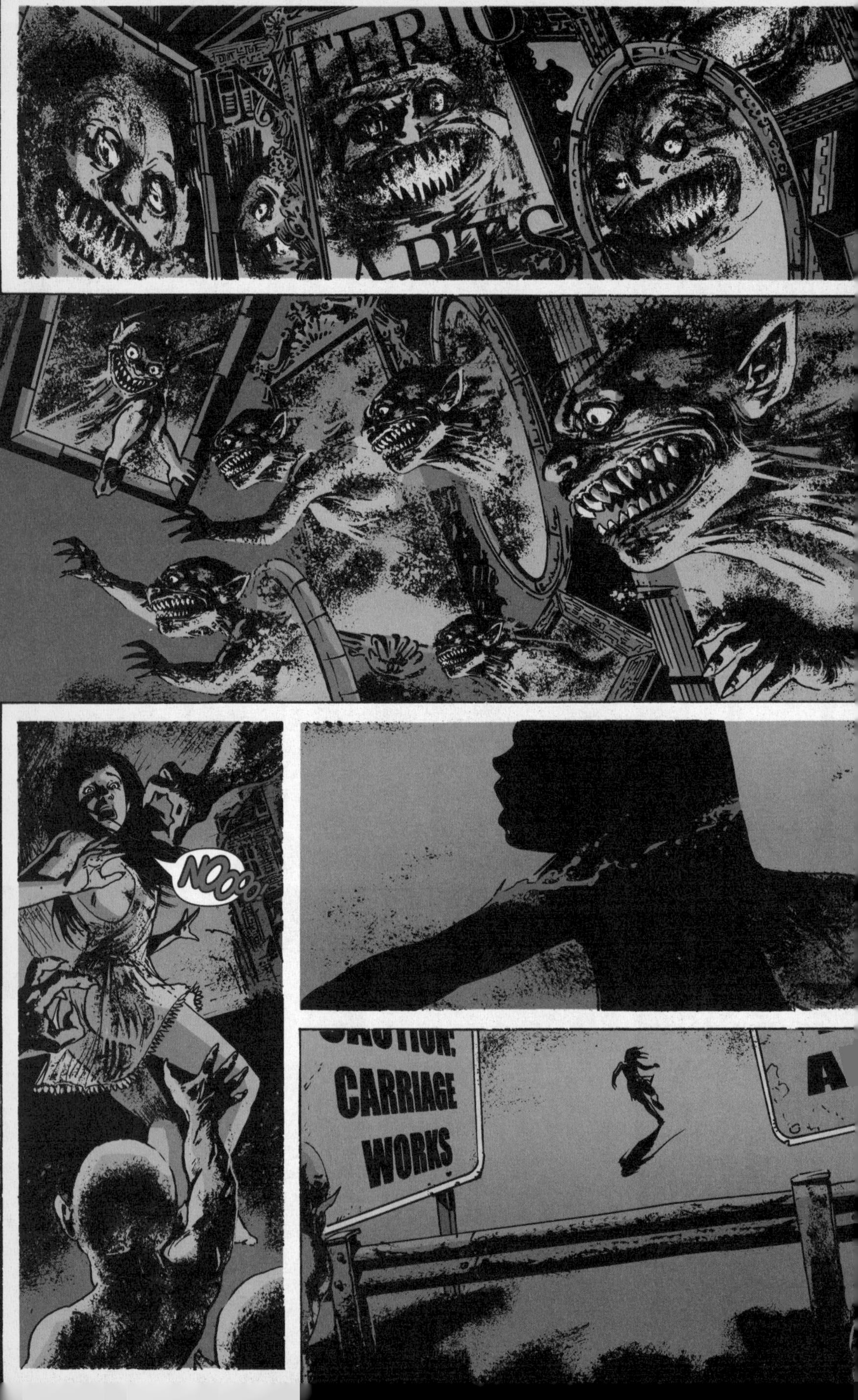
NOOOO!
CARRIAGE
WORKS

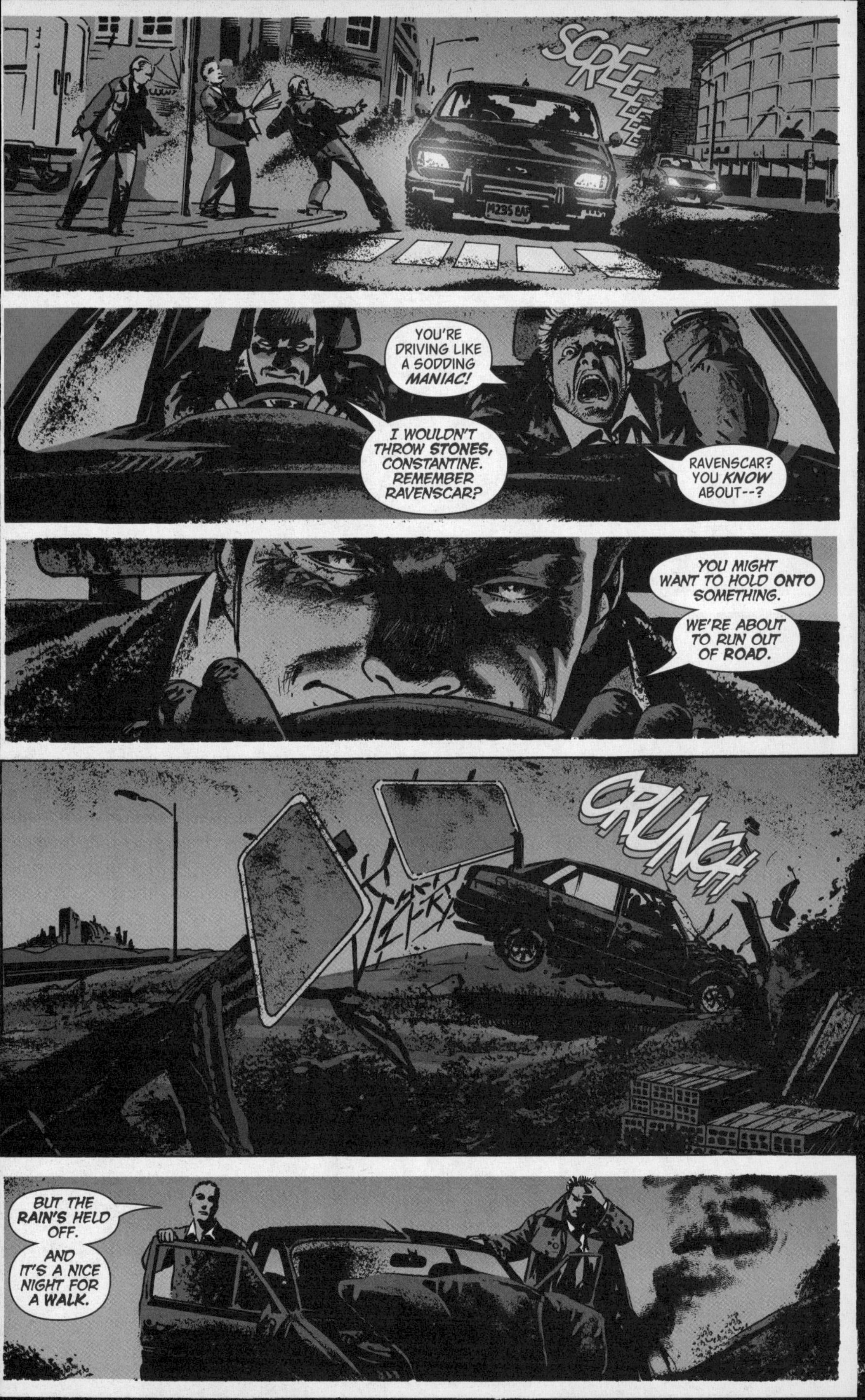
SCREEEEEE
M295 EAF
YOU'RE DRIVING LIKE A SODDING MANIAC!
I WOULDN'T THROW STONES, CONSTANTINE. REMEMBER RAVENSCAR?
RAVENSCAR? YOU KNOW ABOUT--?
YOU MIGHT WANT TO HOLD ONTO SOMETHING.
WE'RE ABOUT TO RUN OUT OF ROAD.
CRUNCH
BUT THE RAIN'S HELD OFF.
AND IT'S A NICE NIGHT FOR A WALK.

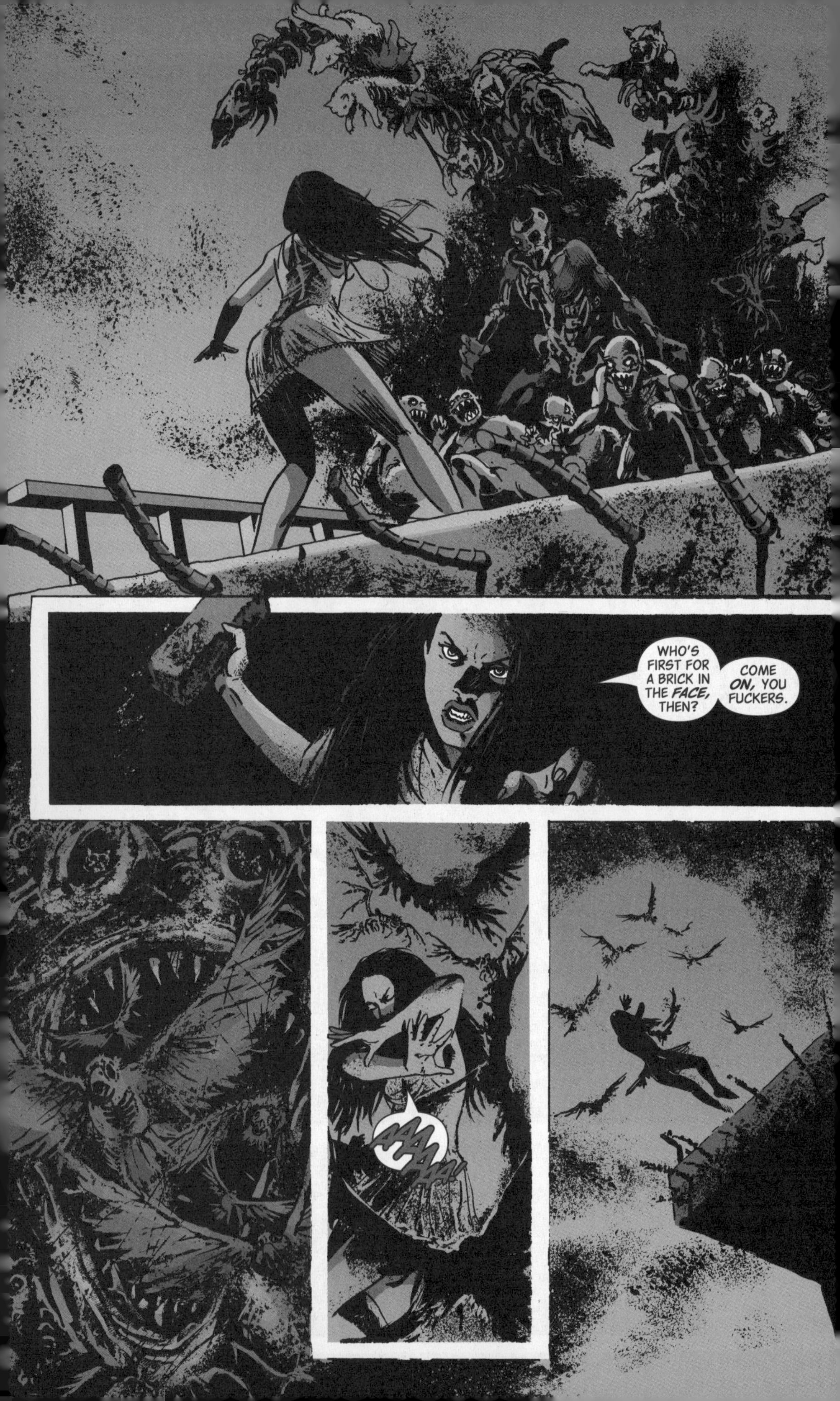
WHO'S FIRST FOR A BRICK IN THE *FACE*, THEN?
COME *ON,* YOU FUCKERS.
AAAAAAA!

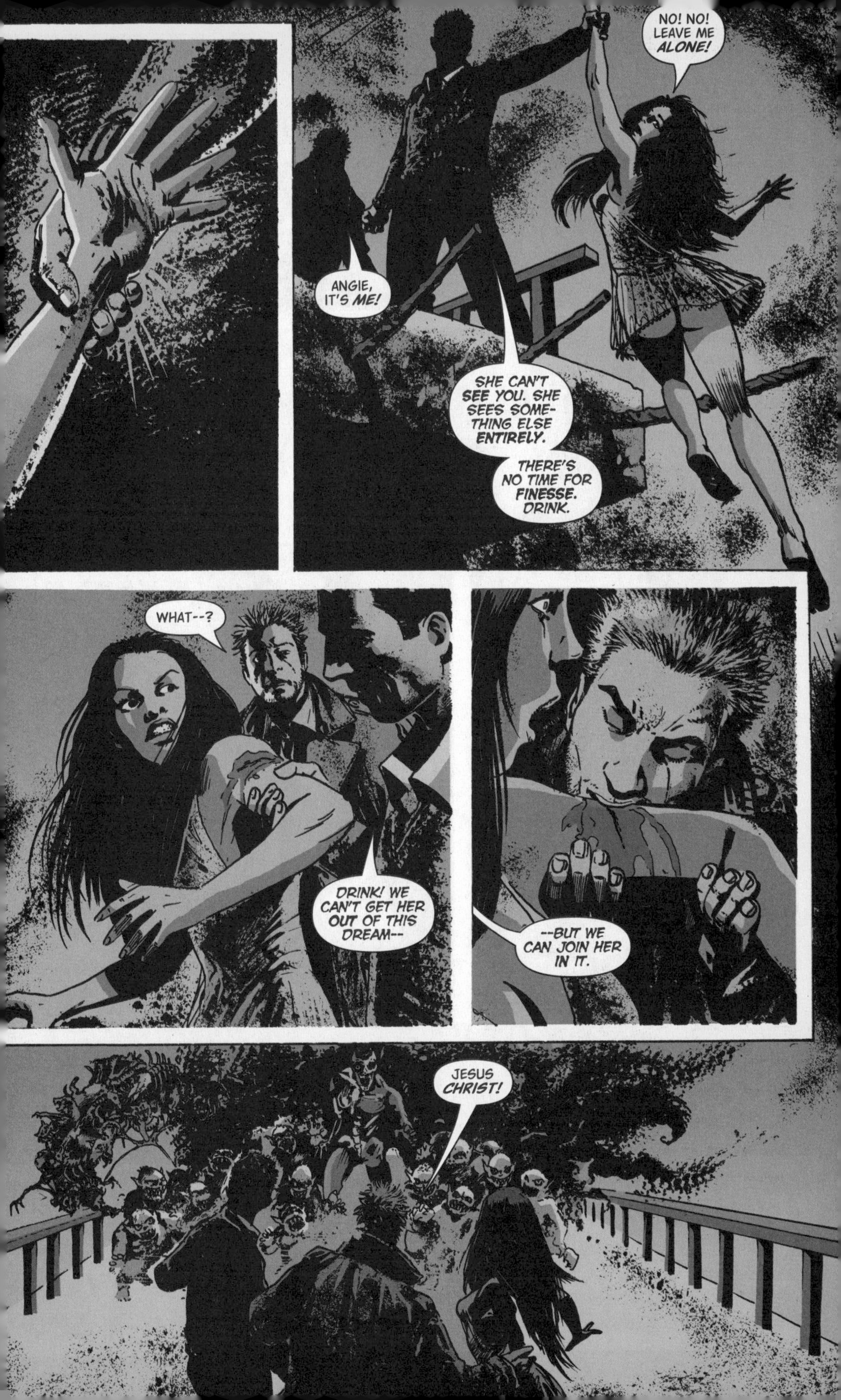
NO! NO! LEAVE ME ALONE!
ANGIE, IT'S ME!
SHE CAN'T SEE YOU. SHE SEES SOME-THING ELSE ENTIRELY.
THERE'S NO TIME FOR FINESSE. DRINK.
WHAT--?
DRINK! WE CAN'T GET HER OUT OF THIS DREAM--
--BUT WE CAN JOIN HER IN IT.
JESUS CHRIST!

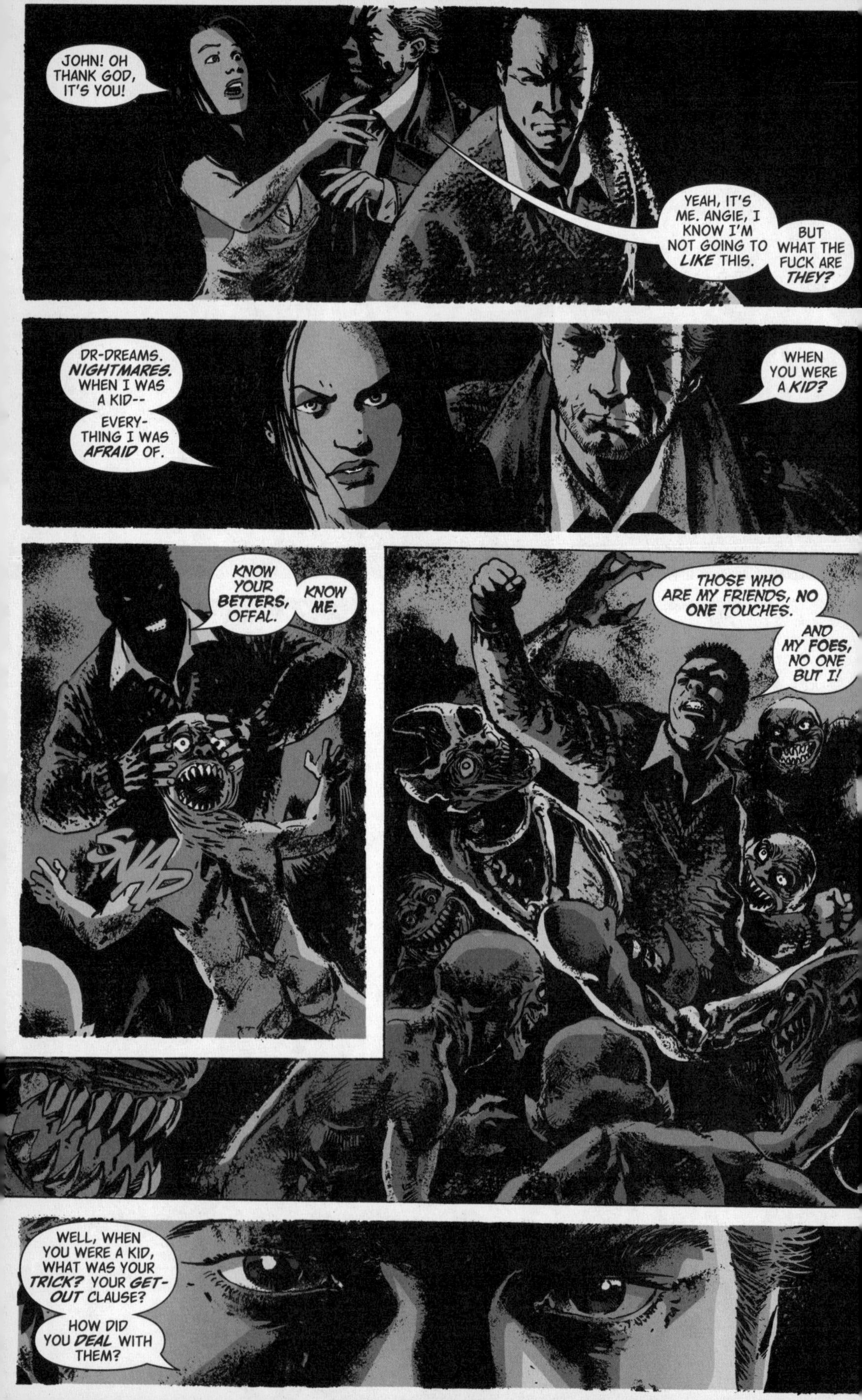
JOHN! OH THANK GOD, IT'S YOU!
YEAH, IT'S ME. ANGIE, I KNOW I'M NOT GOING TO *LIKE* THIS.
BUT WHAT THE FUCK ARE *THEY?*
DR-DREAMS. *NIGHTMARES.* WHEN I WAS A KID--
EVERY-THING I WAS *AFRAID* OF.
WHEN YOU WERE A *KID?*
KNOW YOUR BETTERS, OFFAL.
KNOW ME.
SNAP
THOSE WHO ARE MY FRIENDS, NO ONE TOUCHES.
AND MY FOES, NO ONE BUT I!
WELL, WHEN YOU WERE A KID, WHAT WAS YOUR *TRICK?* YOUR *GET-OUT* CLAUSE?
HOW DID YOU *DEAL* WITH THEM?

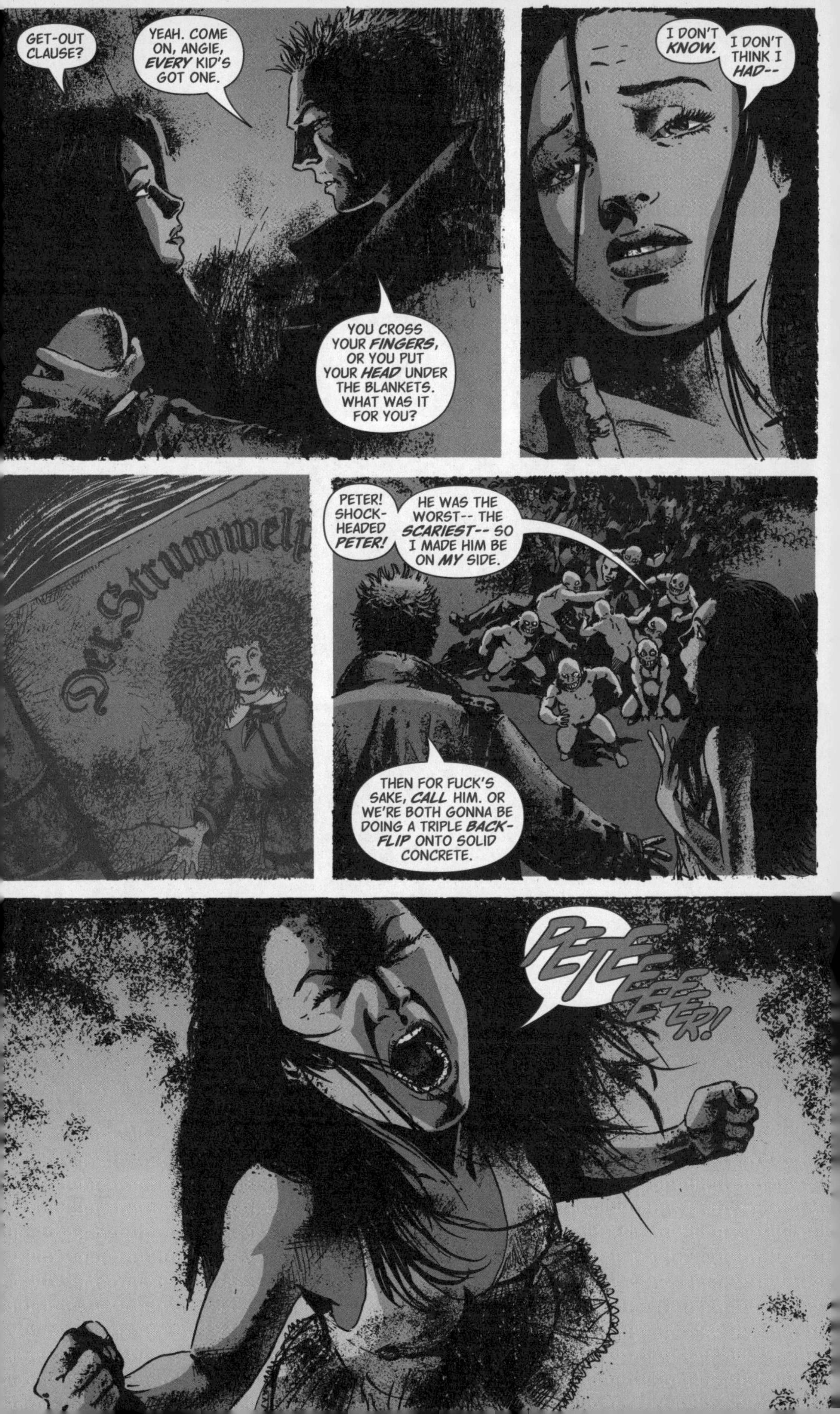
GET-OUT CLAUSE?
YEAH. COME ON, ANGIE, EVERY KID'S GOT ONE.
YOU CROSS YOUR FINGERS, OR YOU PUT YOUR HEAD UNDER THE BLANKETS. WHAT WAS IT FOR YOU?
I DON'T KNOW.
I DON'T THINK I HAD--
Der Struwwelp
PETER! SHOCK-HEADED PETER!
HE WAS THE WORST-- THE SCARIEST-- SO I MADE HIM BE ON MY SIDE.
THEN FOR FUCK'S SAKE, CALL HIM. OR WE'RE BOTH GONNA BE DOING A TRIPLE BACK-FLIP ONTO SOLID CONCRETE.
PETEEEEER!

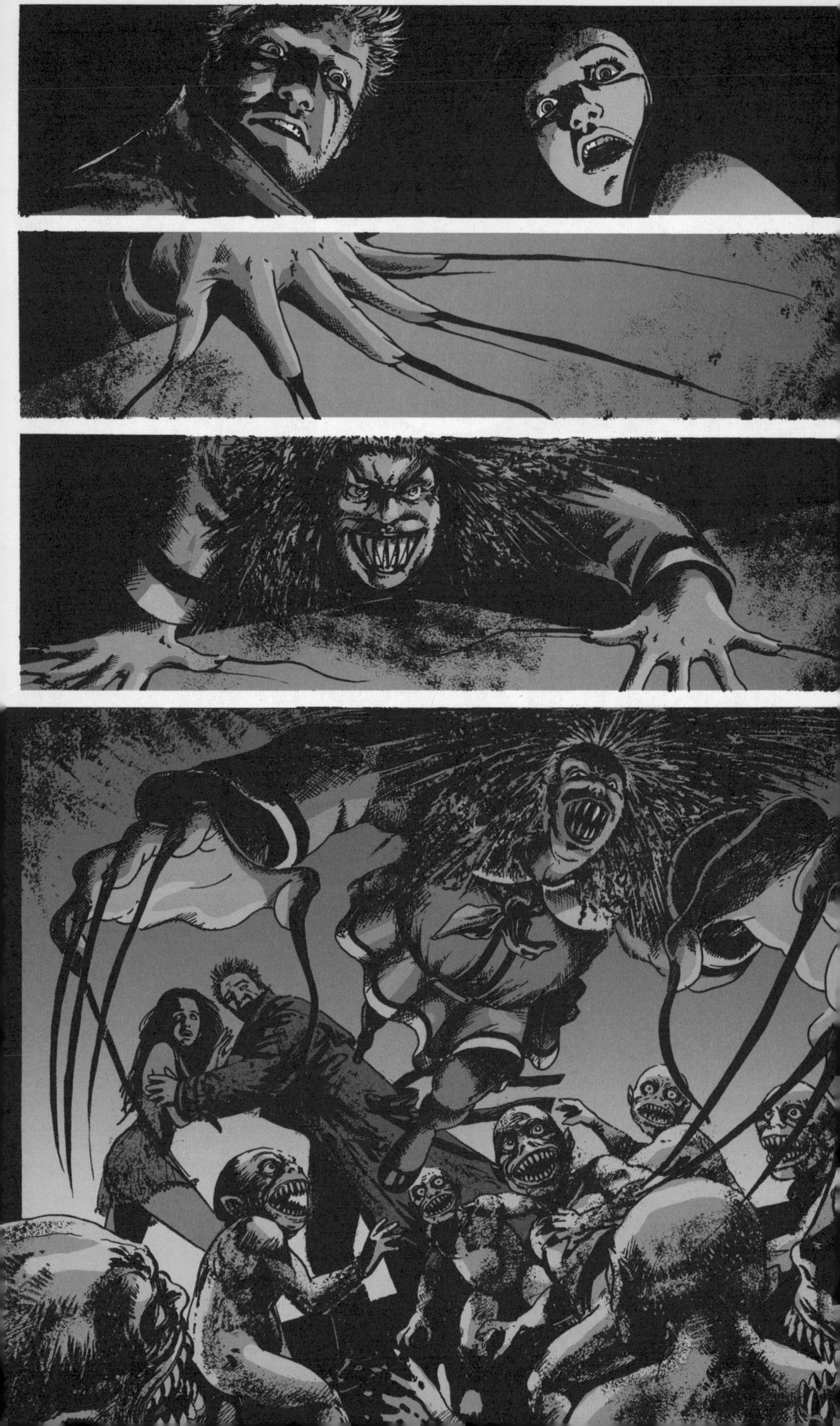

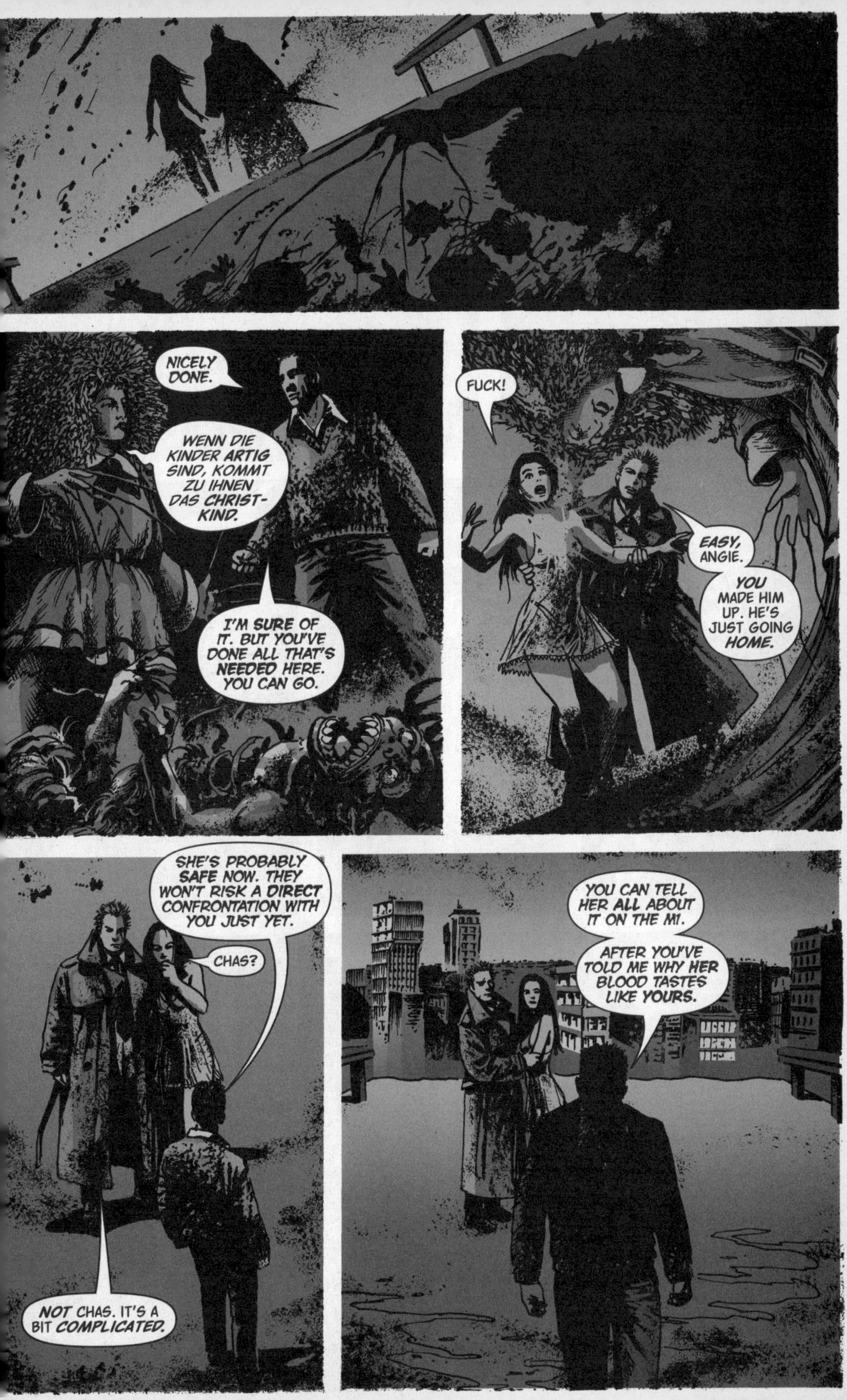
NICELY DONE.
WENN DIE KINDER ARTIG SIND, KOMMT ZU IHNEN DAS CHRIST-KIND.
I'M SURE OF IT. BUT YOU'VE DONE ALL THAT'S NEEDED HERE. YOU CAN GO.
FUCK!
EASY, ANGIE.
YOU MADE HIM UP. HE'S JUST GOING HOME.
SHE'S PROBABLY SAFE NOW. THEY WON'T RISK A DIRECT CONFRONTATION WITH YOU JUST YET.
CHAS?
NOT CHAS. IT'S A BIT COMPLICATED.
YOU CAN TELL HER ALL ABOUT IT ON THE M1.
AFTER YOU'VE TOLD ME WHY HER BLOOD TASTES LIKE YOURS.

"I'M SURE WE'RE ALL IN THE MOOD FOR ANOTHER BEDTIME STORY."

DING DING

HELLO, MR. MASTERS. IS GEMMA READY?

SHE'S JUST DRYING HER HAIR.

I SUPPOSE YOU'D BEST COME IN AND WAIT.

I'LL HANG THIS UP, IF YOU LIKE. SHE COULD BE HALF AN HOUR, YET.

NO! THERE'S NO NEED.

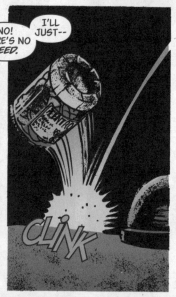

I'LL JUST--

CLINK

LOOK OUT, LAD. YOU DON'T WANT TO BE LOSING THESE.

ON MEDICATION, ARE YOU?

NOSE BLEEDS. THEY'RE FOR-- I GET NOSE BLEEDS, SOMETIMES.

OH YES? THEY'VE A PILL FOR THAT NOW, HAVE THEY?

WHAT'S IT CALLED?

IT'S-- WELL, IT'S AN HERBAL--

--HOMEO-PATHIC--

SIMON!

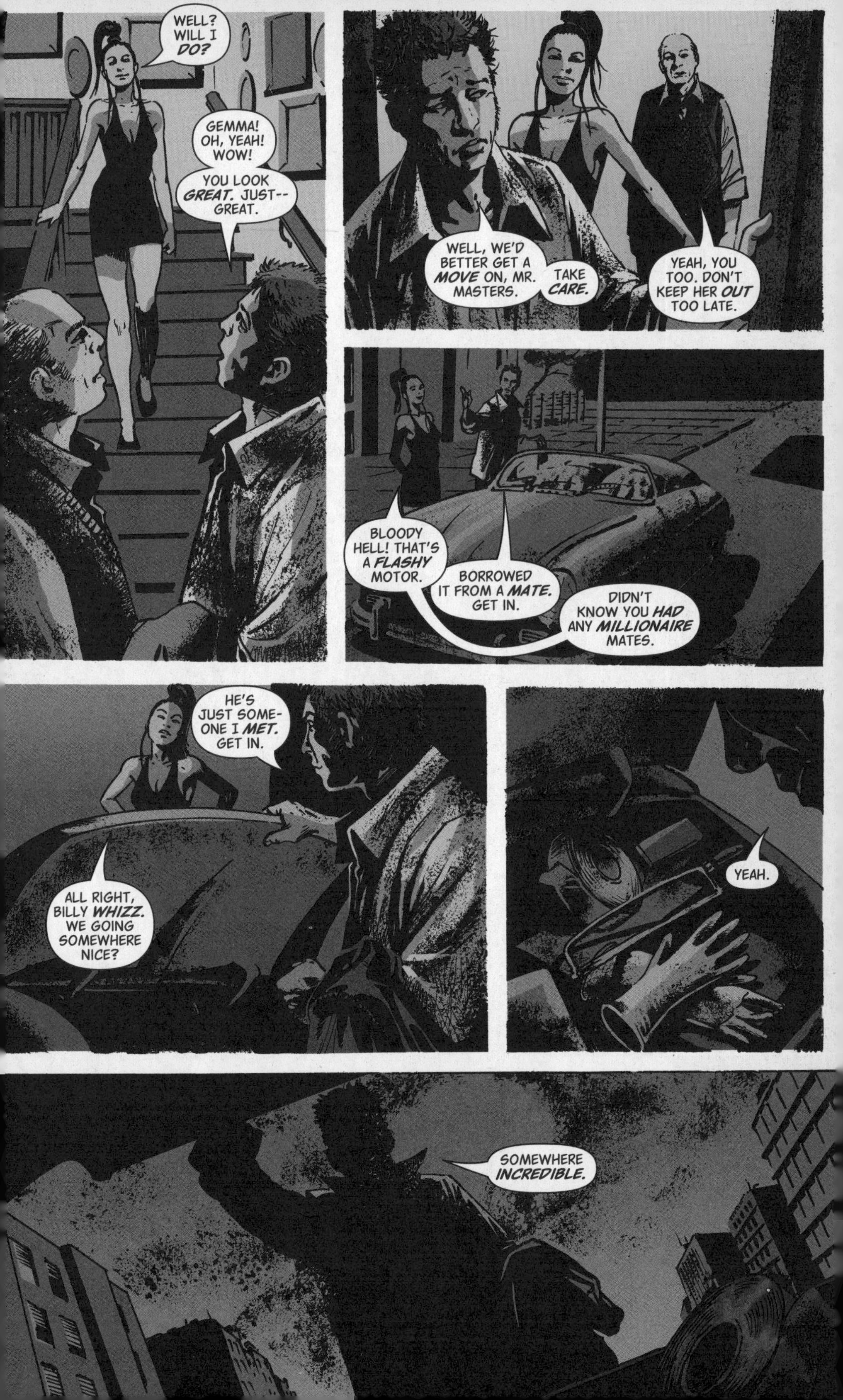
WELL? WILL I *DO?*
GEMMA! OH, YEAH! WOW!
YOU LOOK *GREAT.* JUST--GREAT.
WELL, WE'D BETTER GET A *MOVE* ON, MR. MASTERS.
TAKE *CARE.*
YEAH, YOU TOO. DON'T KEEP HER *OUT* TOO LATE.
BLOODY HELL! THAT'S A *FLASHY* MOTOR.
BORROWED IT FROM A *MATE.* GET IN.
DIDN'T KNOW YOU *HAD* ANY *MILLIONAIRE* MATES.
HE'S JUST SOME-ONE I *MET.* GET IN.
ALL RIGHT, BILLY *WHIZZ.* WE GOING SOMEWHERE NICE?
YEAH.
SOMEWHERE *INCREDIBLE.*

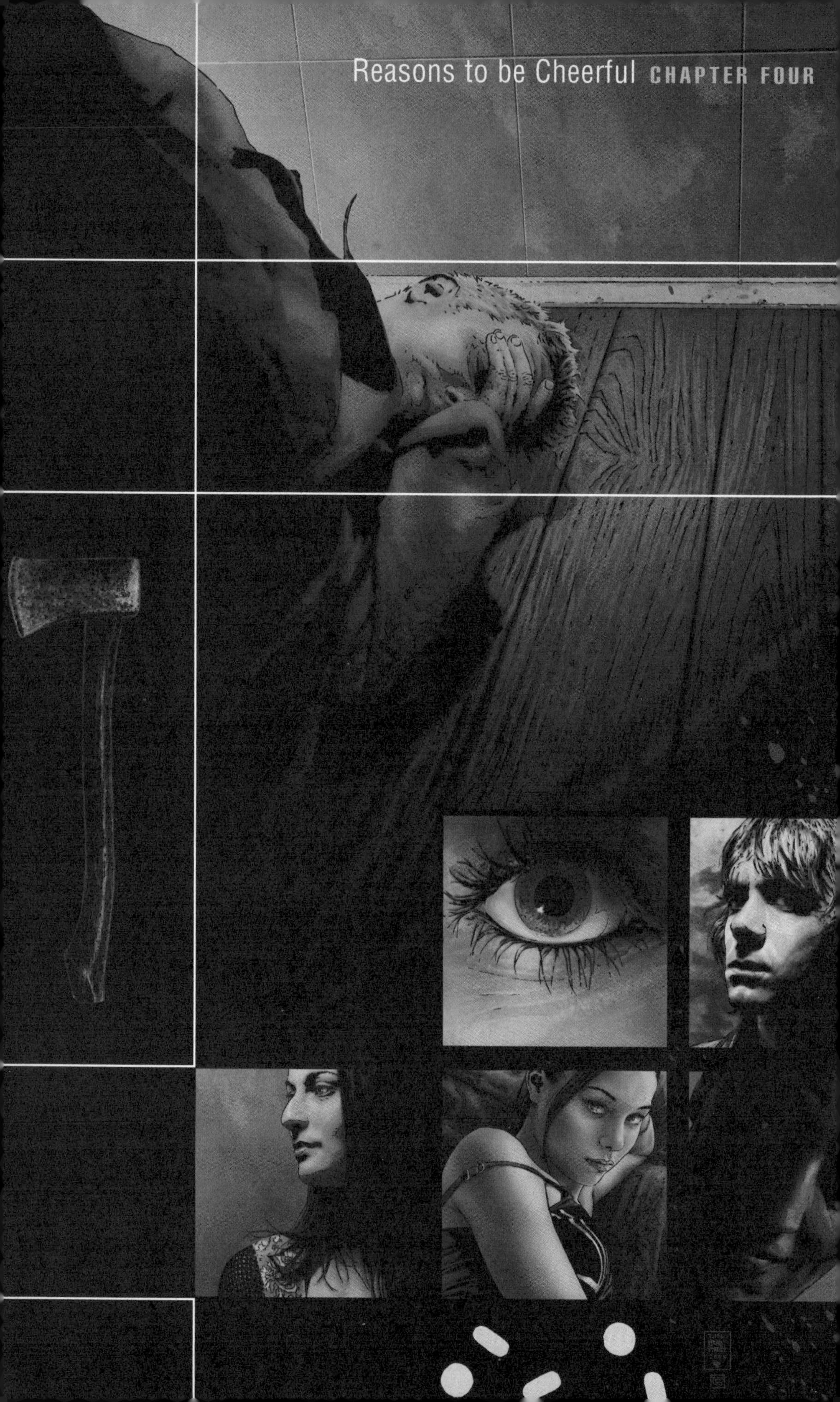
Reasons to be Cheerful CHAPTER FOUR

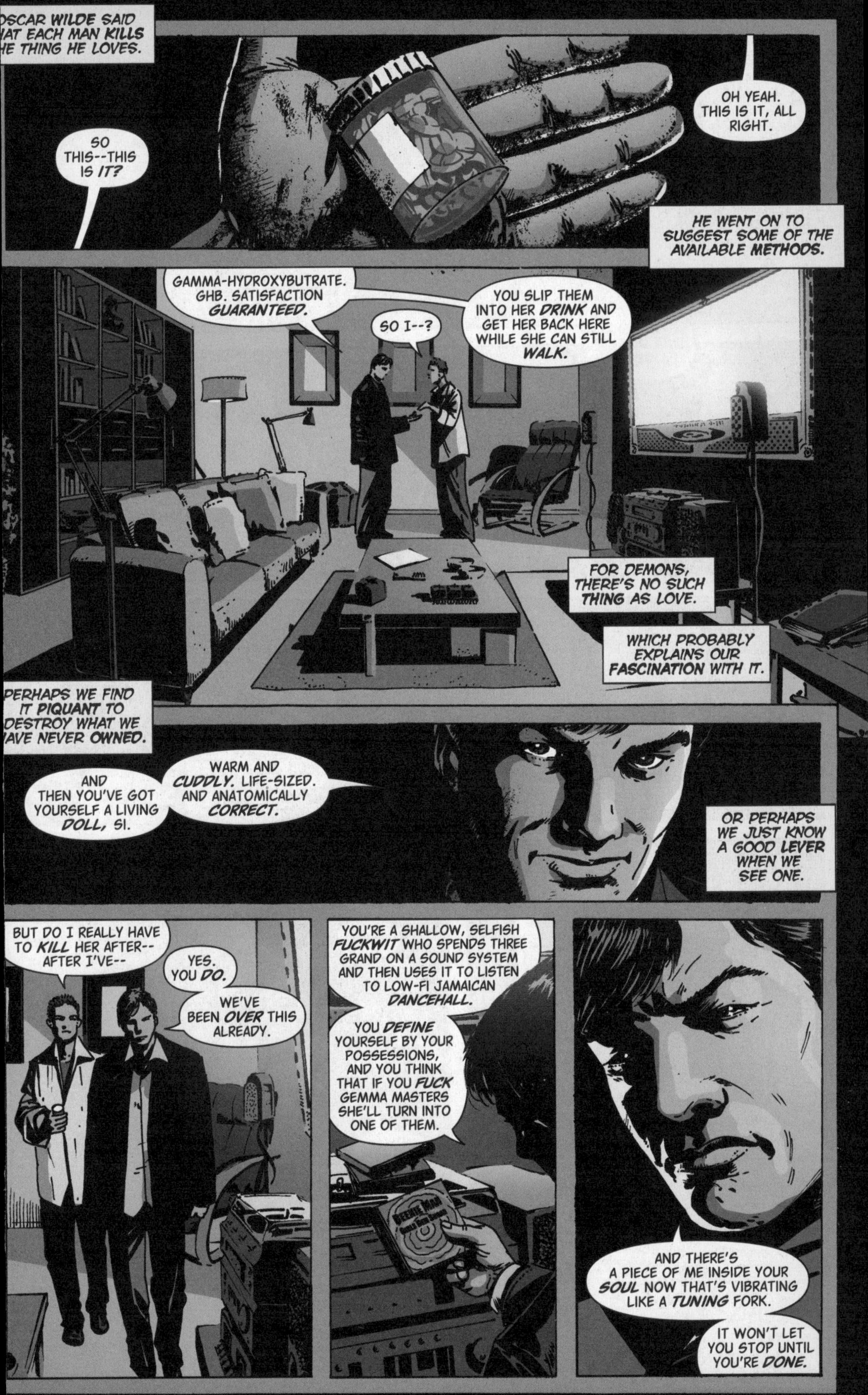
OSCAR WILDE SAID
AT EACH MAN KILLS
E THING HE LOVES.
SO THIS--THIS IS IT?
OH YEAH. THIS IS IT, ALL RIGHT.
HE WENT ON TO SUGGEST SOME OF THE AVAILABLE METHODS.
GAMMA-HYDROXYBUTRATE. GHB. SATISFACTION GUARANTEED.
SO I--?
YOU SLIP THEM INTO HER DRINK AND GET HER BACK HERE WHILE SHE CAN STILL WALK.
FOR DEMONS, THERE'S NO SUCH THING AS LOVE.
WHICH PROBABLY EXPLAINS OUR FASCINATION WITH IT.
PERHAPS WE FIND
IT PIQUANT TO
DESTROY WHAT WE
AVE NEVER OWNED.
AND THEN YOU'VE GOT YOURSELF A LIVING DOLL, SI.
WARM AND CUDDLY. LIFE-SIZED. AND ANATOMICALLY CORRECT.
OR PERHAPS WE JUST KNOW A GOOD LEVER WHEN WE SEE ONE.
BUT DO I REALLY HAVE TO KILL HER AFTER--AFTER I'VE--
YES. YOU DO.
WE'VE BEEN OVER THIS ALREADY.
YOU'RE A SHALLOW, SELFISH FUCKWIT WHO SPENDS THREE GRAND ON A SOUND SYSTEM AND THEN USES IT TO LISTEN TO LOW-FI JAMAICAN DANCEHALL.
YOU DEFINE YOURSELF BY YOUR POSSESSIONS, AND YOU THINK THAT IF YOU FUCK GEMMA MASTERS SHE'LL TURN INTO ONE OF THEM.
BEENIE MAN
AND THERE'S A PIECE OF ME INSIDE YOUR SOUL NOW THAT'S VIBRATING LIKE A TUNING FORK.
IT WON'T LET YOU STOP UNTIL YOU'RE DONE.

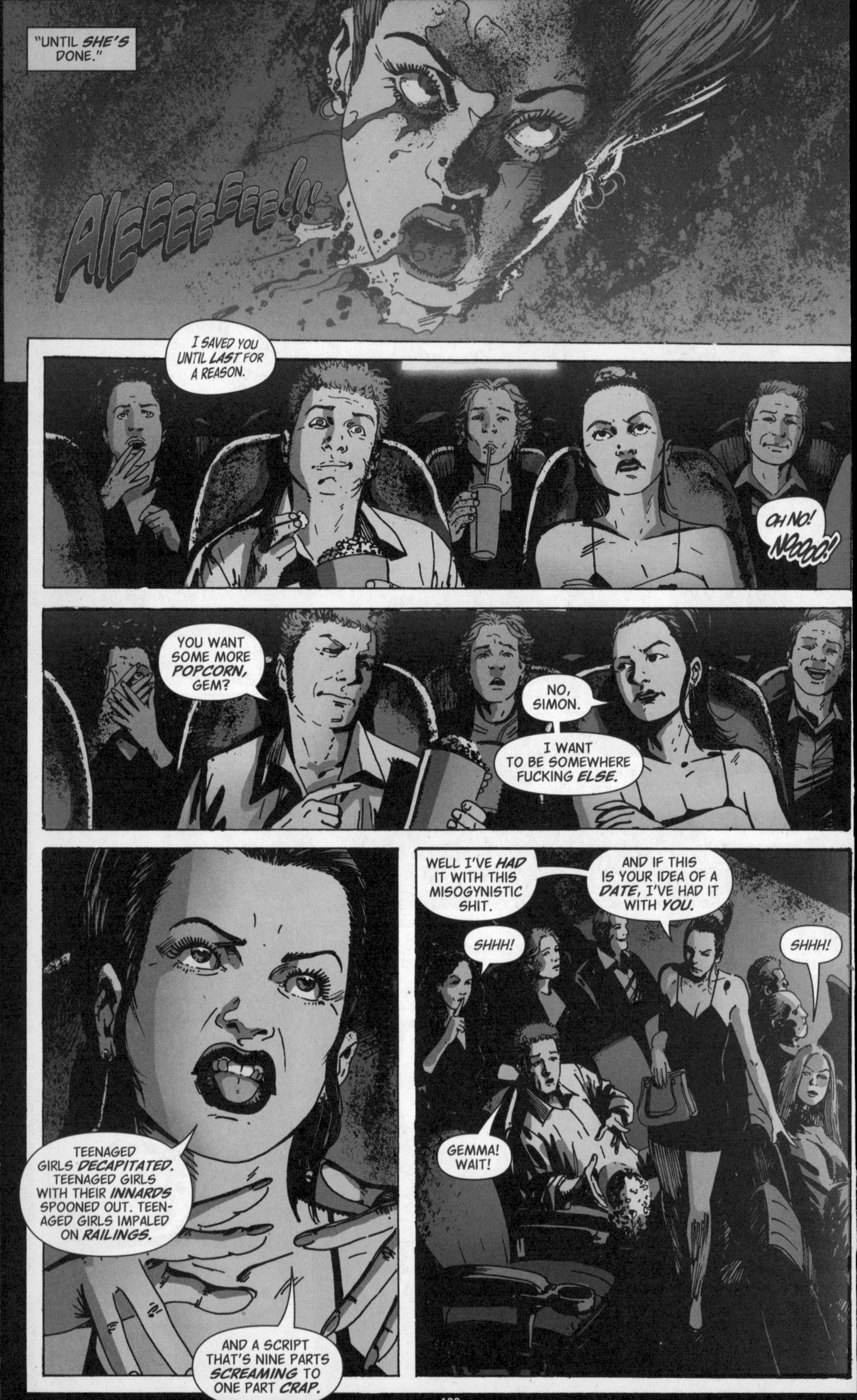

"UNTIL SHE'S DONE."
AIEEEEEEEE!!!
I SAVED YOU UNTIL LAST FOR A REASON.
OH NO! NOOOOO!
YOU WANT SOME MORE POPCORN, GEM?
NO, SIMON.
I WANT TO BE SOMEWHERE FUCKING ELSE.
TEENAGED GIRLS DECAPITATED. TEENAGED GIRLS WITH THEIR INNARDS SPOONED OUT. TEEN-AGED GIRLS IMPALED ON RAILINGS.
AND A SCRIPT THAT'S NINE PARTS SCREAMING TO ONE PART CRAP.
WELL I'VE HAD IT WITH THIS MISOGYNISTIC SHIT.
AND IF THIS IS YOUR IDEA OF A DATE, I'VE HAD IT WITH YOU.
SHHH!
SHHH!
GEMMA! WAIT!

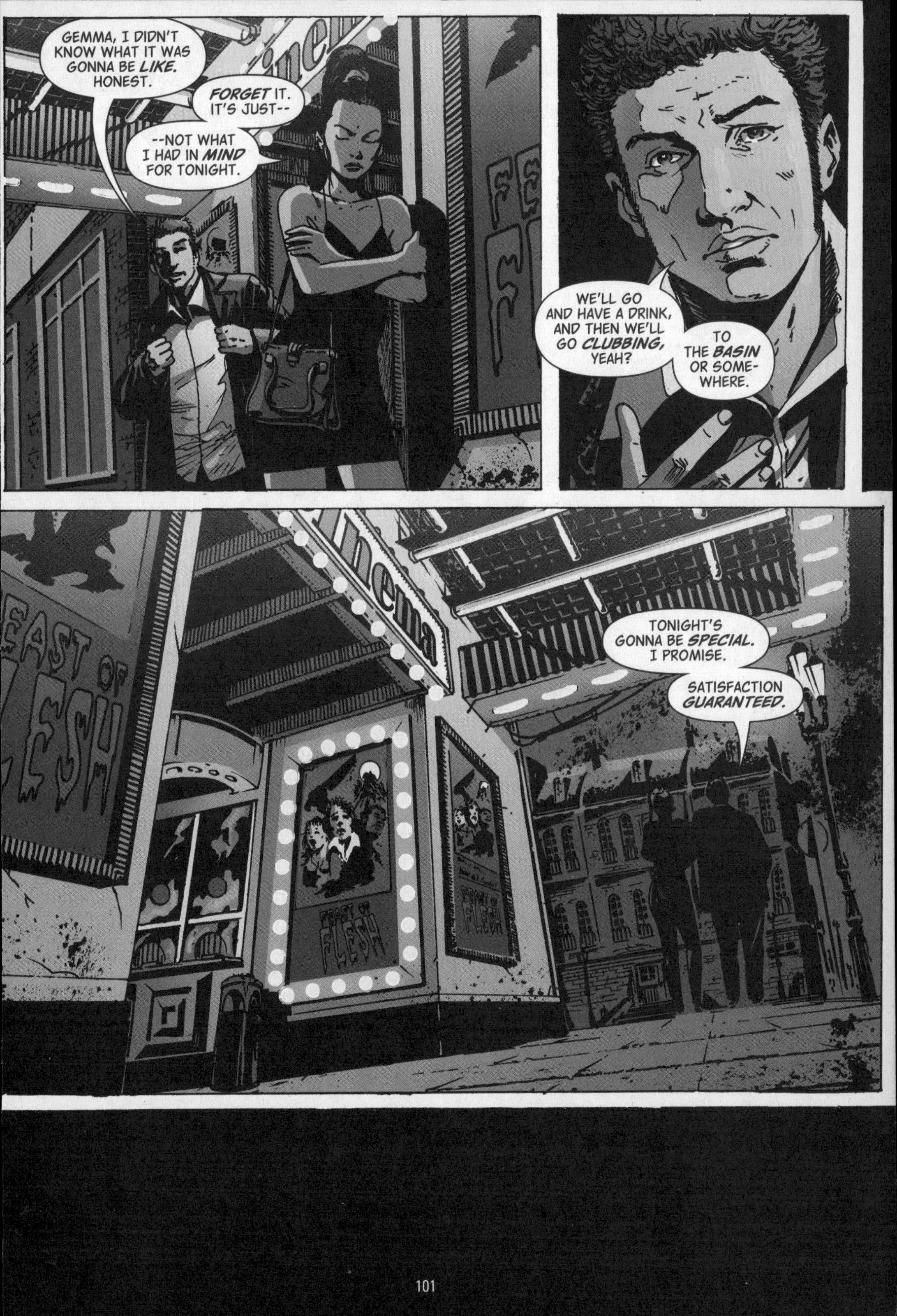
GEMMA, I DIDN'T KNOW WHAT IT WAS GONNA BE LIKE. HONEST.
FORGET IT. IT'S JUST--
--NOT WHAT I HAD IN MIND FOR TONIGHT.
WE'LL GO AND HAVE A DRINK, AND THEN WE'LL GO CLUBBING, YEAH?
TO THE BASIN OR SOME-WHERE.
FEAST OF FLESH
TONIGHT'S GONNA BE SPECIAL. I PROMISE.
SATISFACTION GUARANTEED.

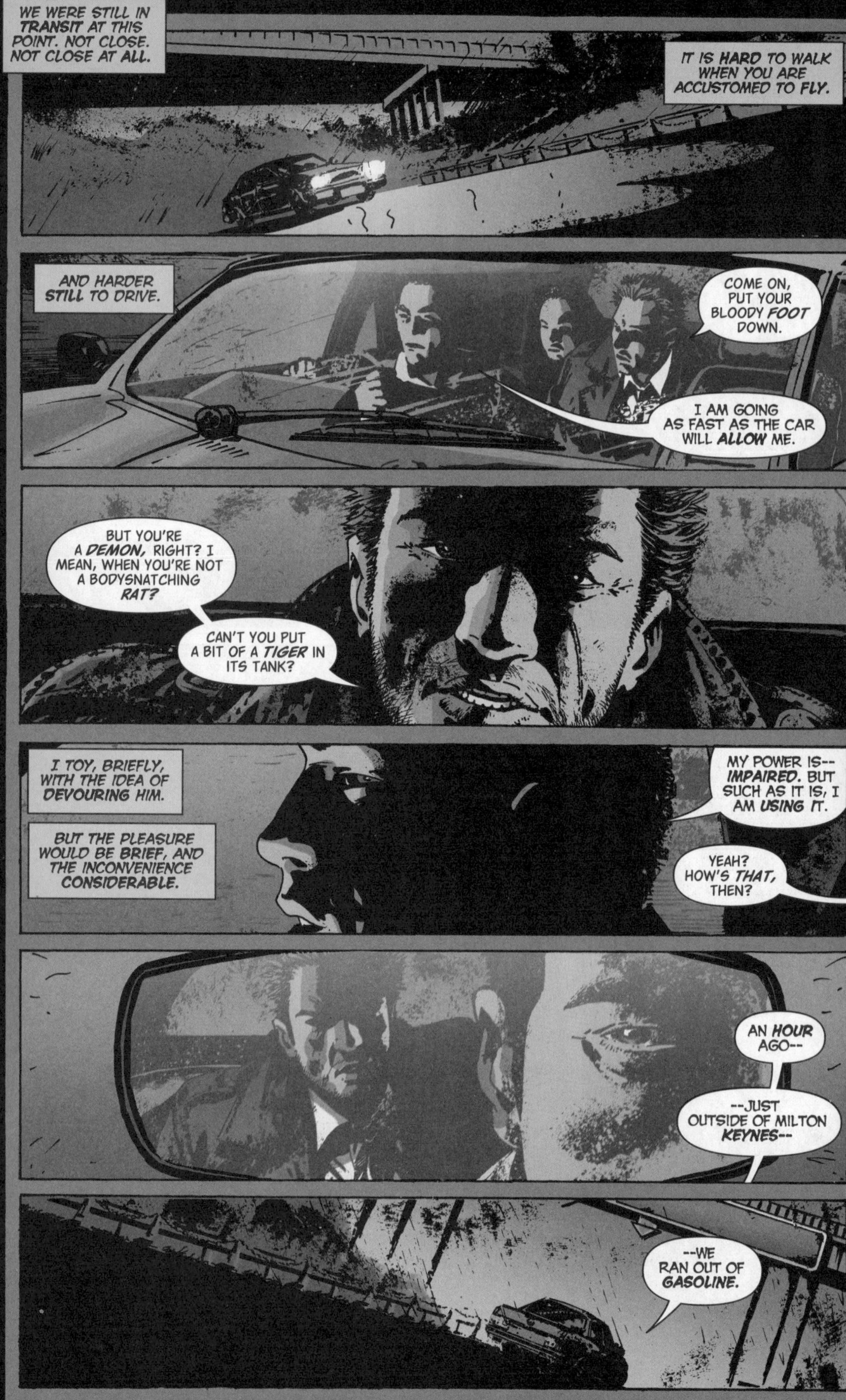
WE WERE STILL IN TRANSIT AT THIS POINT. NOT CLOSE. NOT CLOSE AT ALL.
IT IS HARD TO WALK WHEN YOU ARE ACCUSTOMED TO FLY.
AND HARDER STILL TO DRIVE.
COME ON, PUT YOUR BLOODY FOOT DOWN.
I AM GOING AS FAST AS THE CAR WILL ALLOW ME.
BUT YOU'RE A DEMON, RIGHT? I MEAN, WHEN YOU'RE NOT A BODYSNATCHING RAT?
CAN'T YOU PUT A BIT OF A TIGER IN ITS TANK?
I TOY, BRIEFLY, WITH THE IDEA OF DEVOURING HIM.
BUT THE PLEASURE WOULD BE BRIEF, AND THE INCONVENIENCE CONSIDERABLE.
MY POWER IS-- IMPAIRED. BUT SUCH AS IT IS, I AM USING IT.
YEAH? HOW'S THAT, THEN?
AN HOUR AGO--
--JUST OUTSIDE OF MILTON KEYNES--
--WE RAN OUT OF GASOLINE.

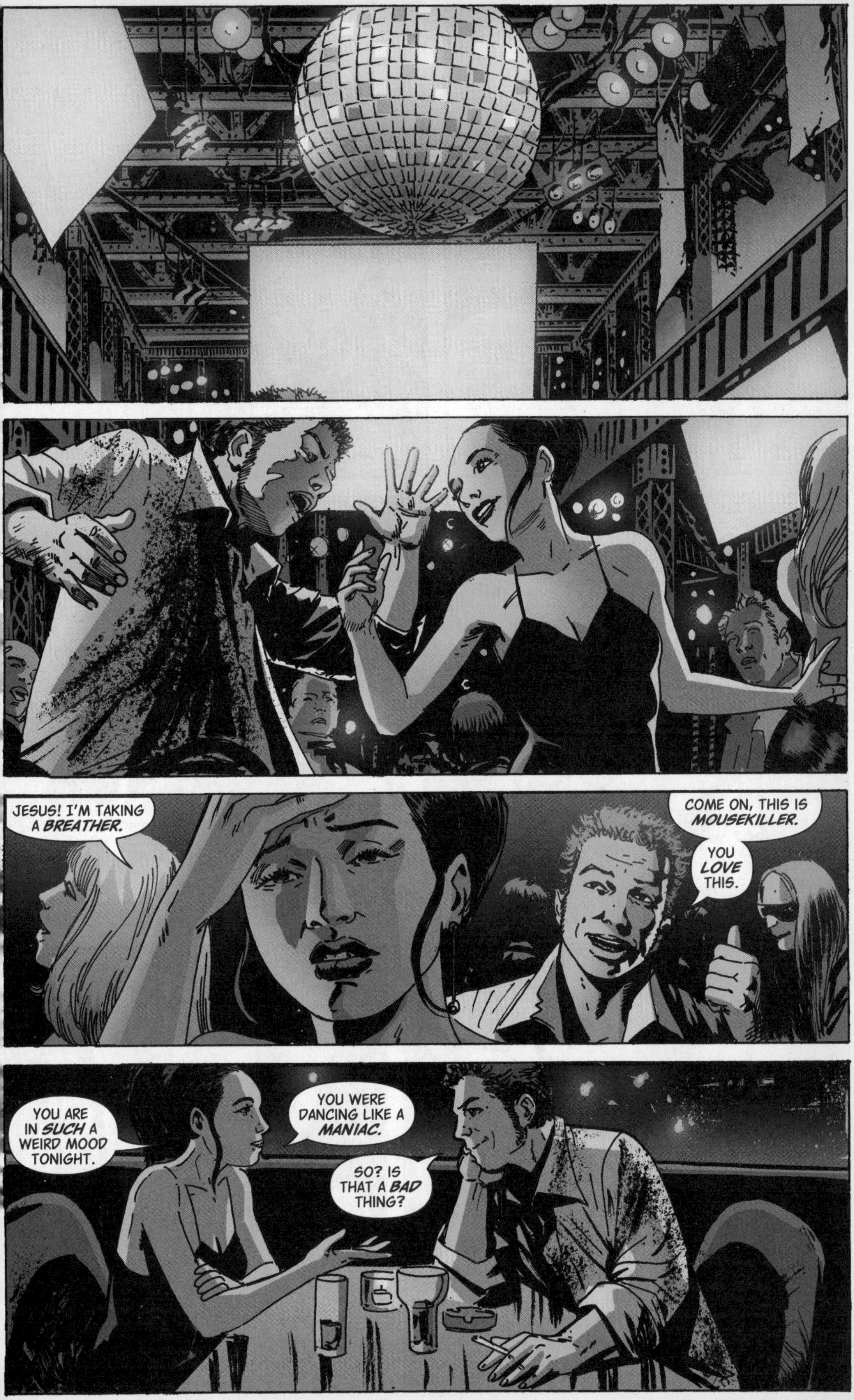
JESUS! I'M TAKING A BREATHER.
COME ON, THIS IS MOUSEKILLER.
YOU LOVE THIS.
YOU ARE IN SUCH A WEIRD MOOD TONIGHT.
YOU WERE DANCING LIKE A MANIAC.
SO? IS THAT A BAD THING?

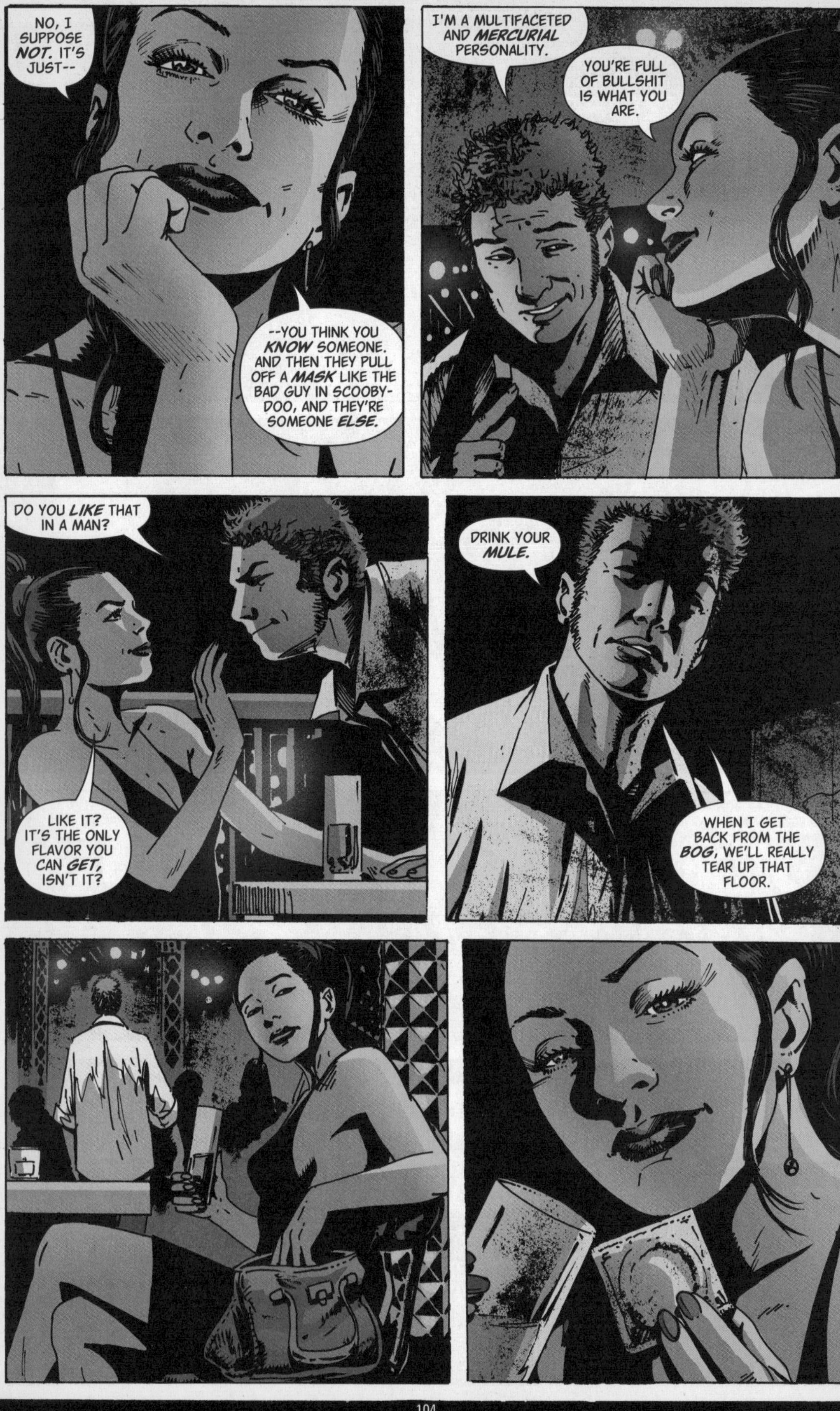
NO, I SUPPOSE NOT. IT'S JUST--
--YOU THINK YOU KNOW SOMEONE. AND THEN THEY PULL OFF A MASK LIKE THE BAD GUY IN SCOOBY-DOO, AND THEY'RE SOMEONE ELSE.
I'M A MULTIFACETED AND MERCURIAL PERSONALITY.
YOU'RE FULL OF BULLSHIT IS WHAT YOU ARE.
DO YOU LIKE THAT IN A MAN?
LIKE IT? IT'S THE ONLY FLAVOR YOU CAN GET, ISN'T IT?
DRINK YOUR MULE.
WHEN I GET BACK FROM THE BOG, WE'LL REALLY TEAR UP THAT FLOOR.

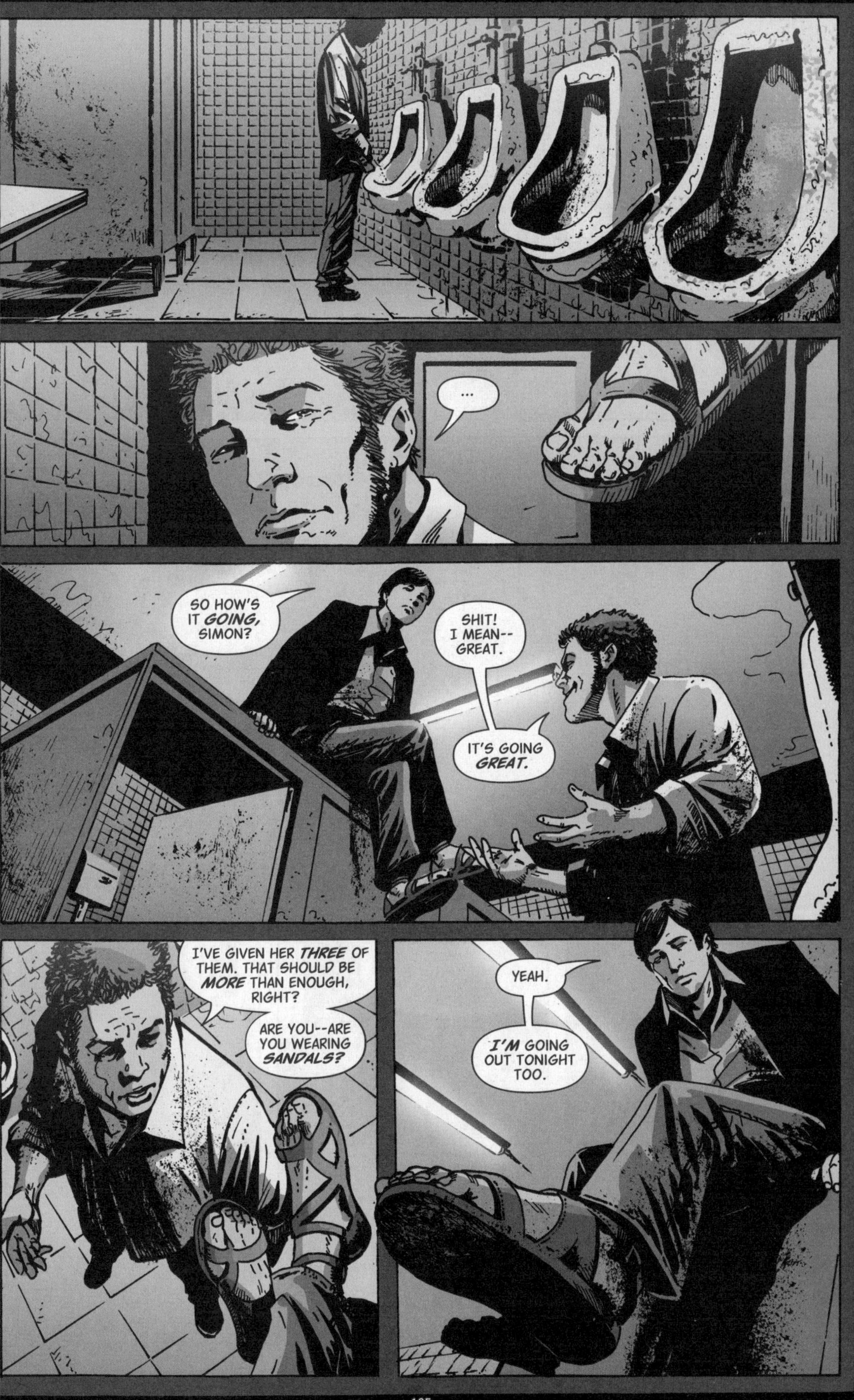
...
SO HOW'S IT GOING, SIMON?
SHIT! I MEAN-- GREAT.
IT'S GOING GREAT.
I'VE GIVEN HER THREE OF THEM. THAT SHOULD BE MORE THAN ENOUGH, RIGHT?
ARE YOU--ARE YOU WEARING SANDALS?
YEAH.
I'M GOING OUT TONIGHT TOO.

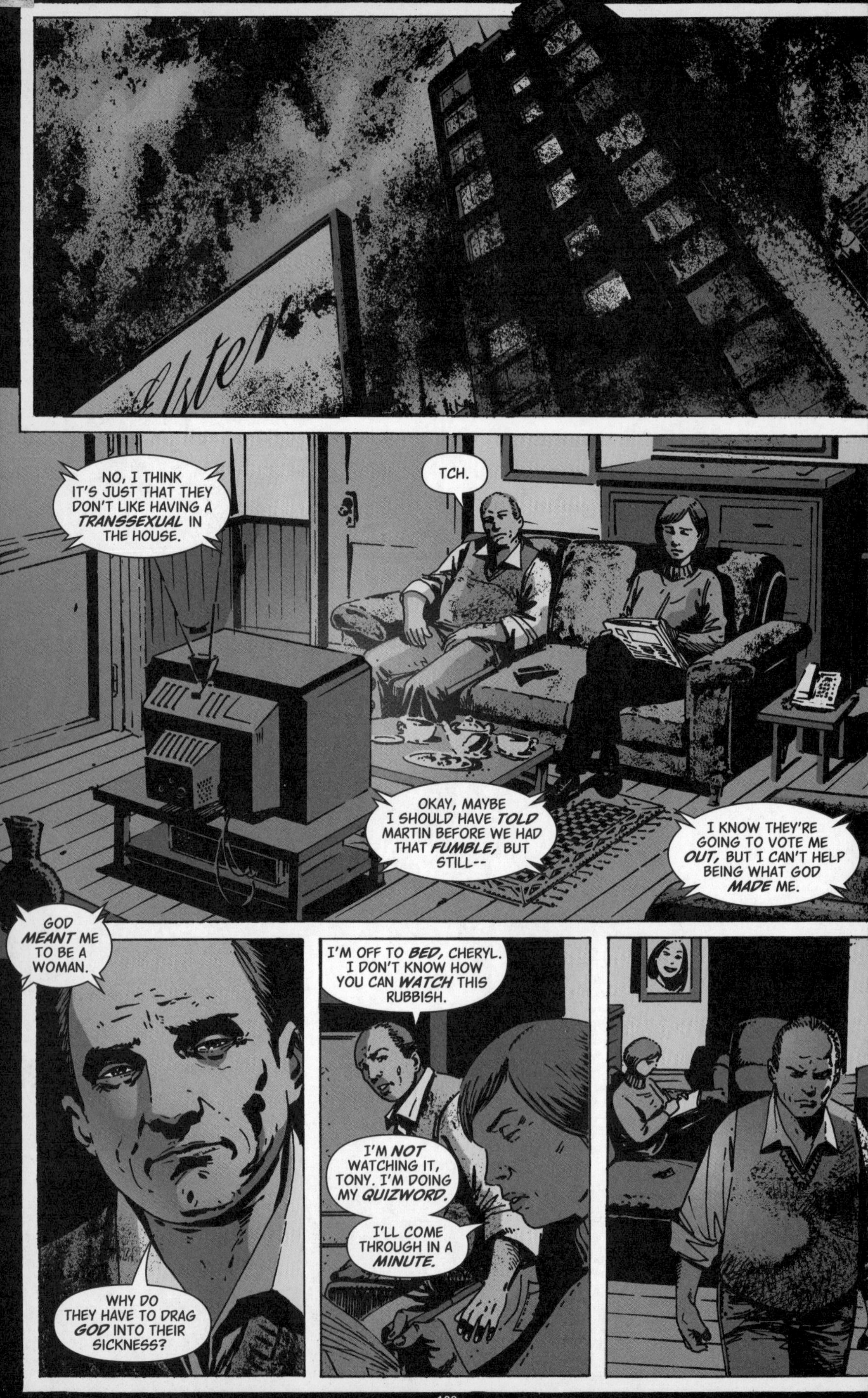
NO, I THINK IT'S JUST THAT THEY DON'T LIKE HAVING A *TRANSSEXUAL* IN THE HOUSE.
TCH.
OKAY, MAYBE I SHOULD HAVE *TOLD* MARTIN BEFORE WE HAD THAT *FUMBLE,* BUT STILL--
I KNOW THEY'RE GOING TO VOTE ME *OUT,* BUT I CAN'T HELP BEING WHAT GOD *MADE* ME.
GOD *MEANT* ME TO BE A WOMAN.
WHY DO THEY HAVE TO DRAG *GOD* INTO THEIR SICKNESS?
I'M OFF TO *BED,* CHERYL. I DON'T KNOW HOW YOU CAN *WATCH* THIS RUBBISH.
I'M *NOT* WATCHING IT, TONY. I'M DOING MY *QUIZWORD.*
I'LL COME THROUGH IN A *MINUTE.*

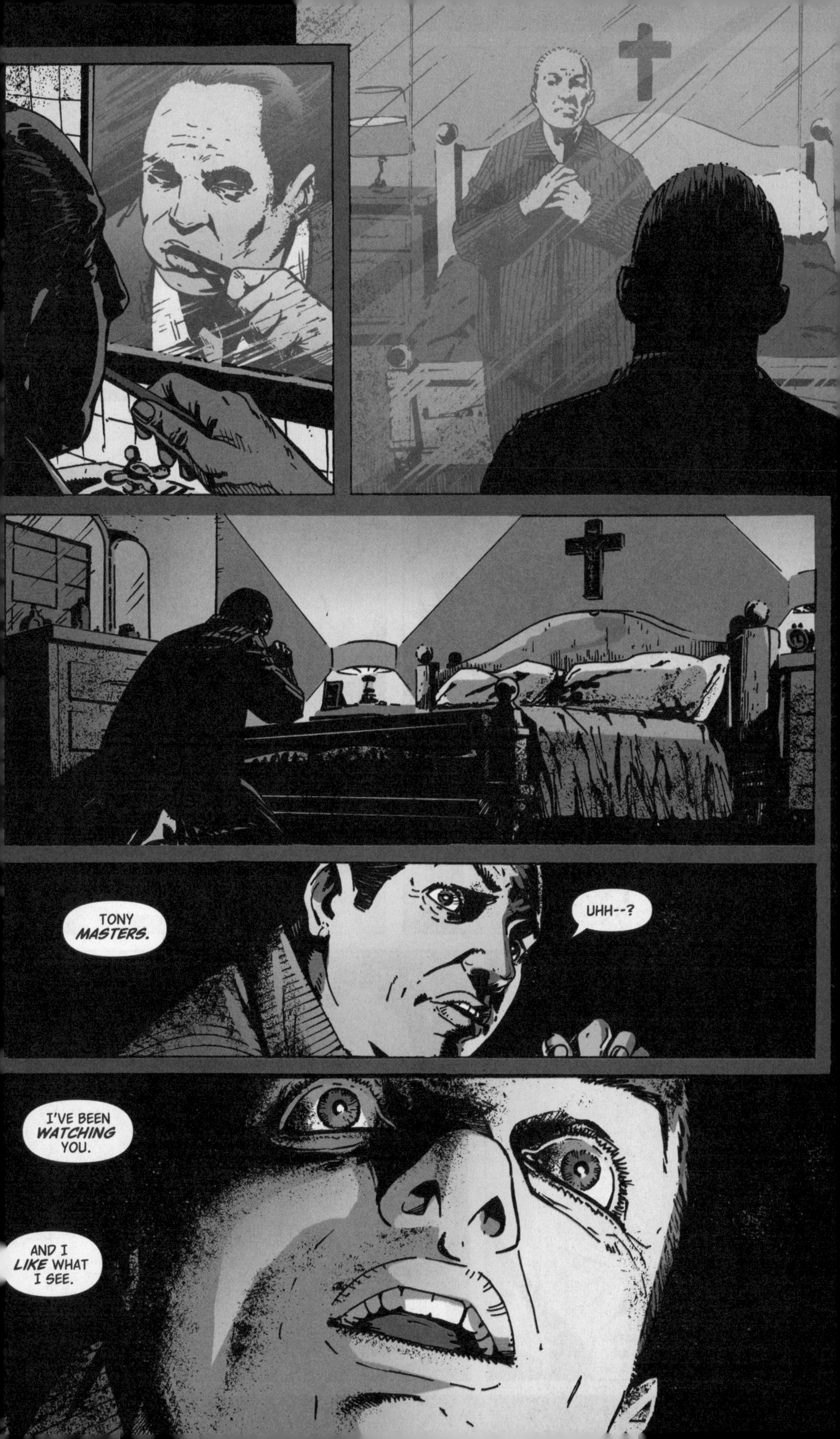
TONY MASTERS.
UHH--?
I'VE BEEN WATCHING YOU.
AND I LIKE WHAT I SEE.

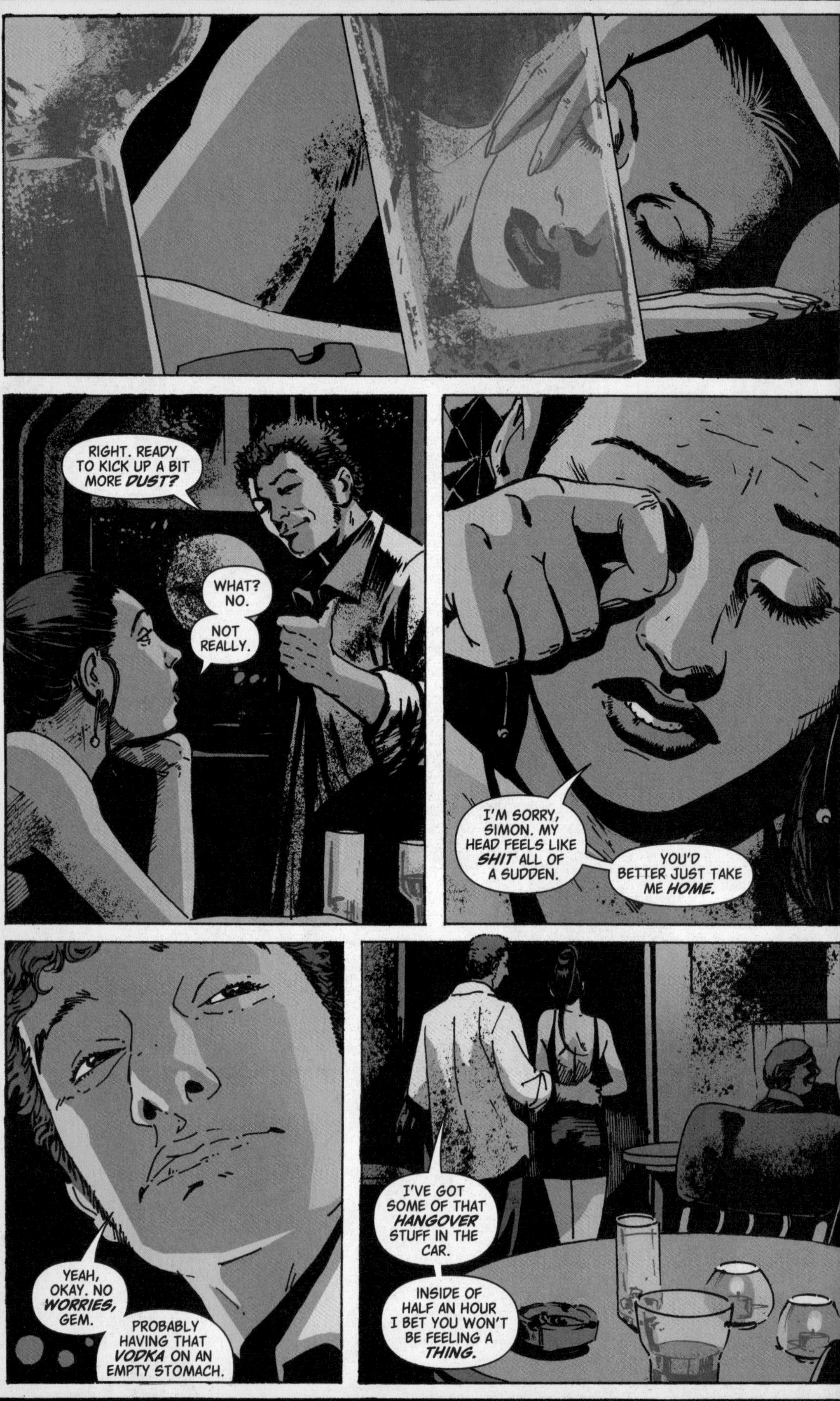
RIGHT. READY TO KICK UP A BIT MORE DUST?
WHAT? NO.
NOT REALLY.
I'M SORRY, SIMON. MY HEAD FEELS LIKE SHIT ALL OF A SUDDEN.
YOU'D BETTER JUST TAKE ME HOME.
YEAH, OKAY. NO WORRIES, GEM.
PROBABLY HAVING THAT VODKA ON AN EMPTY STOMACH.
I'VE GOT SOME OF THAT HANGOVER STUFF IN THE CAR.
INSIDE OF HALF AN HOUR I BET YOU WON'T BE FEELING A THING.

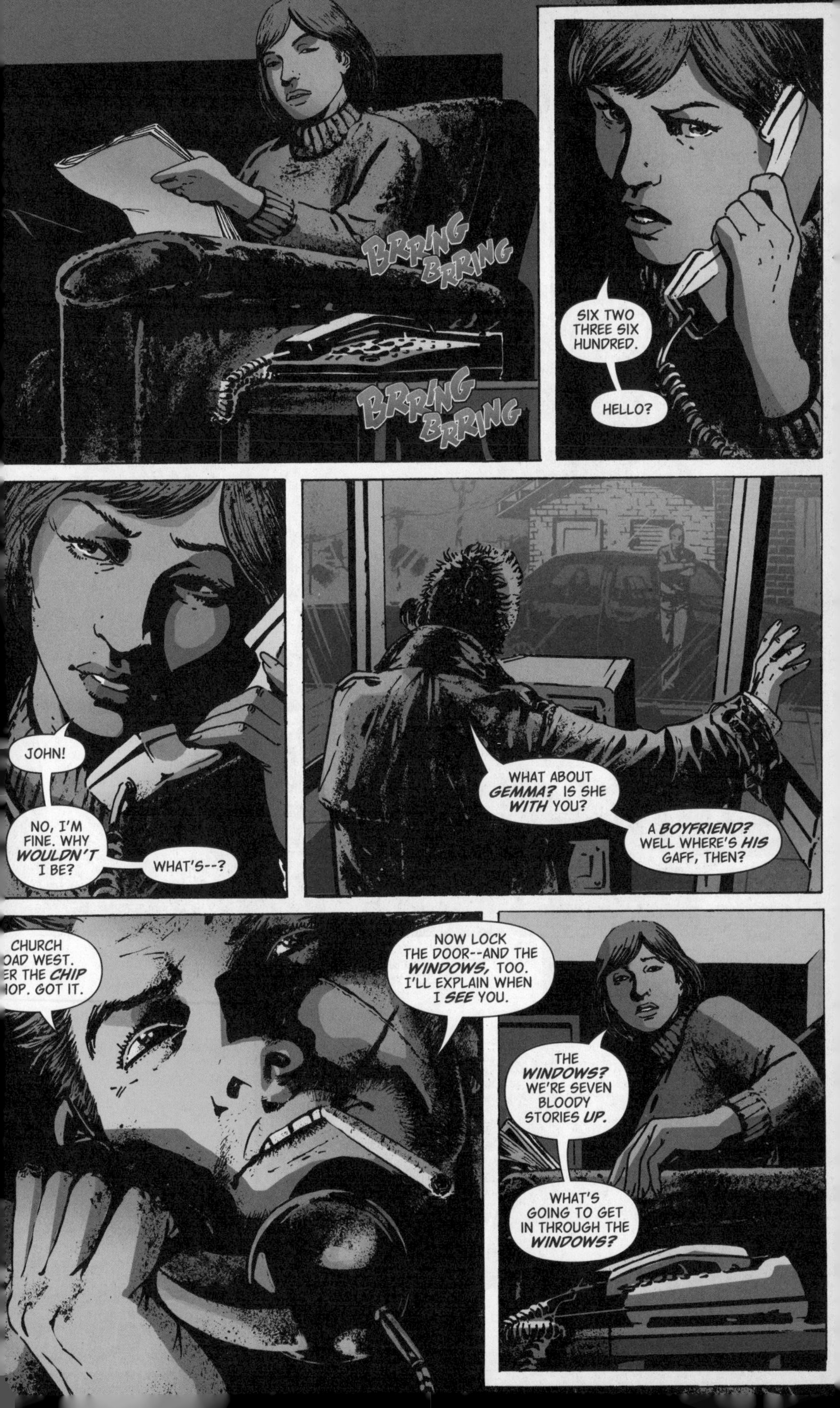

BRRING BRRING
BRRING BRRING
SIX TWO THREE SIX HUNDRED.
HELLO?
JOHN!
NO, I'M FINE. WHY WOULDN'T I BE?
WHAT'S--?
WHAT ABOUT GEMMA? IS SHE WITH YOU?
A BOYFRIEND? WELL WHERE'S HIS GAFF, THEN?
CHURCH
OAD WEST.
ER THE CHIP
IOP. GOT IT.
NOW LOCK THE DOOR--AND THE WINDOWS, TOO. I'LL EXPLAIN WHEN I SEE YOU.
THE WINDOWS? WE'RE SEVEN BLOODY STORIES UP.
WHAT'S GOING TO GET IN THROUGH THE WINDOWS?

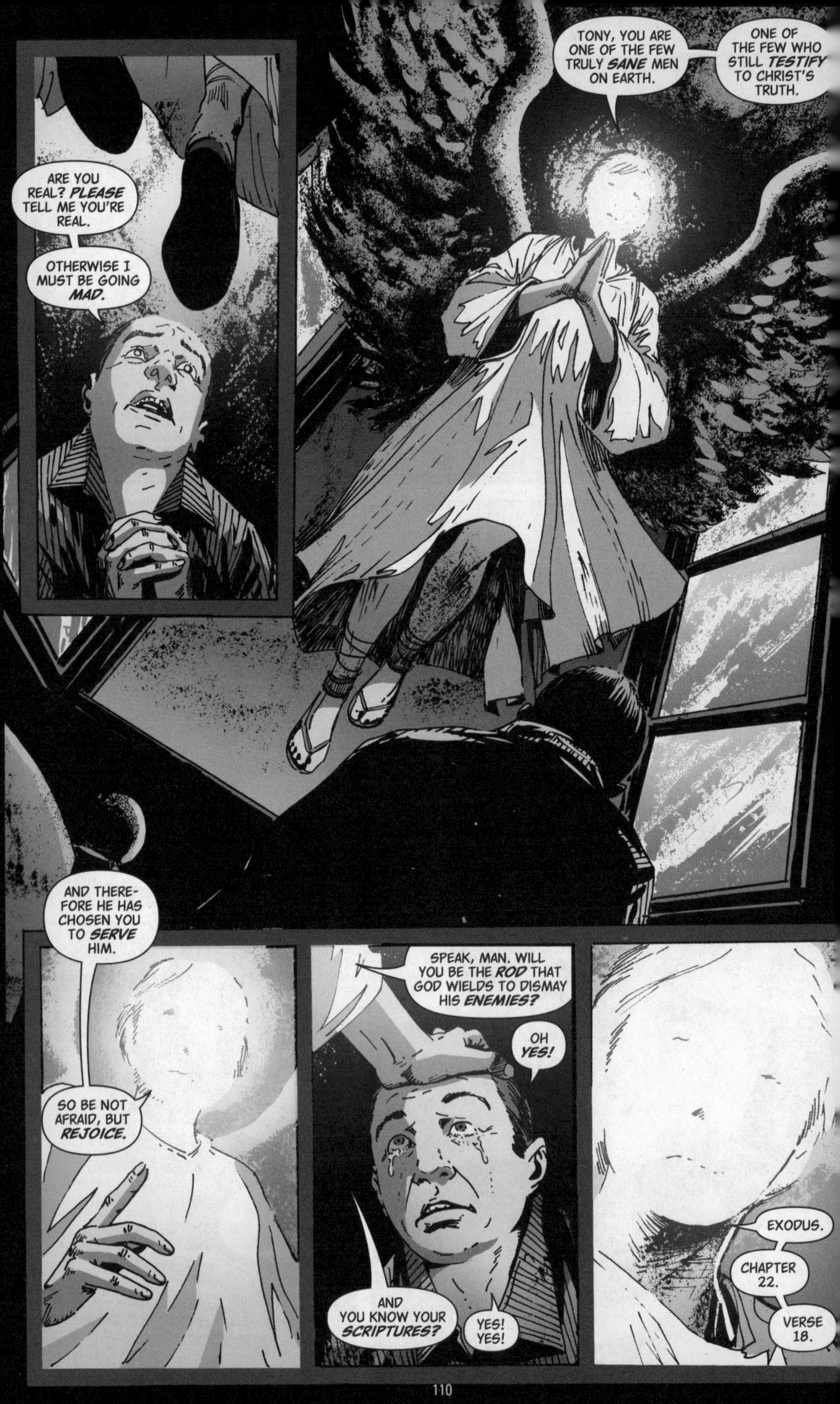

ARE YOU REAL? PLEASE TELL ME YOU'RE REAL.
OTHERWISE I MUST BE GOING MAD.
TONY, YOU ARE ONE OF THE FEW TRULY SANE MEN ON EARTH.
ONE OF THE FEW WHO STILL TESTIFY TO CHRIST'S TRUTH.
AND THEREFORE HE HAS CHOSEN YOU TO SERVE HIM.
SO BE NOT AFRAID, BUT REJOICE.
SPEAK, MAN. WILL YOU BE THE ROD THAT GOD WIELDS TO DISMAY HIS ENEMIES?
OH YES!
AND YOU KNOW YOUR SCRIPTURES?
YES! YES!
EXODUS.
CHAPTER 22.
VERSE 18.

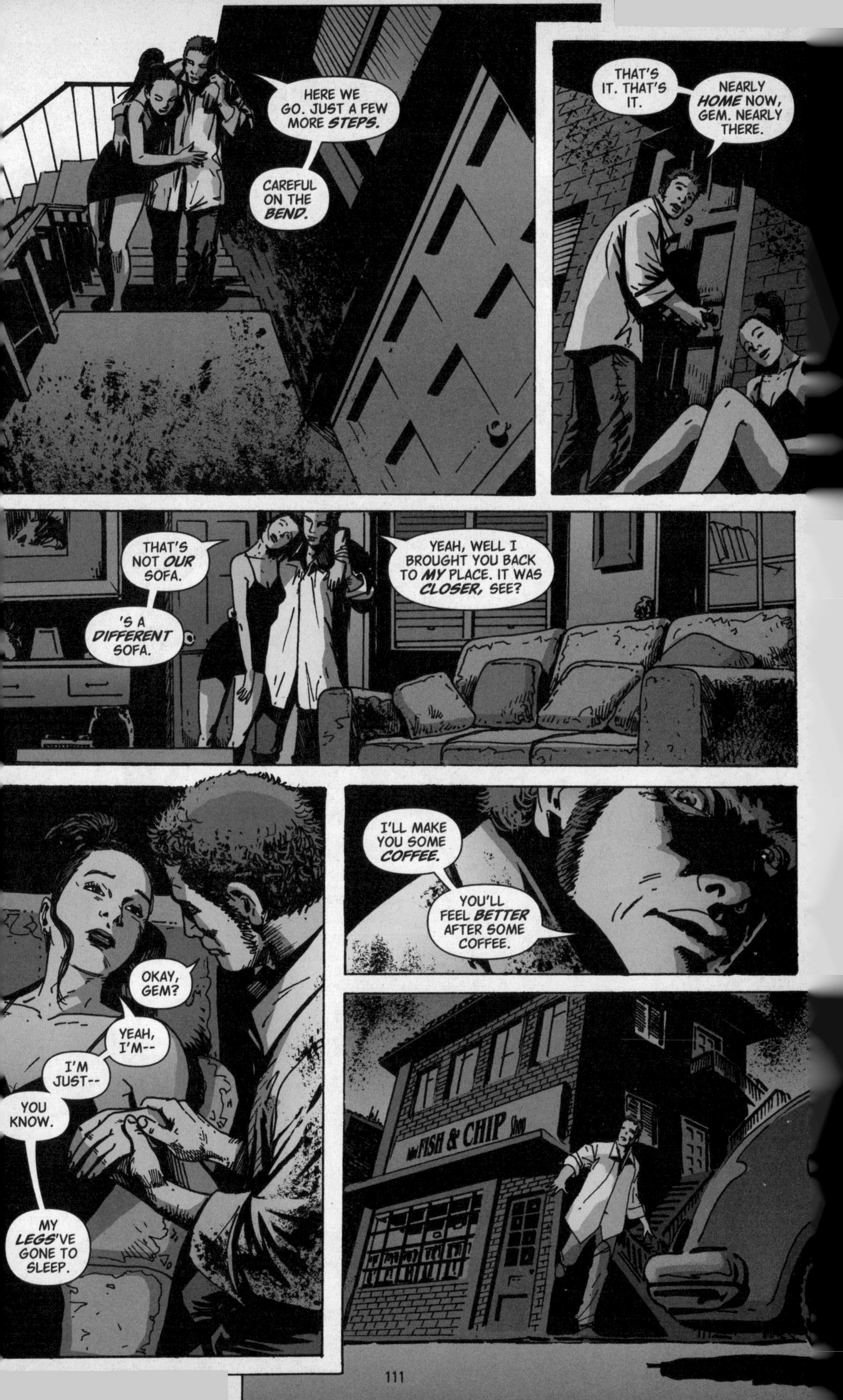
HERE WE GO. JUST A FEW MORE STEPS.
CAREFUL ON THE BEND.
THAT'S IT. THAT'S IT.
NEARLY HOME NOW, GEM. NEARLY THERE.
THAT'S NOT OUR SOFA.
'S A DIFFERENT SOFA.
YEAH, WELL I BROUGHT YOU BACK TO MY PLACE. IT WAS CLOSER, SEE?
OKAY, GEM?
YEAH, I'M--
I'M JUST--
YOU KNOW.
MY LEGS'VE GONE TO SLEEP.
I'LL MAKE YOU SOME COFFEE.
YOU'LL FEEL BETTER AFTER SOME COFFEE.
FISH & CHIP Shop

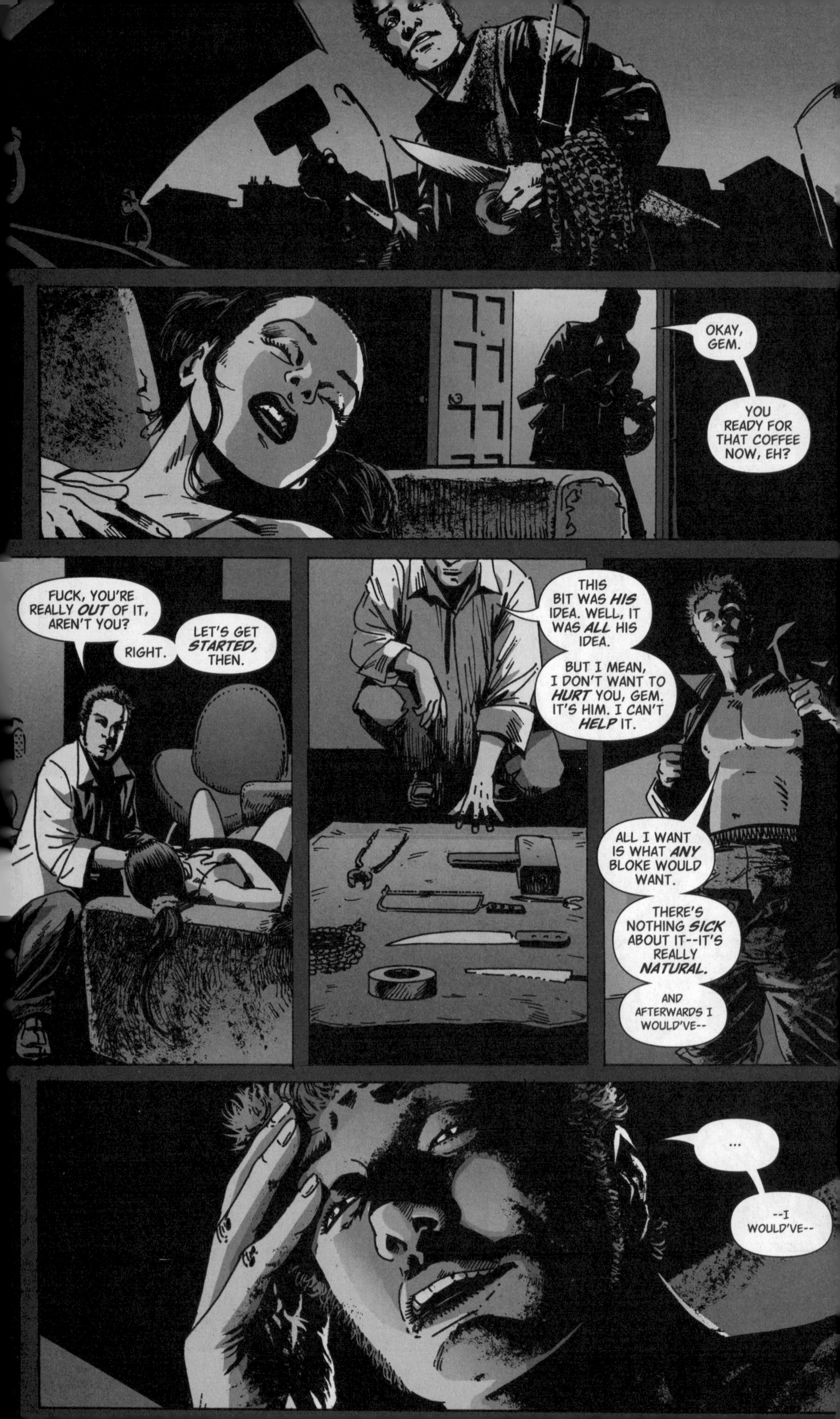

OKAY, GEM.
YOU READY FOR THAT COFFEE NOW, EH?
FUCK, YOU'RE REALLY OUT OF IT, AREN'T YOU?
RIGHT.
LET'S GET STARTED, THEN.
THIS BIT WAS HIS IDEA. WELL, IT WAS ALL HIS IDEA.
BUT I MEAN, I DON'T WANT TO HURT YOU, GEM. IT'S HIM. I CAN'T HELP IT.
ALL I WANT IS WHAT ANY BLOKE WOULD WANT.
THERE'S NOTHING SICK ABOUT IT--IT'S REALLY NATURAL.
AND AFTERWARDS I WOULD'VE--
...
--I WOULD'VE--

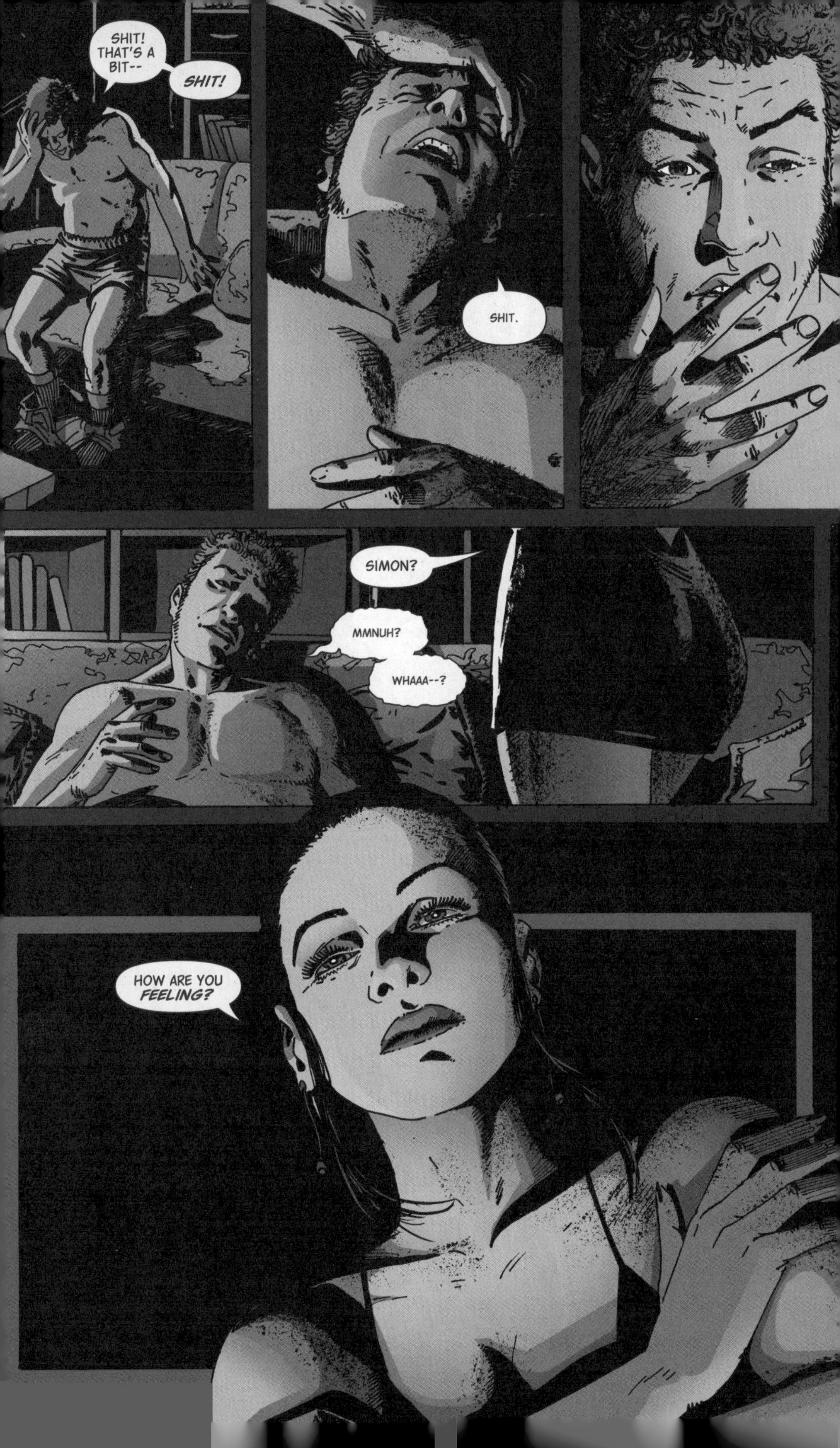
SHIT! THAT'S A BIT--
SHIT!
SHIT.
SIMON?
MMNUH?
WHAAA--?
HOW ARE YOU FEELING?

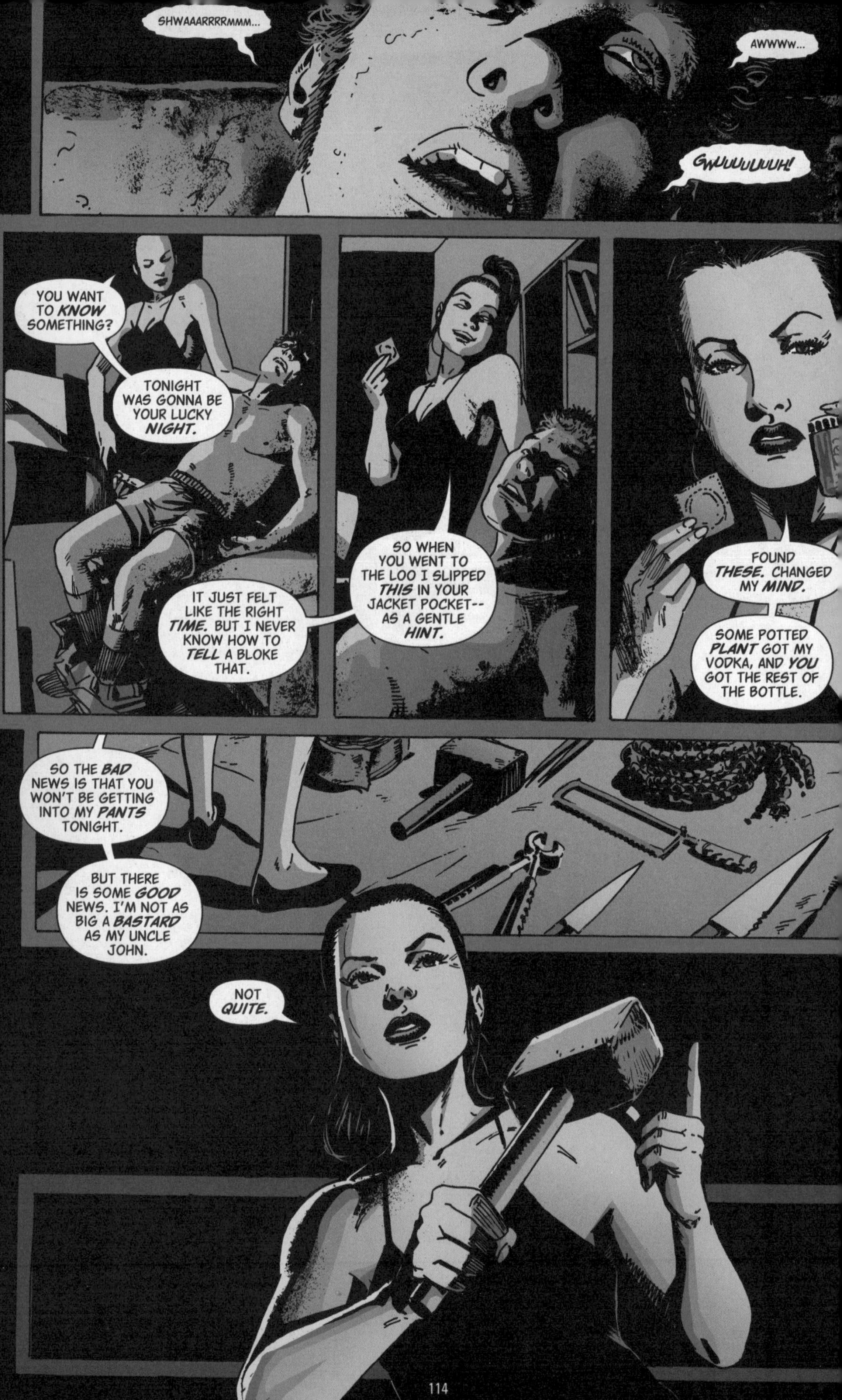
SHWAAARRRRMMM...
AWWWW...
GWUUUUUUH!
YOU WANT TO KNOW SOMETHING?
TONIGHT WAS GONNA BE YOUR LUCKY NIGHT.
IT JUST FELT LIKE THE RIGHT TIME. BUT I NEVER KNOW HOW TO TELL A BLOKE THAT.
SO WHEN YOU WENT TO THE LOO I SLIPPED THIS IN YOUR JACKET POCKET-- AS A GENTLE HINT.
FOUND THESE. CHANGED MY MIND.
SOME POTTED PLANT GOT MY VODKA, AND YOU GOT THE REST OF THE BOTTLE.
SO THE BAD NEWS IS THAT YOU WON'T BE GETTING INTO MY PANTS TONIGHT.
BUT THERE IS SOME GOOD NEWS. I'M NOT AS BIG A BASTARD AS MY UNCLE JOHN.
NOT QUITE.

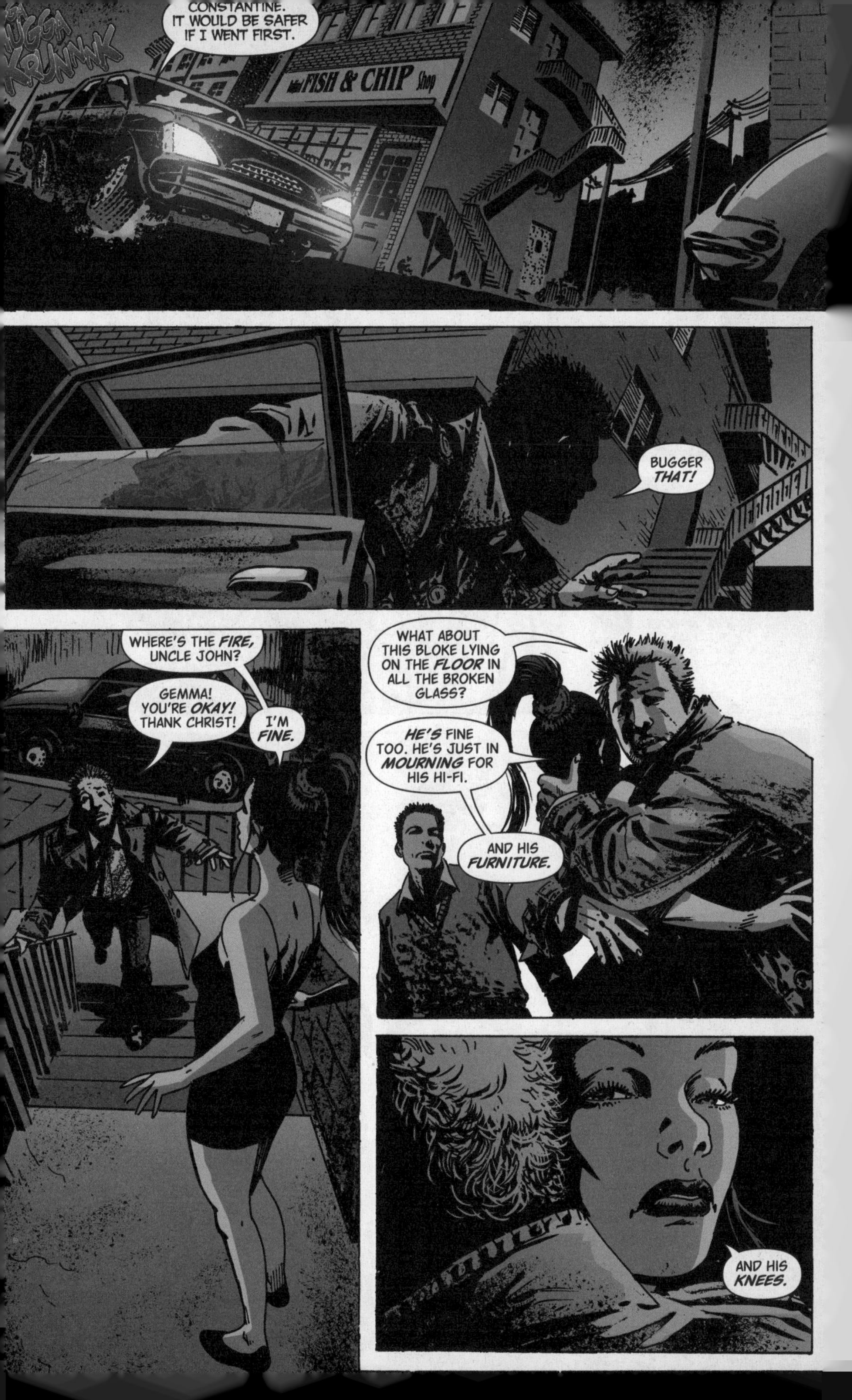
KRUNNNK
CONSTANTINE. IT WOULD BE SAFER IF I WENT FIRST.
FISH & CHIP Shop
BUGGER *THAT!*
WHERE'S THE *FIRE,* UNCLE JOHN?
GEMMA! YOU'RE *OKAY!* THANK CHRIST!
I'M *FINE.*
WHAT ABOUT THIS BLOKE LYING ON THE *FLOOR* IN ALL THE BROKEN GLASS?
HE'S FINE TOO. HE'S JUST IN *MOURNING* FOR HIS HI-FI.
AND HIS *FURNITURE.*
AND HIS *KNEES.*

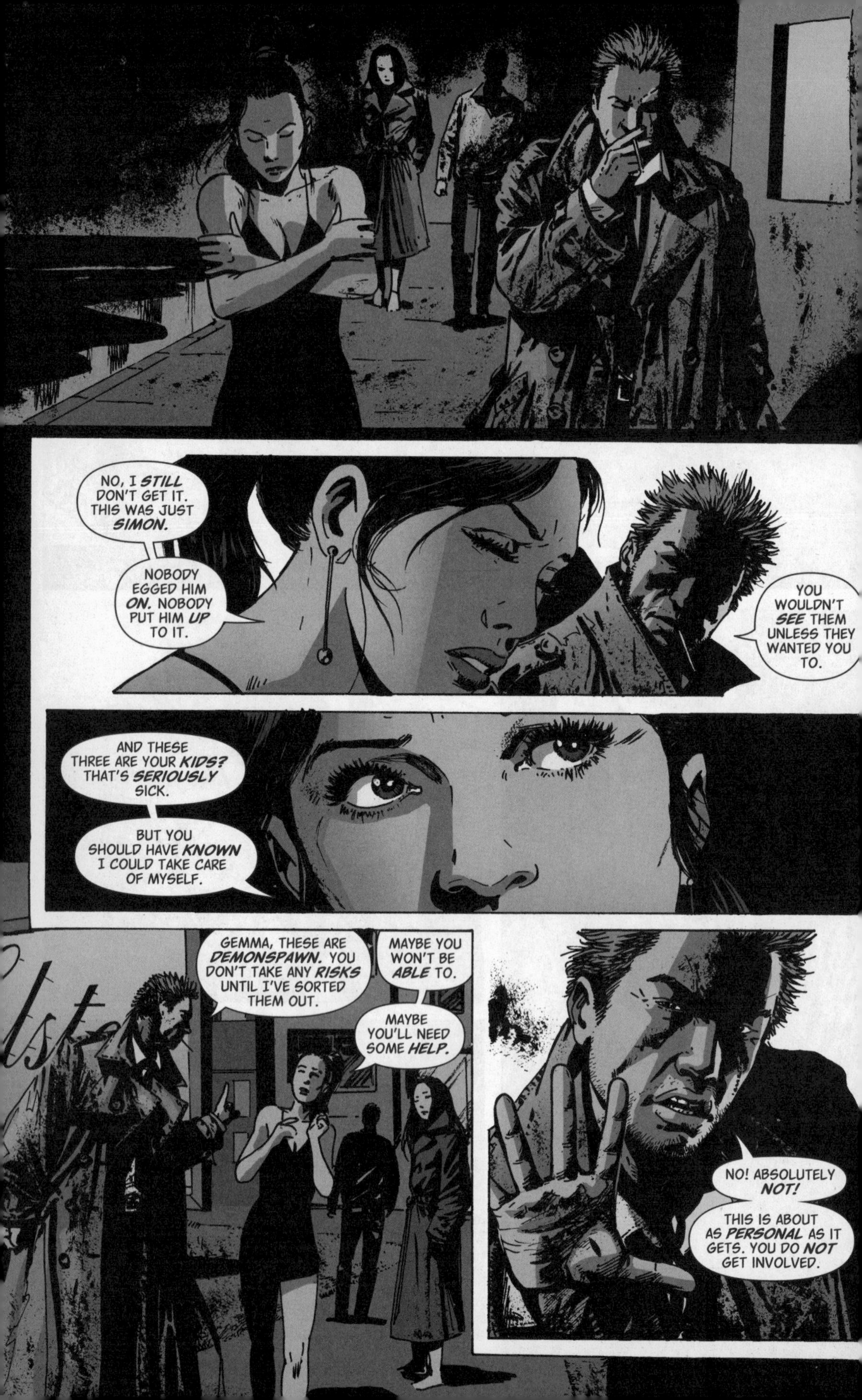
NO, I STILL DON'T GET IT. THIS WAS JUST SIMON.
NOBODY EGGED HIM ON. NOBODY PUT HIM UP TO IT.
YOU WOULDN'T SEE THEM UNLESS THEY WANTED YOU TO.
AND THESE THREE ARE YOUR KIDS? THAT'S SERIOUSLY SICK.
BUT YOU SHOULD HAVE KNOWN I COULD TAKE CARE OF MYSELF.
GEMMA, THESE ARE DEMONSPAWN. YOU DON'T TAKE ANY RISKS UNTIL I'VE SORTED THEM OUT.
MAYBE YOU WON'T BE ABLE TO.
MAYBE YOU'LL NEED SOME HELP.
NO! ABSOLUTELY NOT!
THIS IS ABOUT AS PERSONAL AS IT GETS. YOU DO NOT GET INVOLVED.

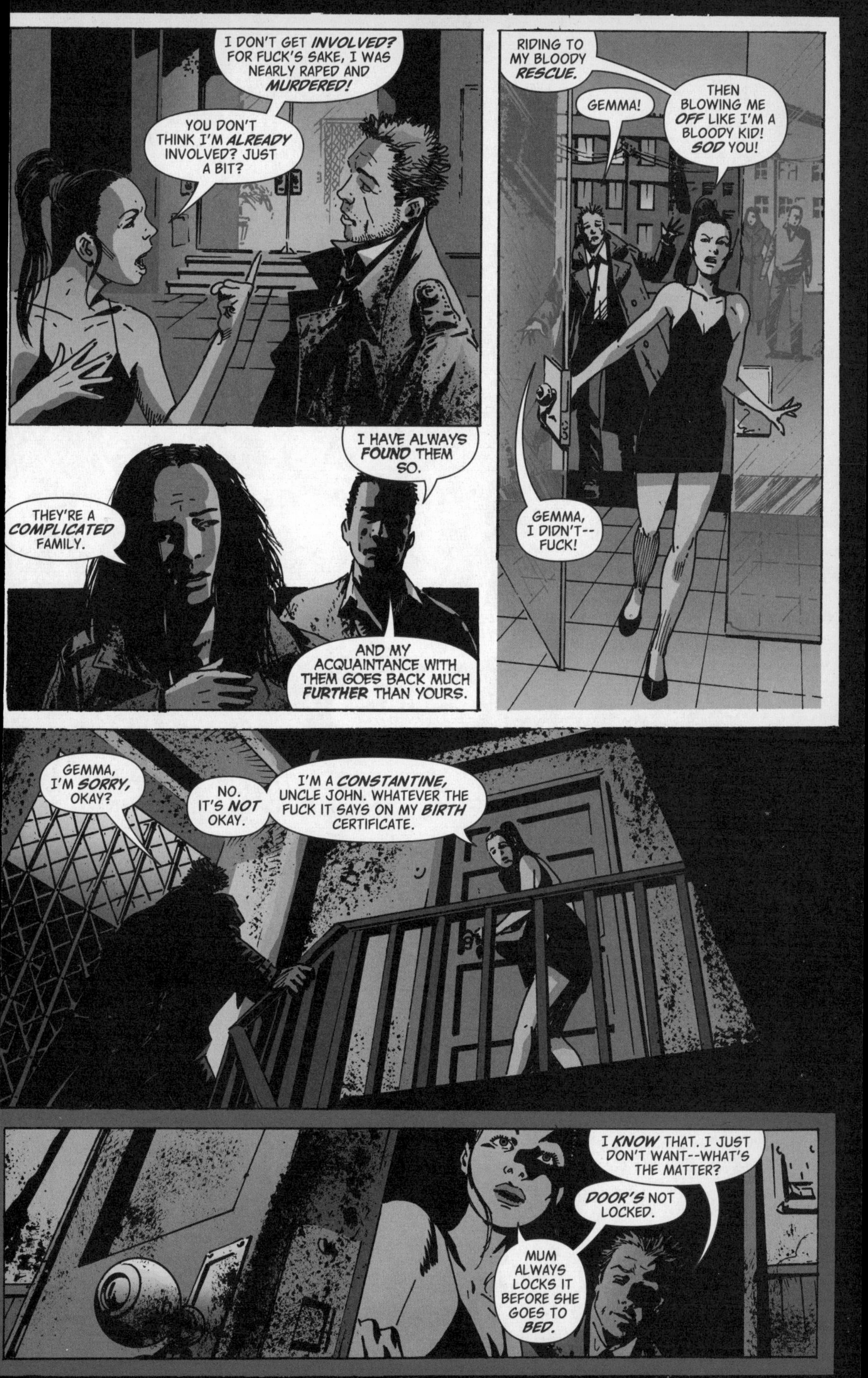
I DON'T GET INVOLVED? FOR FUCK'S SAKE, I WAS NEARLY RAPED AND MURDERED!
YOU DON'T THINK I'M ALREADY INVOLVED? JUST A BIT?
RIDING TO MY BLOODY RESCUE.
GEMMA!
THEN BLOWING ME OFF LIKE I'M A BLOODY KID! SOD YOU!
GEMMA, I DIDN'T-- FUCK!
THEY'RE A COMPLICATED FAMILY.
I HAVE ALWAYS FOUND THEM SO.
AND MY ACQUAINTANCE WITH THEM GOES BACK MUCH FURTHER THAN YOURS.
GEMMA, I'M SORRY, OKAY?
NO. IT'S NOT OKAY.
I'M A CONSTANTINE, UNCLE JOHN. WHATEVER THE FUCK IT SAYS ON MY BIRTH CERTIFICATE.
I KNOW THAT. I JUST DON'T WANT--WHAT'S THE MATTER?
DOOR'S NOT LOCKED.
MUM ALWAYS LOCKS IT BEFORE SHE GOES TO BED.

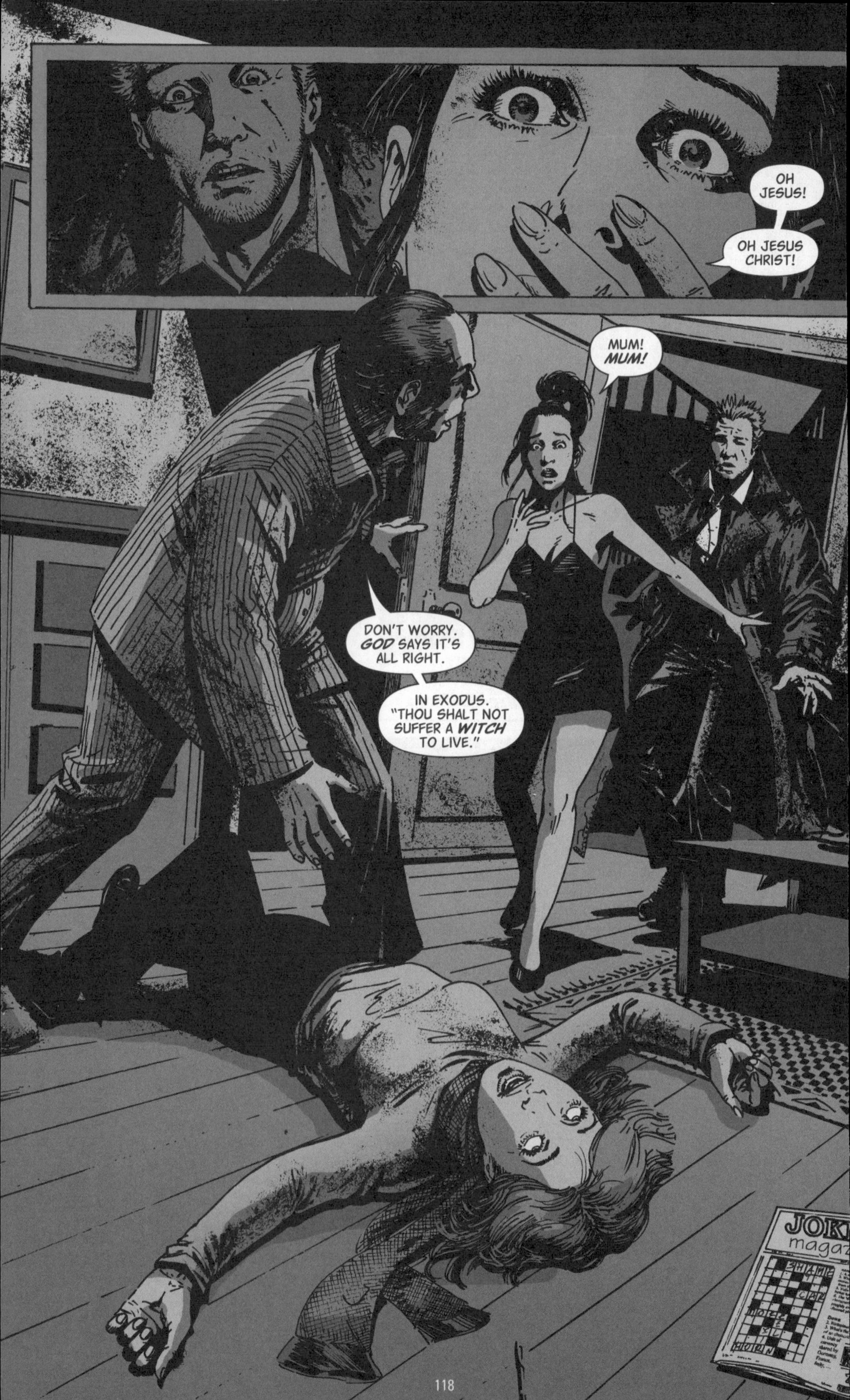
OH JESUS!
OH JESUS CHRIST!
MUM! MUM!
DON'T WORRY. GOD SAYS IT'S ALL RIGHT.
IN EXODUS. "THOU SHALT NOT SUFFER A WITCH TO LIVE."
JOK
magaz

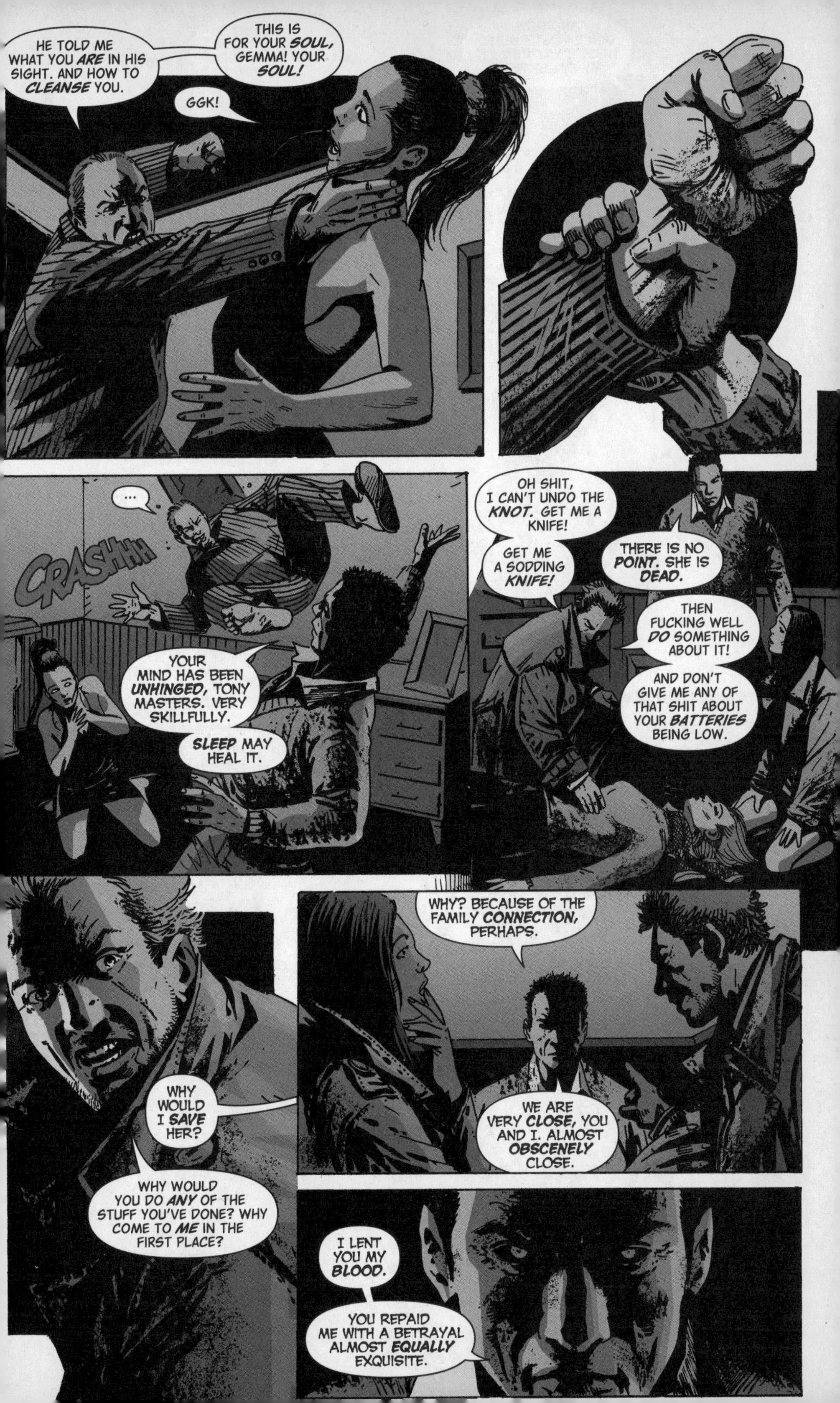

HE TOLD ME WHAT YOU ARE IN HIS SIGHT. AND HOW TO CLEANSE YOU.
THIS IS FOR YOUR SOUL, GEMMA! YOUR SOUL!
GGK!
...
CRASHHH
YOUR MIND HAS BEEN UNHINGED, TONY MASTERS. VERY SKILLFULLY.
SLEEP MAY HEAL IT.
OH SHIT, I CAN'T UNDO THE KNOT. GET ME A KNIFE!
GET ME A SODDING KNIFE!
THERE IS NO POINT. SHE IS DEAD.
THEN FUCKING WELL DO SOMETHING ABOUT IT!
AND DON'T GIVE ME ANY OF THAT SHIT ABOUT YOUR BATTERIES BEING LOW.
WHY WOULD I SAVE HER?
WHY WOULD YOU DO ANY OF THE STUFF YOU'VE DONE? WHY COME TO ME IN THE FIRST PLACE?
WHY? BECAUSE OF THE FAMILY CONNECTION, PERHAPS.
WE ARE VERY CLOSE, YOU AND I. ALMOST OBSCENELY CLOSE.
I LENT YOU MY BLOOD.
YOU REPAID ME WITH A BETRAYAL ALMOST EQUALLY EXQUISITE.

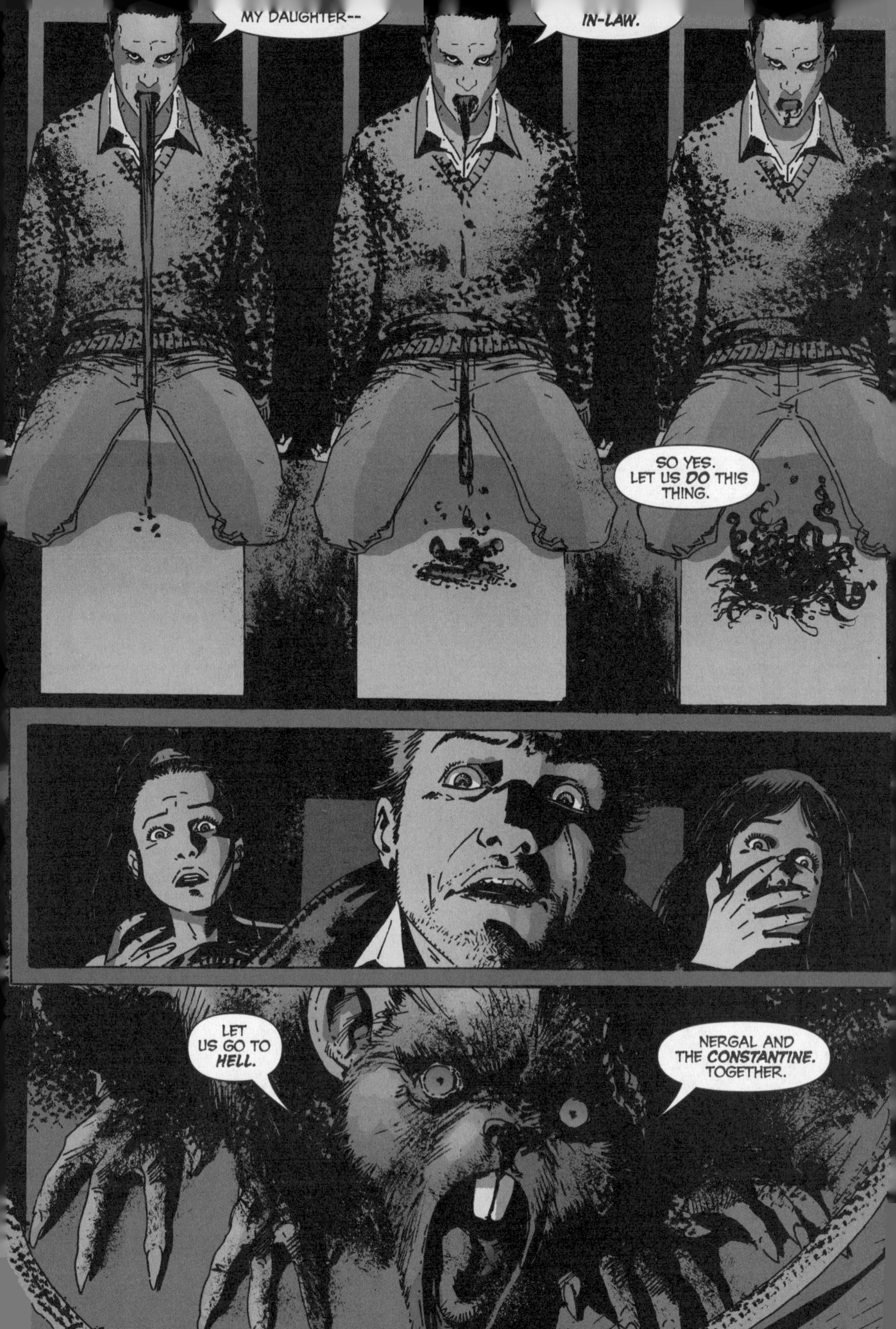
MY DAUGHTER--
IN-LAW.
SO YES. LET US DO THIS THING.
LET US GO TO HELL.
NERGAL AND THE CONSTANTINE. TOGETHER.

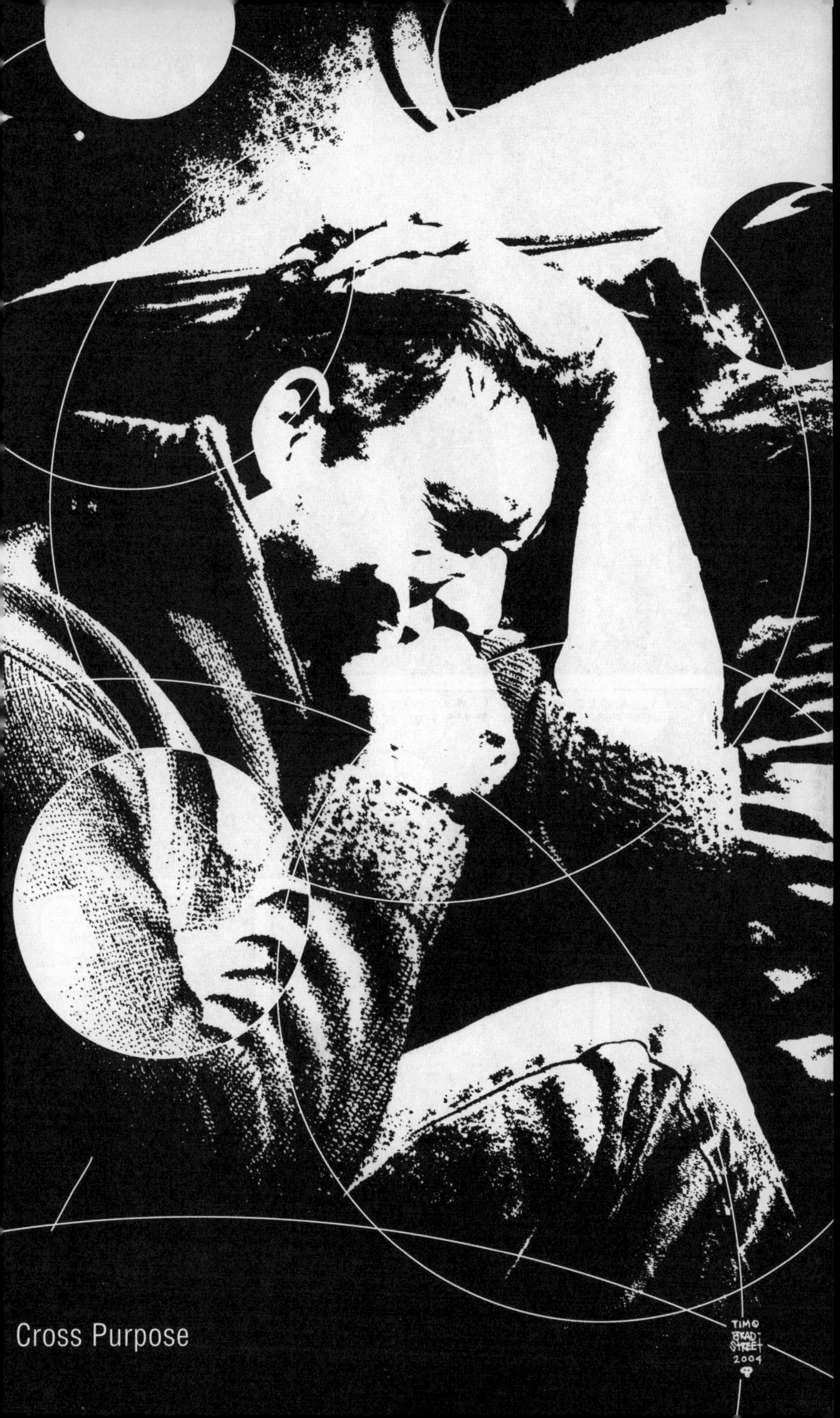
TIMO BRAD-STREET 2004

Cross Purpose

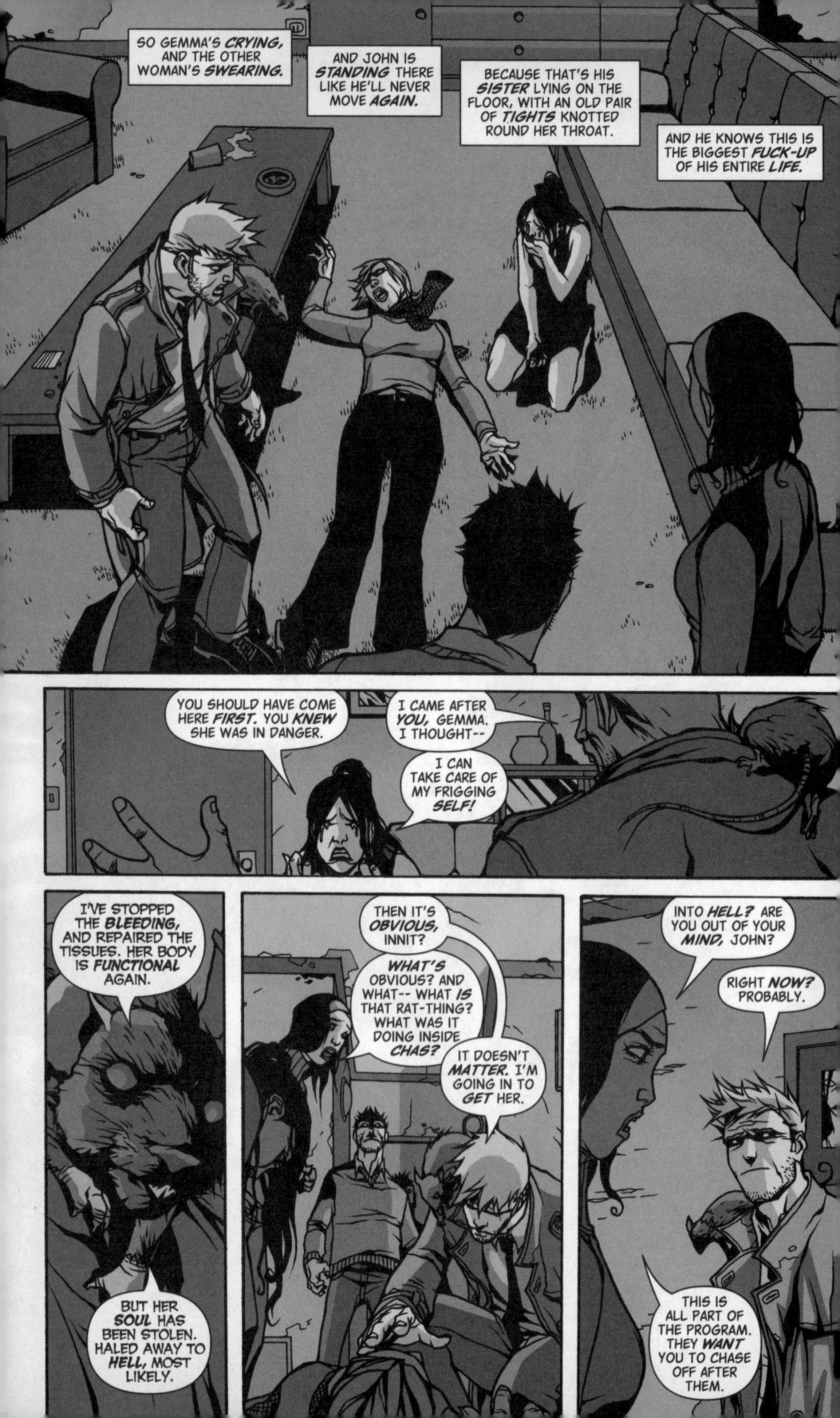

SO GEMMA'S CRYING, AND THE OTHER WOMAN'S SWEARING.
AND JOHN IS STANDING THERE LIKE HE'LL NEVER MOVE AGAIN.
BECAUSE THAT'S HIS SISTER LYING ON THE FLOOR, WITH AN OLD PAIR OF TIGHTS KNOTTED ROUND HER THROAT.
AND HE KNOWS THIS IS THE BIGGEST FUCK-UP OF HIS ENTIRE LIFE.
YOU SHOULD HAVE COME HERE FIRST. YOU KNEW SHE WAS IN DANGER.
I CAME AFTER YOU, GEMMA. I THOUGHT--
I CAN TAKE CARE OF MY FRIGGING SELF!
I'VE STOPPED THE BLEEDING, AND REPAIRED THE TISSUES. HER BODY IS FUNCTIONAL AGAIN.
BUT HER SOUL HAS BEEN STOLEN. HALED AWAY TO HELL, MOST LIKELY.
THEN IT'S OBVIOUS, INNIT?
WHAT'S OBVIOUS? AND WHAT-- WHAT IS THAT RAT-THING? WHAT WAS IT DOING INSIDE CHAS?
IT DOESN'T MATTER. I'M GOING IN TO GET HER.
INTO HELL? ARE YOU OUT OF YOUR MIND, JOHN?
RIGHT NOW? PROBABLY.
THIS IS ALL PART OF THE PROGRAM. THEY WANT YOU TO CHASE OFF AFTER THEM.

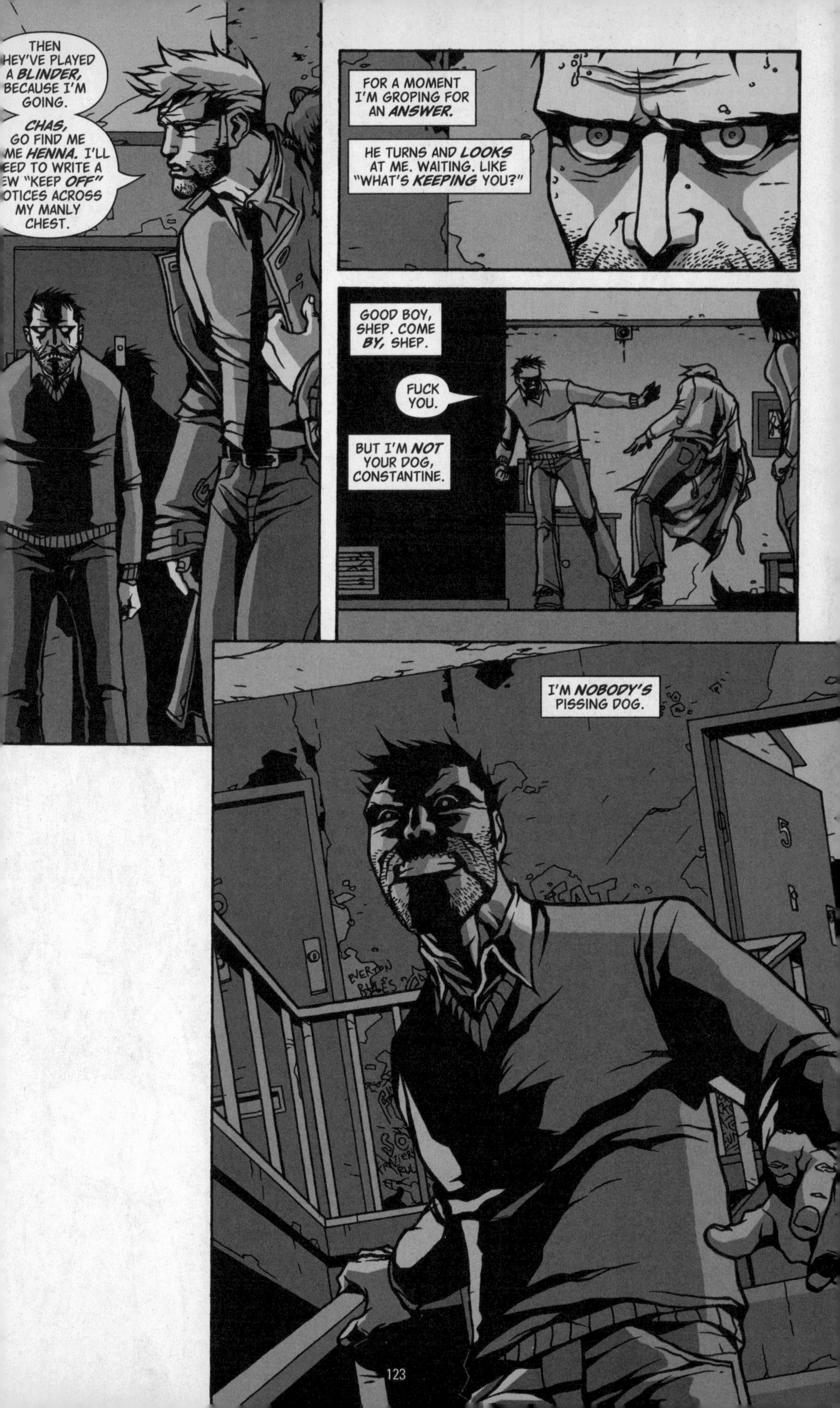
THEN HEY'VE PLAYED A BLINDER, BECAUSE I'M GOING.
CHAS, GO FIND ME ME HENNA. I'LL EED TO WRITE A EW "KEEP OFF" OTICES ACROSS MY MANLY CHEST.
FOR A MOMENT I'M GROPING FOR AN ANSWER.
HE TURNS AND LOOKS AT ME. WAITING. LIKE "WHAT'S KEEPING YOU?"
GOOD BOY, SHEP. COME BY, SHEP.
FUCK YOU.
BUT I'M NOT YOUR DOG, CONSTANTINE.
I'M NOBODY'S PISSING DOG.
EVERTON RULES
5

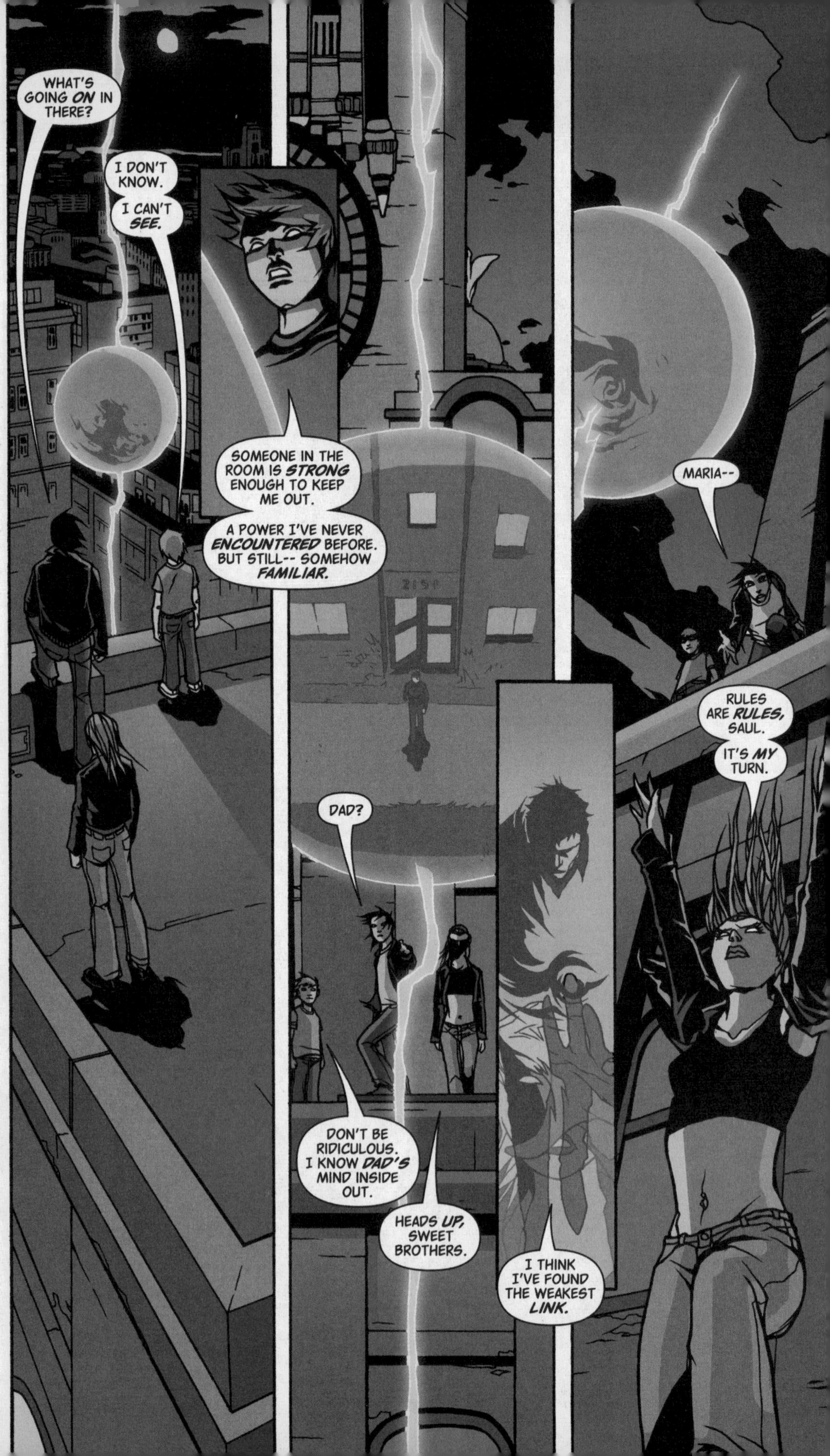
WHAT'S GOING ON IN THERE?
I DON'T KNOW.
I CAN'T SEE.
SOMEONE IN THE ROOM IS STRONG ENOUGH TO KEEP ME OUT.
A POWER I'VE NEVER ENCOUNTERED BEFORE. BUT STILL-- SOMEHOW FAMILIAR.
DAD?
DON'T BE RIDICULOUS. I KNOW DAD'S MIND INSIDE OUT.
HEADS UP, SWEET BROTHERS.
I THINK I'VE FOUND THE WEAKEST LINK.
MARIA--
RULES ARE RULES, SAUL.
IT'S MY TURN.

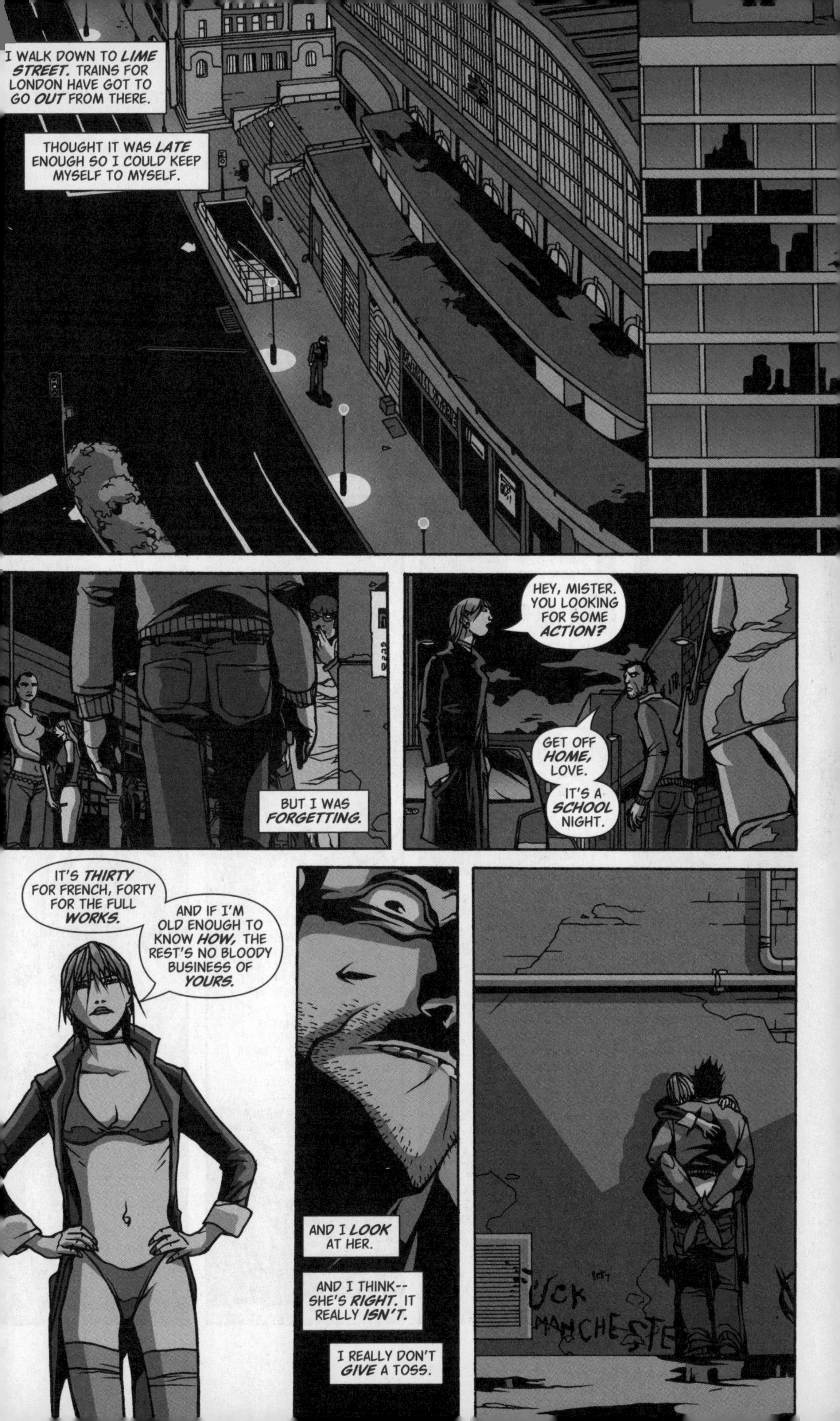
I WALK DOWN TO *LIME STREET.* TRAINS FOR LONDON HAVE GOT TO GO *OUT* FROM THERE.
THOUGHT IT WAS *LATE* ENOUGH SO I COULD KEEP MYSELF TO MYSELF.
BUT I WAS *FORGETTING.*
HEY, MISTER. YOU LOOKING FOR SOME *ACTION?*
GET OFF *HOME,* LOVE.
IT'S A *SCHOOL* NIGHT.
IT'S *THIRTY* FOR FRENCH, FORTY FOR THE FULL *WORKS.*
AND IF I'M OLD ENOUGH TO KNOW *HOW,* THE REST'S NO BLOODY BUSINESS OF *YOURS.*
AND I *LOOK* AT HER.
AND I THINK-- SHE'S *RIGHT.* IT REALLY *ISN'T.*
I REALLY DON'T *GIVE* A TOSS.

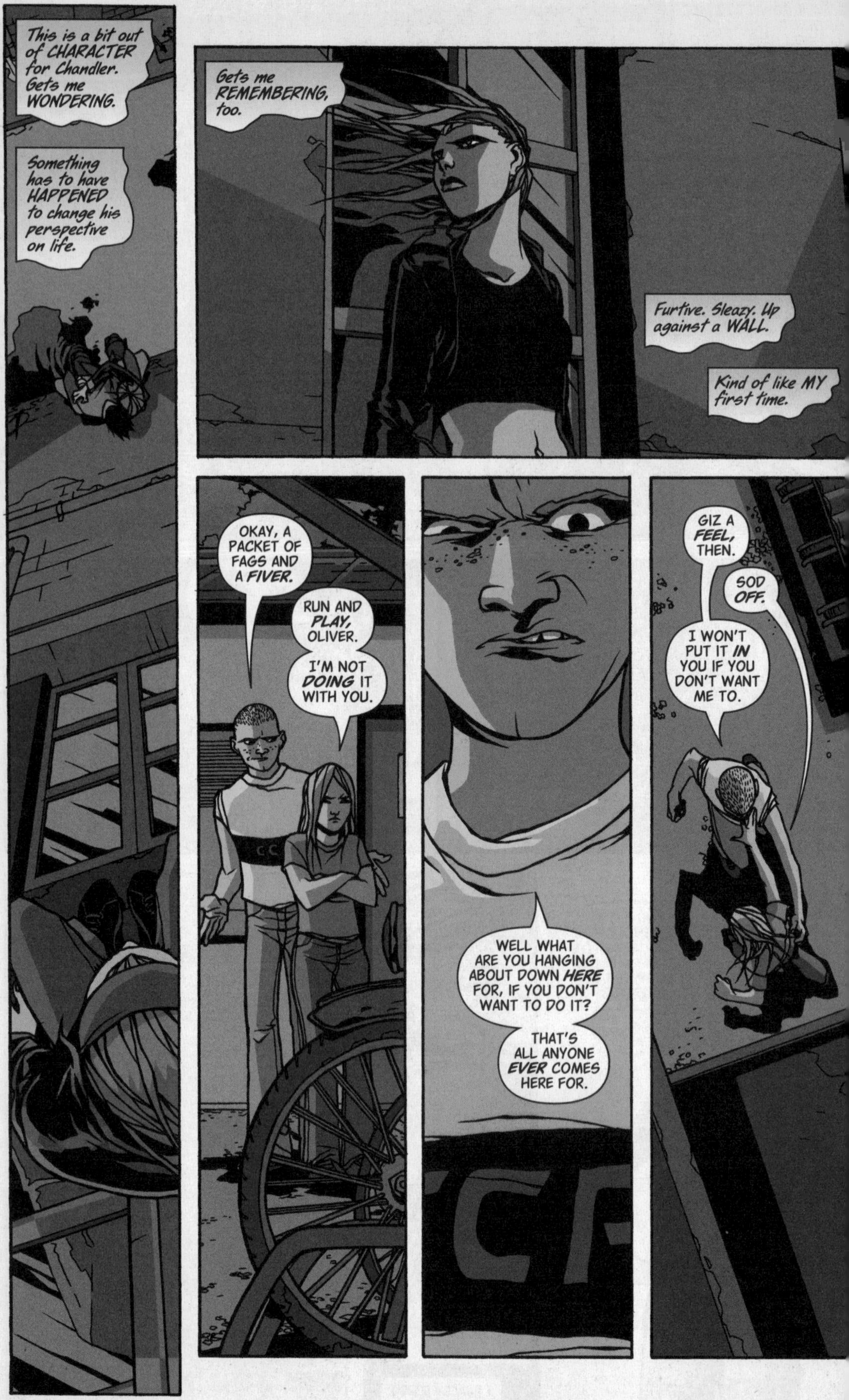
This is a bit out of CHARACTER for Chandler. Gets me WONDERING.
Something has to have HAPPENED to change his perspective on life.
Gets me REMEMBERING, too.
Furtive. Sleazy. Up against a WALL.
Kind of like MY first time.
OKAY, A PACKET OF FAGS AND A FIVER.
RUN AND PLAY, OLIVER.
I'M NOT DOING IT WITH YOU.
WELL WHAT ARE YOU HANGING ABOUT DOWN HERE FOR, IF YOU DON'T WANT TO DO IT?
THAT'S ALL ANYONE EVER COMES HERE FOR.
GIZ A FEEL, THEN.
SOD OFF.
I WON'T PUT IT IN YOU IF YOU DON'T WANT ME TO.

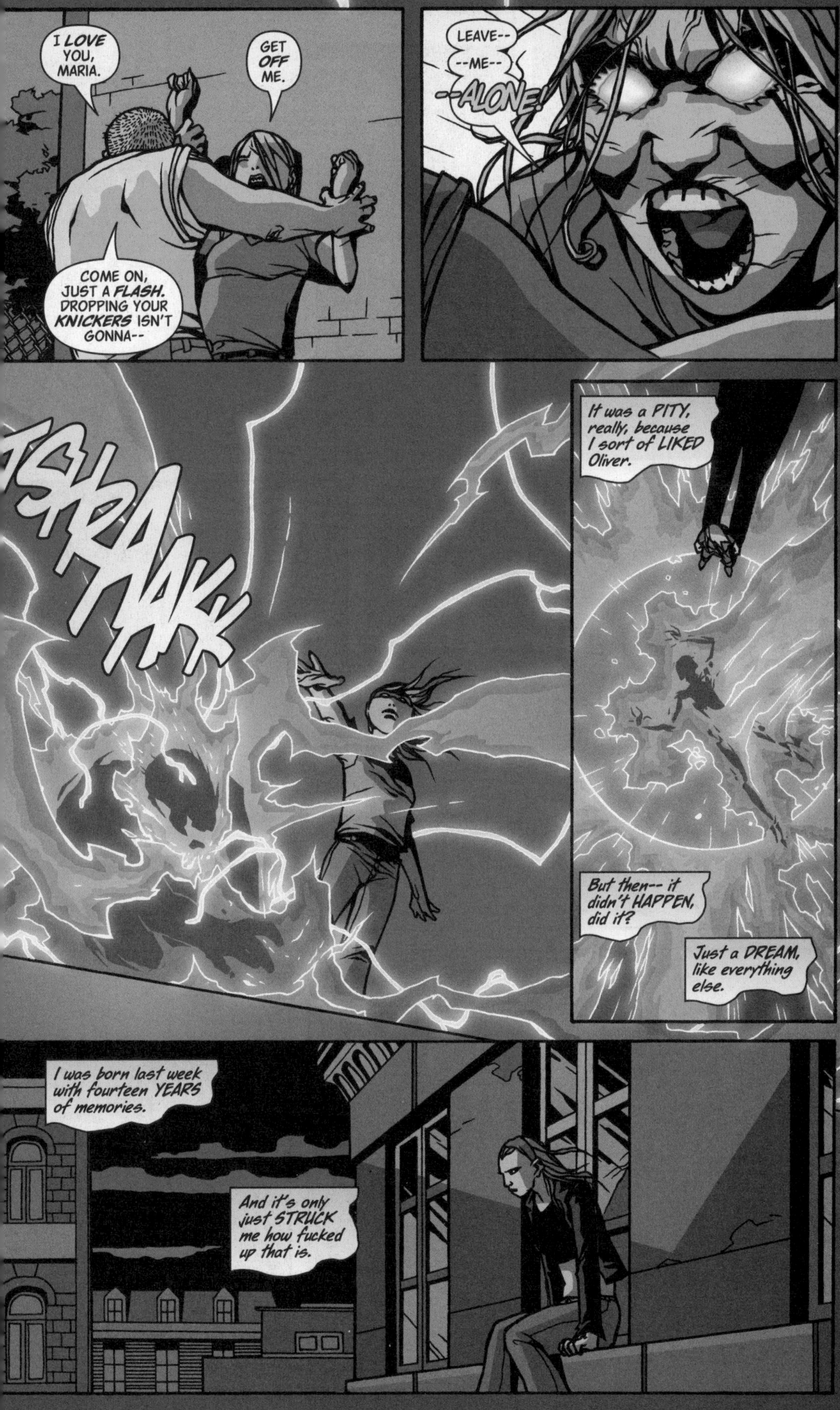
I LOVE YOU, MARIA.
GET OFF ME.
COME ON, JUST A FLASH. DROPPING YOUR KNICKERS ISN'T GONNA--
LEAVE--
--ME--
--ALONE!
TSHRAAKK!
It was a PITY, really, because I sort of LIKED Oliver.
But then-- it didn't HAPPEN, did it?
Just a DREAM, like everything else.
I was born last week with fourteen YEARS of memories.
And it's only just STRUCK me how fucked up that is.

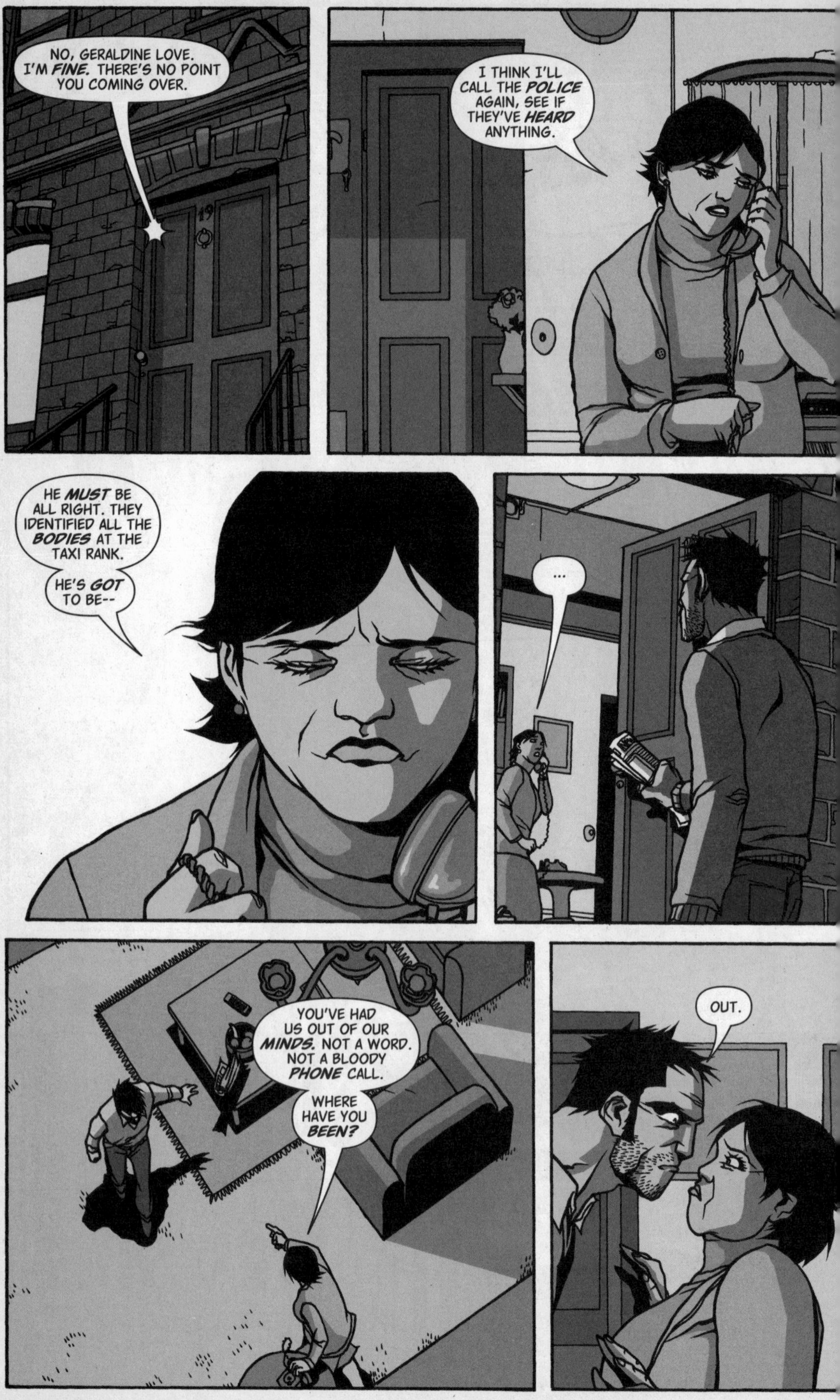

NO, GERALDINE LOVE. I'M FINE. THERE'S NO POINT YOU COMING OVER.
I THINK I'LL CALL THE POLICE AGAIN, SEE IF THEY'VE HEARD ANYTHING.
HE MUST BE ALL RIGHT. THEY IDENTIFIED ALL THE BODIES AT THE TAXI RANK.
HE'S GOT TO BE--
...
YOU'VE HAD US OUT OF OUR MINDS. NOT A WORD. NOT A BLOODY PHONE CALL.
WHERE HAVE YOU BEEN?
OUT.

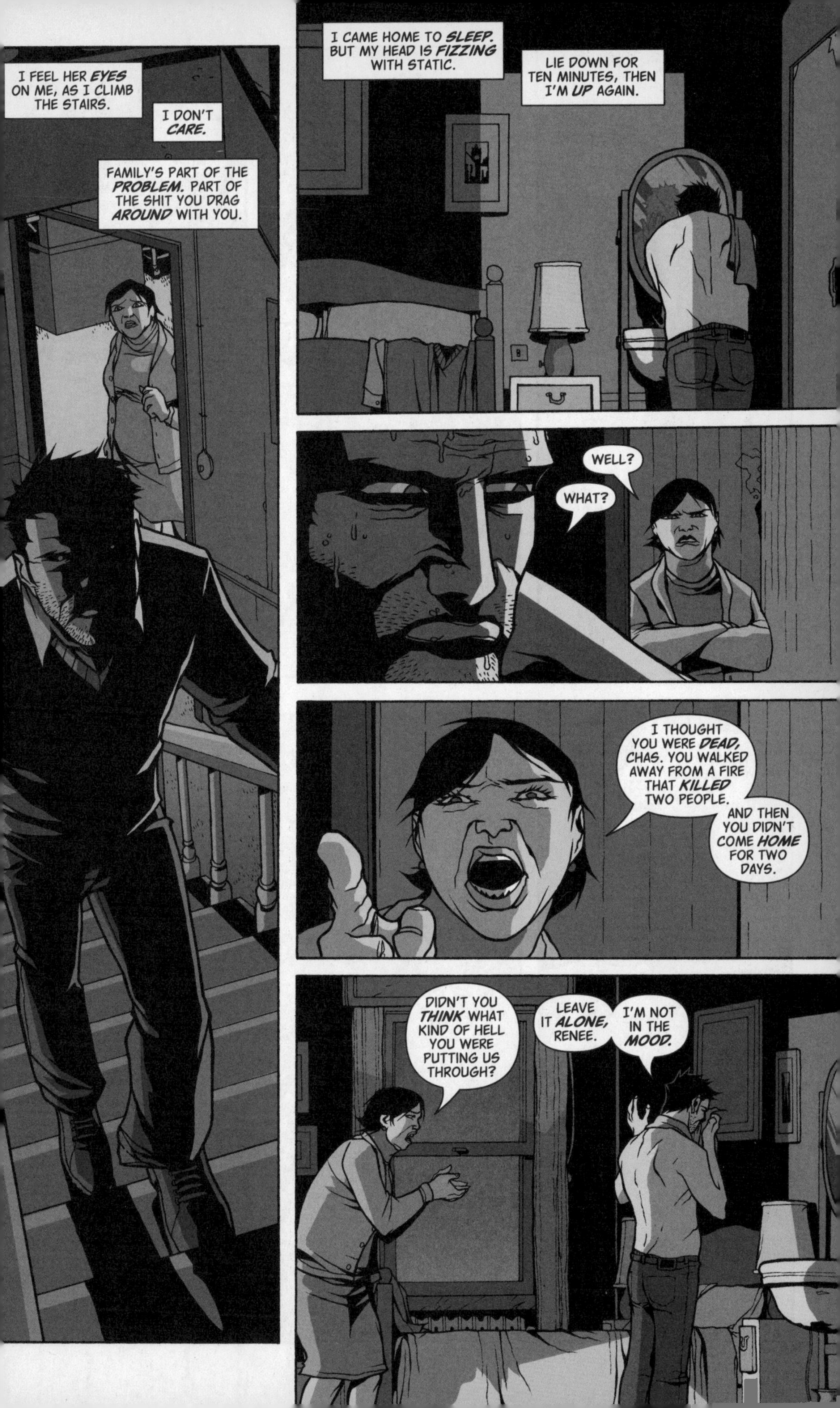
I FEEL HER EYES ON ME, AS I CLIMB THE STAIRS.
I DON'T CARE.
FAMILY'S PART OF THE PROBLEM. PART OF THE SHIT YOU DRAG AROUND WITH YOU.
I CAME HOME TO SLEEP. BUT MY HEAD IS FIZZING WITH STATIC.
LIE DOWN FOR TEN MINUTES, THEN I'M UP AGAIN.
WELL?
WHAT?
I THOUGHT YOU WERE DEAD, CHAS. YOU WALKED AWAY FROM A FIRE THAT KILLED TWO PEOPLE.
AND THEN YOU DIDN'T COME HOME FOR TWO DAYS.
DIDN'T YOU THINK WHAT KIND OF HELL YOU WERE PUTTING US THROUGH?
LEAVE IT ALONE, RENEE.
I'M NOT IN THE MOOD.

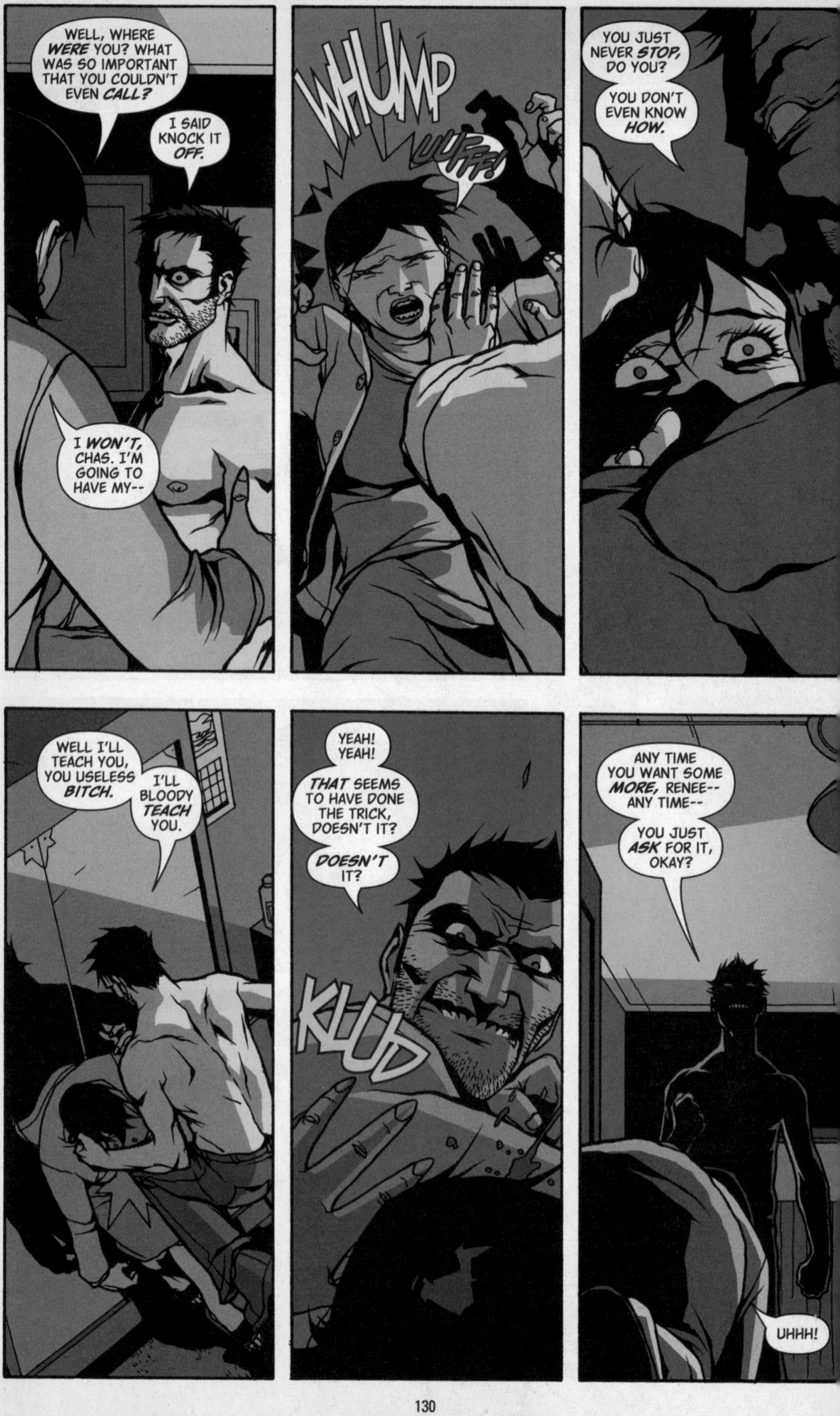
WELL, WHERE WERE YOU? WHAT WAS SO IMPORTANT THAT YOU COULDN'T EVEN CALL?
I SAID KNOCK IT OFF.
I WON'T, CHAS. I'M GOING TO HAVE MY--
WHUMP
UUFF!
YOU JUST NEVER STOP, DO YOU?
YOU DON'T EVEN KNOW HOW.
WELL I'LL TEACH YOU, YOU USELESS BITCH.
I'LL BLOODY TEACH YOU.
YEAH! YEAH!
THAT SEEMS TO HAVE DONE THE TRICK, DOESN'T IT?
DOESN'T IT?
KLUD
ANY TIME YOU WANT SOME MORE, RENEE-- ANY TIME--
YOU JUST ASK FOR IT, OKAY?
UHHH!

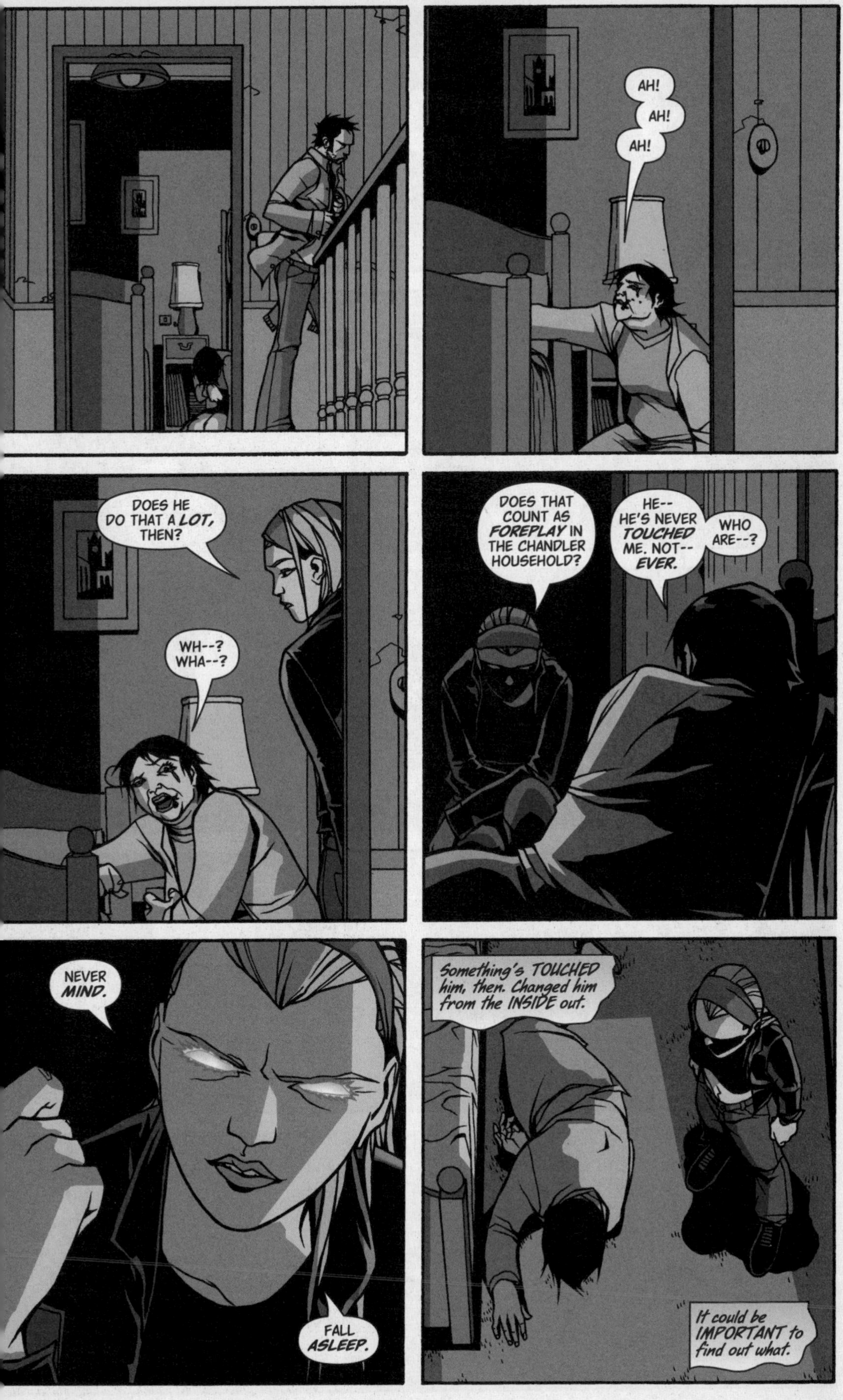
AH!
AH!
AH!
DOES HE DO THAT A *LOT*, THEN?
WH--? WHA--?
DOES THAT COUNT AS *FOREPLAY* IN THE CHANDLER HOUSEHOLD?
HE-- HE'S NEVER *TOUCHED* ME. NOT-- *EVER*.
WHO ARE--?
NEVER *MIND*.
FALL *ASLEEP*.
Something's TOUCHED him, then. Changed him from the INSIDE out.
It could be IMPORTANT to find out what.

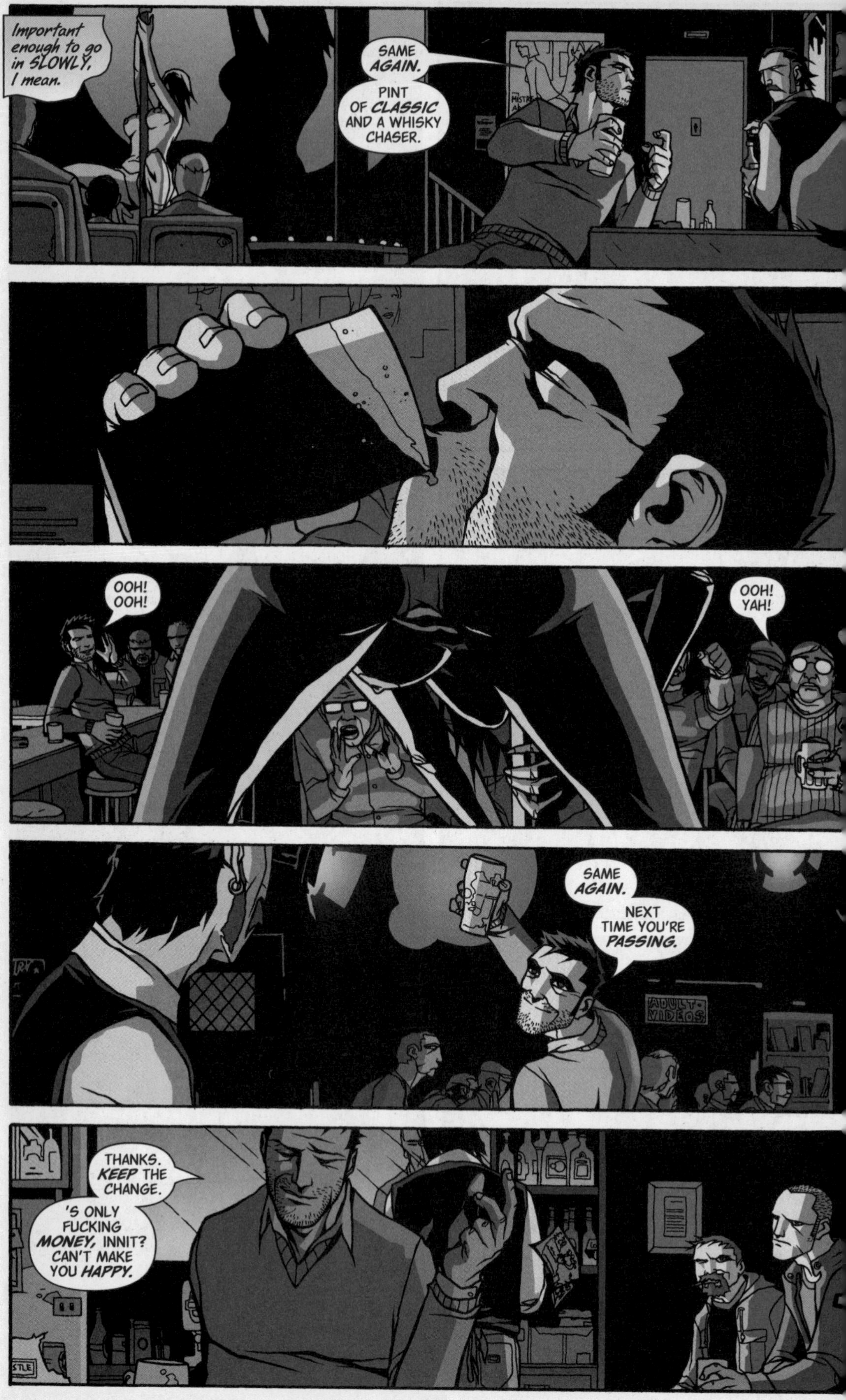
Important enough to go in SLOWLY, I mean.
SAME AGAIN.
PINT OF CLASSIC AND A WHISKY CHASER.
OOH! OOH!
OOH! YAH!
SAME AGAIN.
NEXT TIME YOU'RE PASSING.
ADULT VIDEOS
THANKS. KEEP THE CHANGE.
'S ONLY FUCKING MONEY, INNIT? CAN'T MAKE YOU HAPPY.

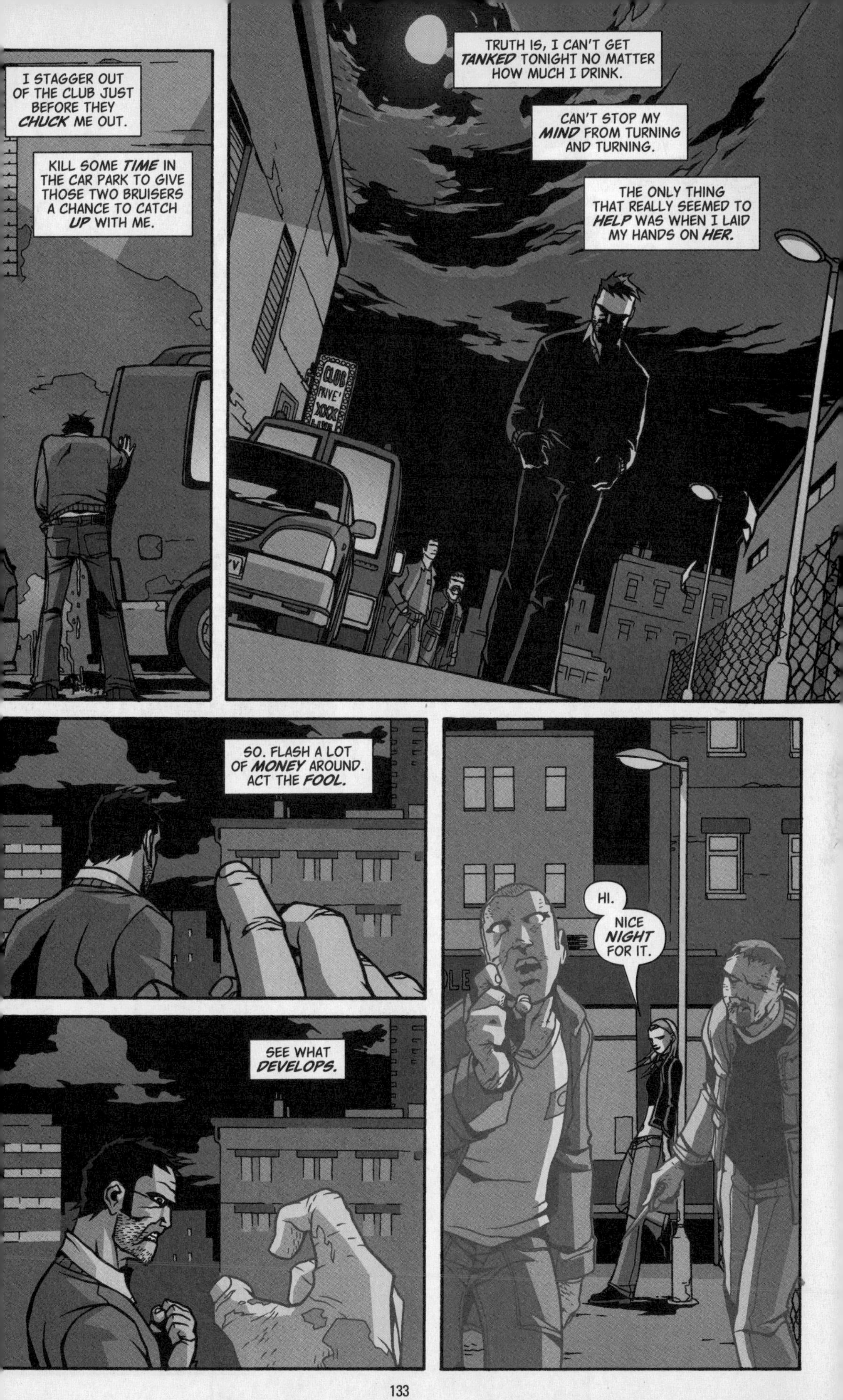

I STAGGER OUT OF THE CLUB JUST BEFORE THEY *CHUCK* ME OUT.
KILL SOME *TIME* IN THE CAR PARK TO GIVE THOSE TWO BRUISERS A CHANCE TO CATCH *UP* WITH ME.
TRUTH IS, I CAN'T GET *TANKED* TONIGHT NO MATTER HOW MUCH I DRINK.
CAN'T STOP MY *MIND* FROM TURNING AND TURNING.
THE ONLY THING THAT REALLY SEEMED TO *HELP* WAS WHEN I LAID MY HANDS ON *HER.*
SO. FLASH A LOT OF *MONEY* AROUND. ACT THE *FOOL.*
SEE WHAT *DEVELOPS.*
HI.
NICE *NIGHT* FOR IT.

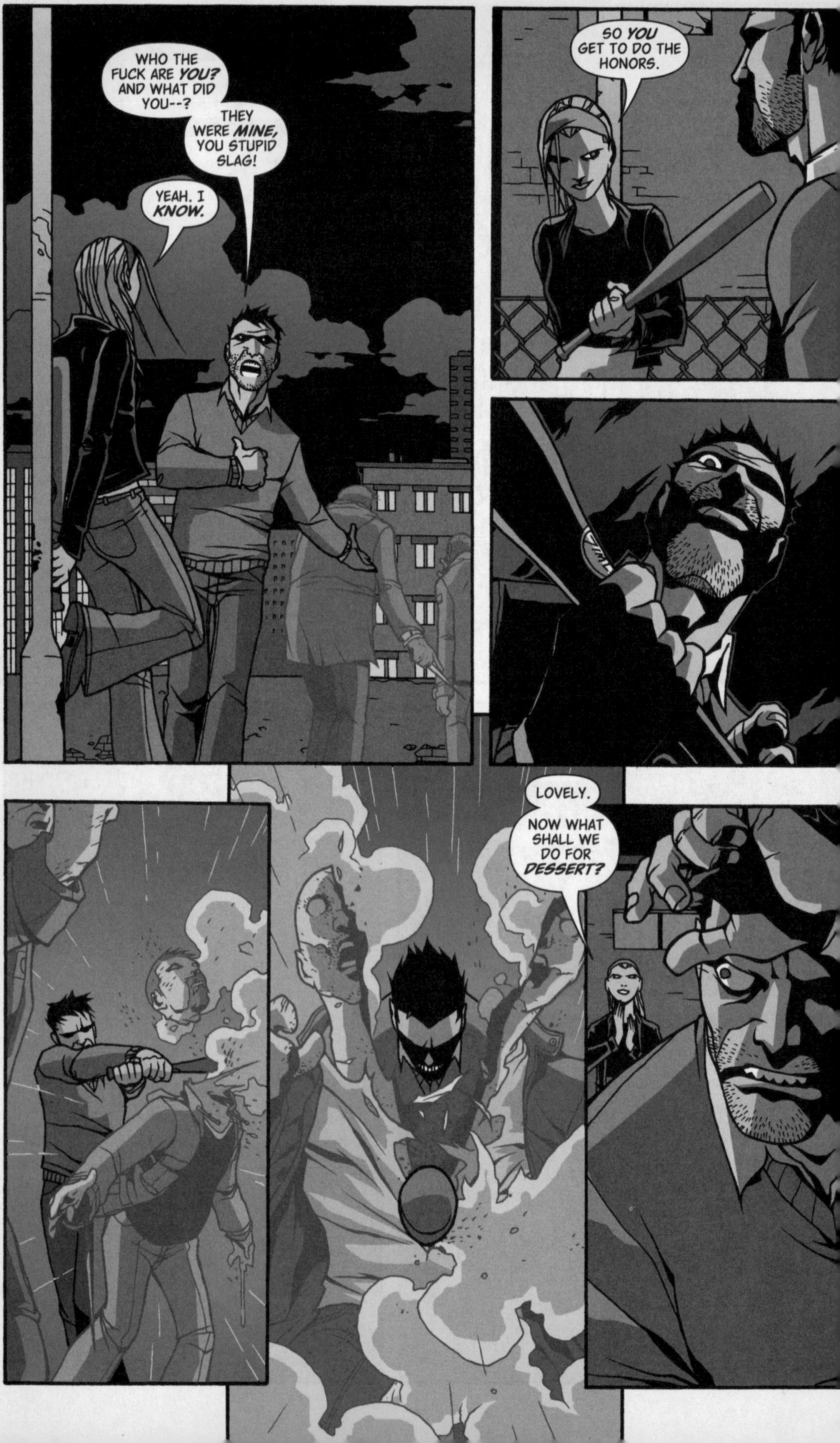
WHO THE FUCK ARE YOU? AND WHAT DID YOU--?
THEY WERE MINE, YOU STUPID SLAG!
YEAH. I KNOW.
SO YOU GET TO DO THE HONORS.
LOVELY.
NOW WHAT SHALL WE DO FOR DESSERT?

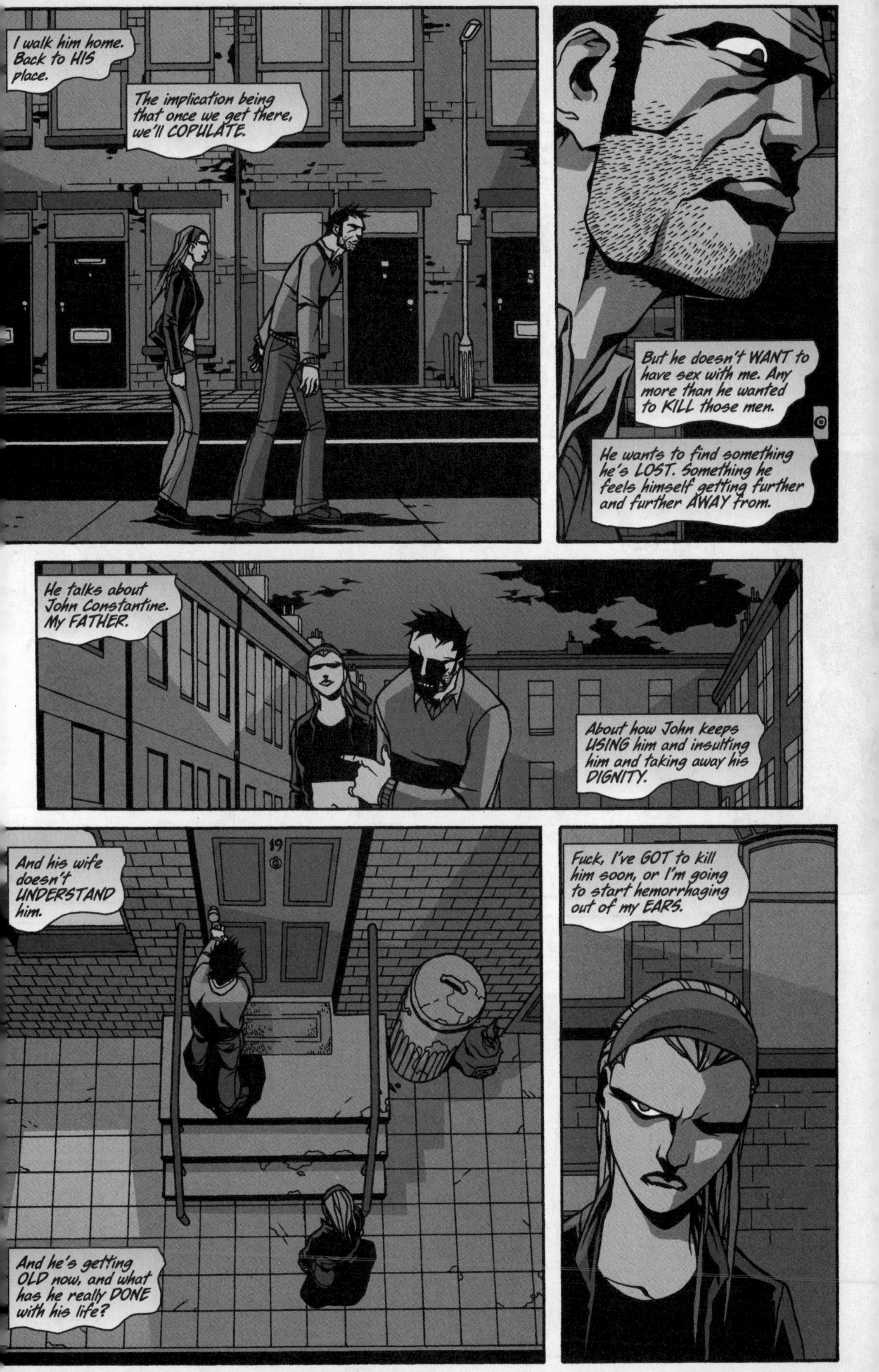
I walk him home. Back to HIS place.
The implication being that once we get there, we'll COPULATE.
But he doesn't WANT to have sex with me. Any more than he wanted to KILL those men.
He wants to find something he's LOST. Something he feels himself getting further and further AWAY from.
He talks about John Constantine. My FATHER.
About how John keeps USING him and insulting him and taking away his DIGNITY.
And his wife doesn't UNDERSTAND him.
19
And he's getting OLD now, and what has he really DONE with his life?
Fuck, I've GOT to kill him soon, or I'm going to start hemorrhaging out of my EARS.

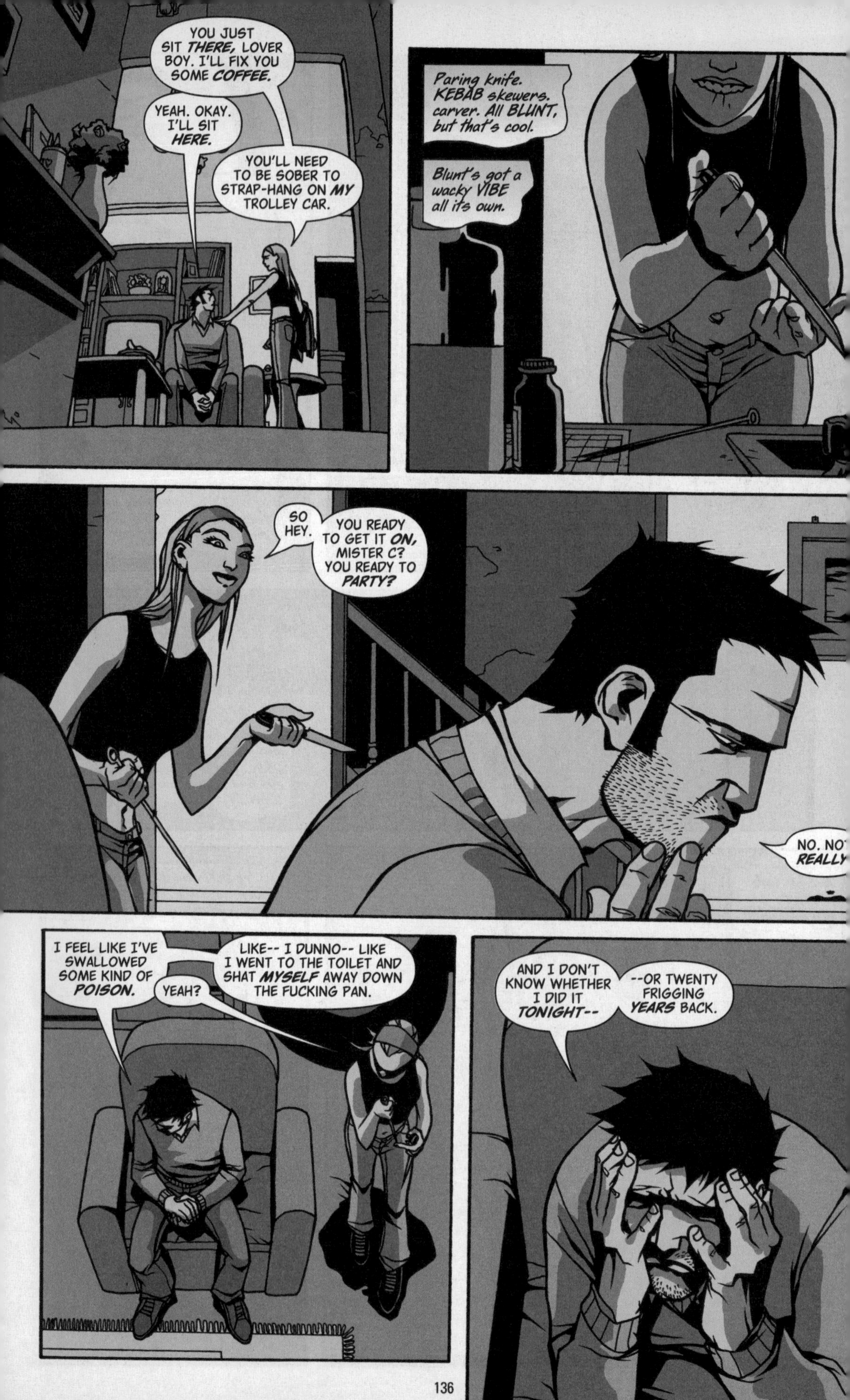
YOU JUST SIT *THERE,* LOVER BOY. I'LL FIX YOU SOME *COFFEE.*
YEAH. OKAY. I'LL SIT *HERE.*
YOU'LL NEED TO BE SOBER TO STRAP-HANG ON *MY* TROLLEY CAR.
Paring knife. KEBAB skewers. carver. All BLUNT, but that's cool.
Blunt's got a wacky VIBE all its own.
SO HEY.
YOU READY TO GET IT *ON,* MISTER C? YOU READY TO *PARTY?*
NO. NOT *REALLY*
I FEEL LIKE I'VE SWALLOWED SOME KIND OF *POISON.*
YEAH?
LIKE-- I DUNNO-- LIKE I WENT TO THE TOILET AND SHAT *MYSELF* AWAY DOWN THE FUCKING PAN.
AND I DON'T KNOW WHETHER I DID IT *TONIGHT--*
--OR TWENTY FRIGGING *YEARS* BACK.

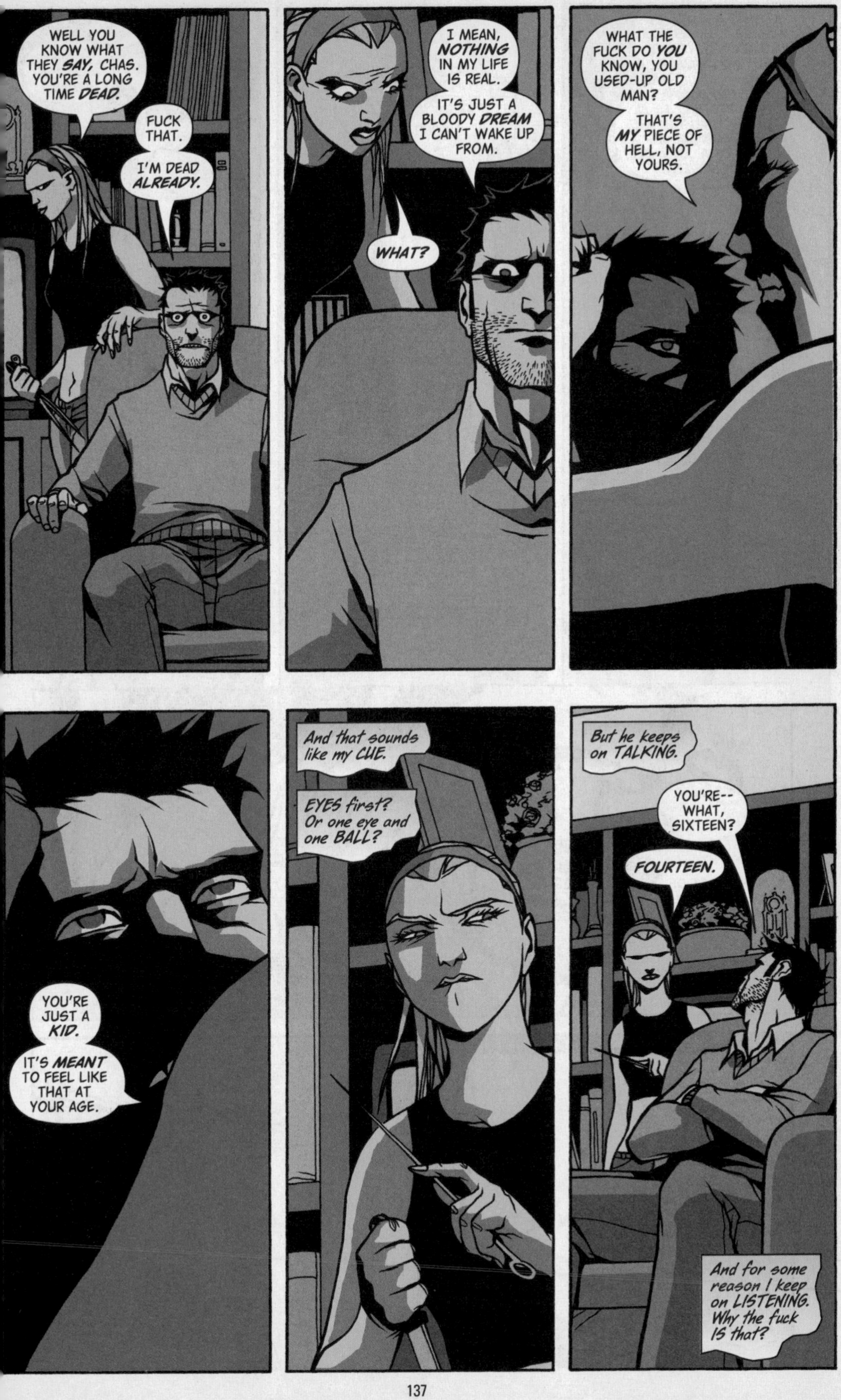
WELL YOU KNOW WHAT THEY SAY, CHAS. YOU'RE A LONG TIME DEAD.
FUCK THAT.
I'M DEAD ALREADY.
I MEAN, NOTHING IN MY LIFE IS REAL.
IT'S JUST A BLOODY DREAM I CAN'T WAKE UP FROM.
WHAT?
WHAT THE FUCK DO YOU KNOW, YOU USED-UP OLD MAN?
THAT'S MY PIECE OF HELL, NOT YOURS.
YOU'RE JUST A KID.
IT'S MEANT TO FEEL LIKE THAT AT YOUR AGE.
And that sounds like my CUE.
EYES first? Or one eye and one BALL?
But he keeps on TALKING.
YOU'RE--WHAT, SIXTEEN?
FOURTEEN.
And for some reason I keep on LISTENING. Why the fuck IS that?

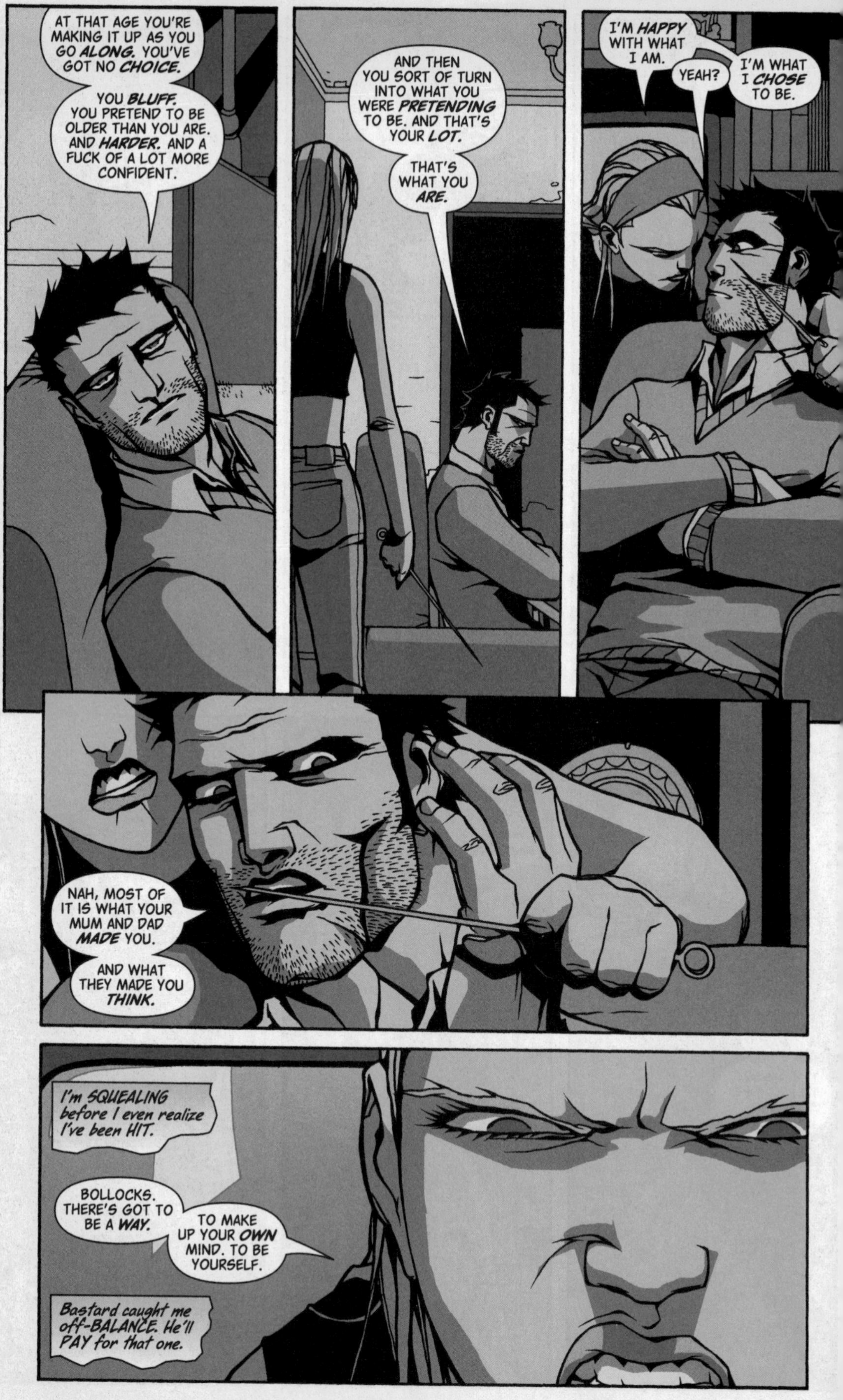
AT THAT AGE YOU'RE MAKING IT UP AS YOU GO ALONG. YOU'VE GOT NO CHOICE.
YOU BLUFF. YOU PRETEND TO BE OLDER THAN YOU ARE. AND HARDER. AND A FUCK OF A LOT MORE CONFIDENT.
AND THEN YOU SORT OF TURN INTO WHAT YOU WERE PRETENDING TO BE. AND THAT'S YOUR LOT.
THAT'S WHAT YOU ARE.
I'M HAPPY WITH WHAT I AM.
YEAH?
I'M WHAT I CHOSE TO BE.
NAH, MOST OF IT IS WHAT YOUR MUM AND DAD MADE YOU.
AND WHAT THEY MADE YOU THINK.
I'm SQUEALING before I even realize I've been HIT.
BOLLOCKS. THERE'S GOT TO BE A WAY.
TO MAKE UP YOUR OWN MIND. TO BE YOURSELF.
Bastard caught me off-BALANCE. He'll PAY for that one.

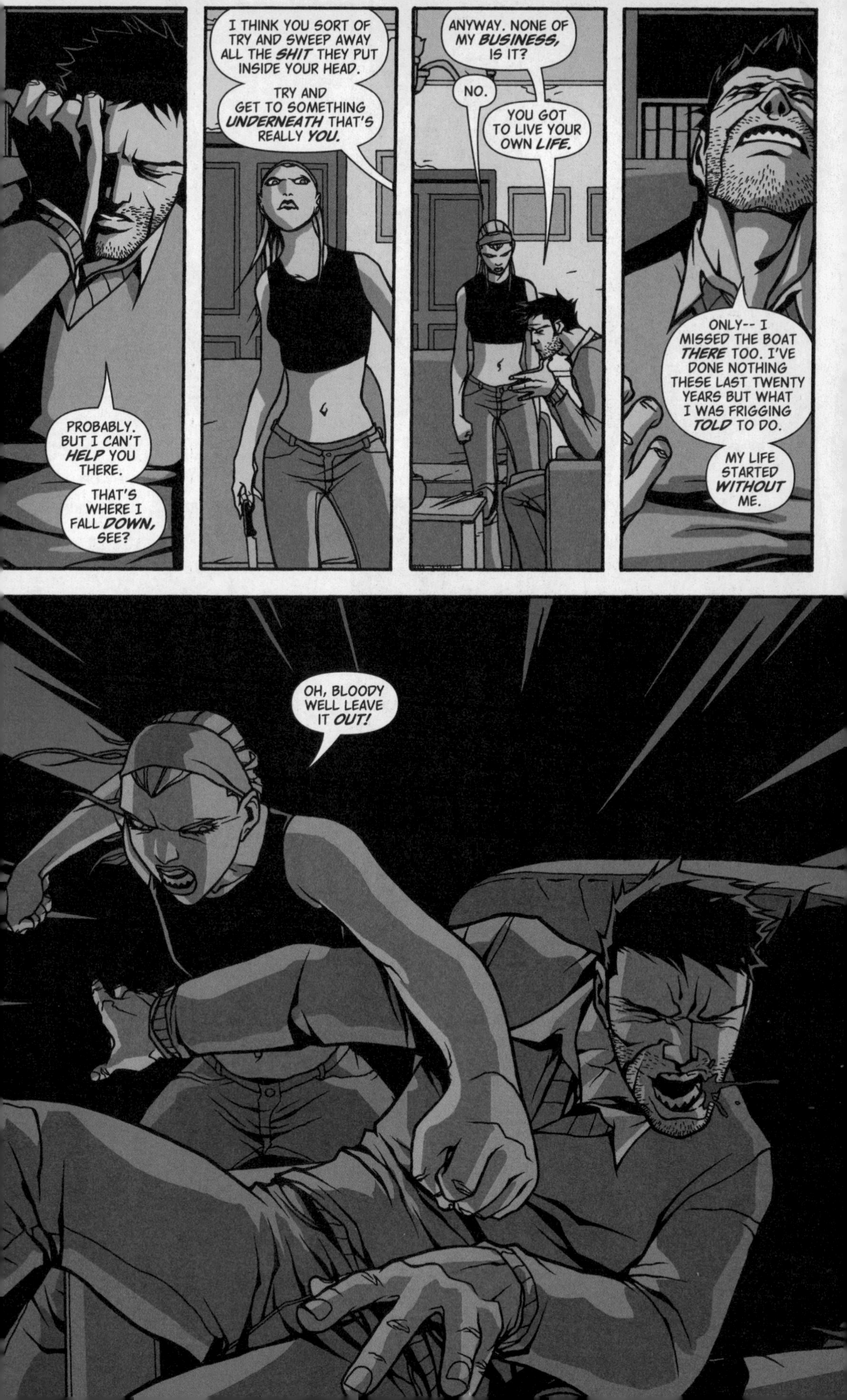
PROBABLY. BUT I CAN'T HELP YOU THERE.
THAT'S WHERE I FALL DOWN, SEE?
I THINK YOU SORT OF TRY AND SWEEP AWAY ALL THE SHIT THEY PUT INSIDE YOUR HEAD.
TRY AND GET TO SOMETHING UNDERNEATH THAT'S REALLY YOU.
ANYWAY. NONE OF MY BUSINESS, IS IT?
NO.
YOU GOT TO LIVE YOUR OWN LIFE.
ONLY-- I MISSED THE BOAT THERE TOO. I'VE DONE NOTHING THESE LAST TWENTY YEARS BUT WHAT I WAS FRIGGING TOLD TO DO.
MY LIFE STARTED WITHOUT ME.
OH, BLOODY WELL LEAVE IT OUT!

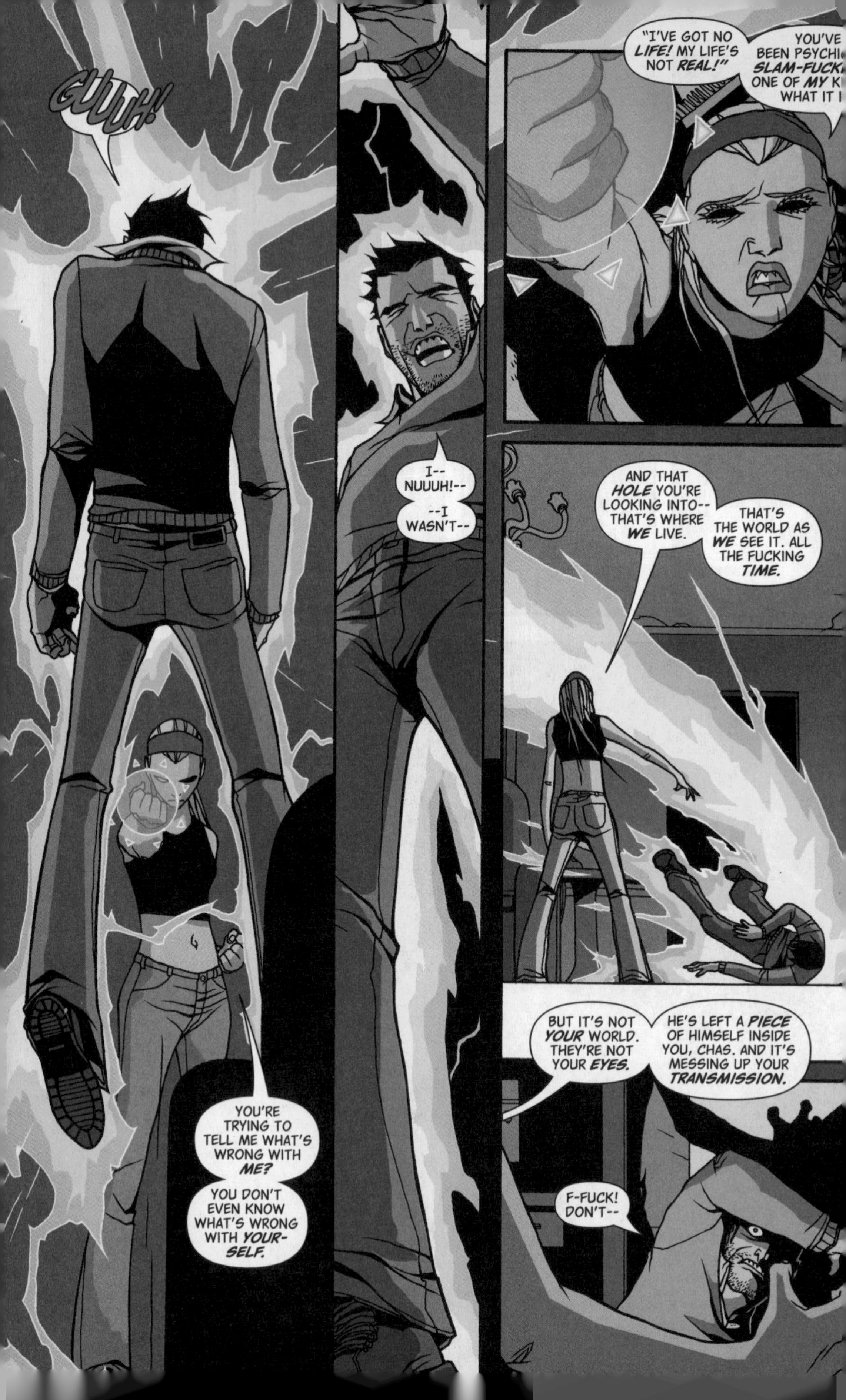
GUUUH!
I-- NUUUH!--
--I WASN'T--
"I'VE GOT NO LIFE! MY LIFE'S NOT REAL!"
AND THAT HOLE YOU'RE LOOKING INTO-- THAT'S WHERE WE LIVE.
THAT'S THE WORLD AS WE SEE IT. ALL THE FUCKING TIME.
BUT IT'S NOT YOUR WORLD. THEY'RE NOT YOUR EYES.
HE'S LEFT A PIECE OF HIMSELF INSIDE YOU, CHAS. AND IT'S MESSING UP YOUR TRANSMISSION.
F-FUCK! DON'T--
YOU'RE TRYING TO TELL ME WHAT'S WRONG WITH ME?
YOU DON'T EVEN KNOW WHAT'S WRONG WITH YOURSELF.

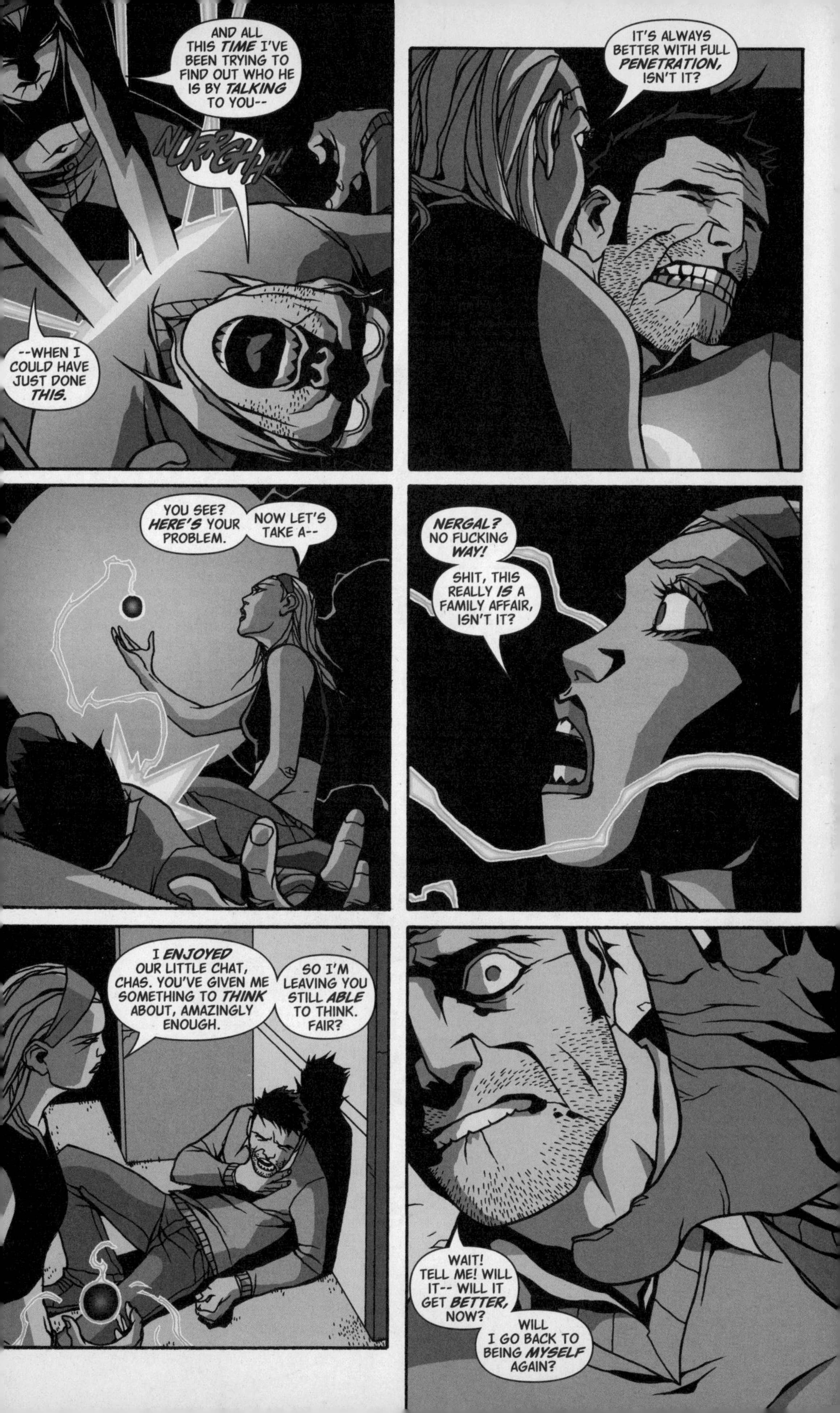
AND ALL THIS TIME I'VE BEEN TRYING TO FIND OUT WHO HE IS BY TALKING TO YOU--
NURRGHHH!
--WHEN I COULD HAVE JUST DONE THIS.
IT'S ALWAYS BETTER WITH FULL PENETRATION, ISN'T IT?
YOU SEE? HERE'S YOUR PROBLEM.
NOW LET'S TAKE A--
NERGAL? NO FUCKING WAY!
SHIT, THIS REALLY IS A FAMILY AFFAIR, ISN'T IT?
I ENJOYED OUR LITTLE CHAT, CHAS. YOU'VE GIVEN ME SOMETHING TO THINK ABOUT, AMAZINGLY ENOUGH.
SO I'M LEAVING YOU STILL ABLE TO THINK. FAIR?
WAIT! TELL ME! WILL IT-- WILL IT GET BETTER, NOW?
WILL I GO BACK TO BEING MYSELF AGAIN?

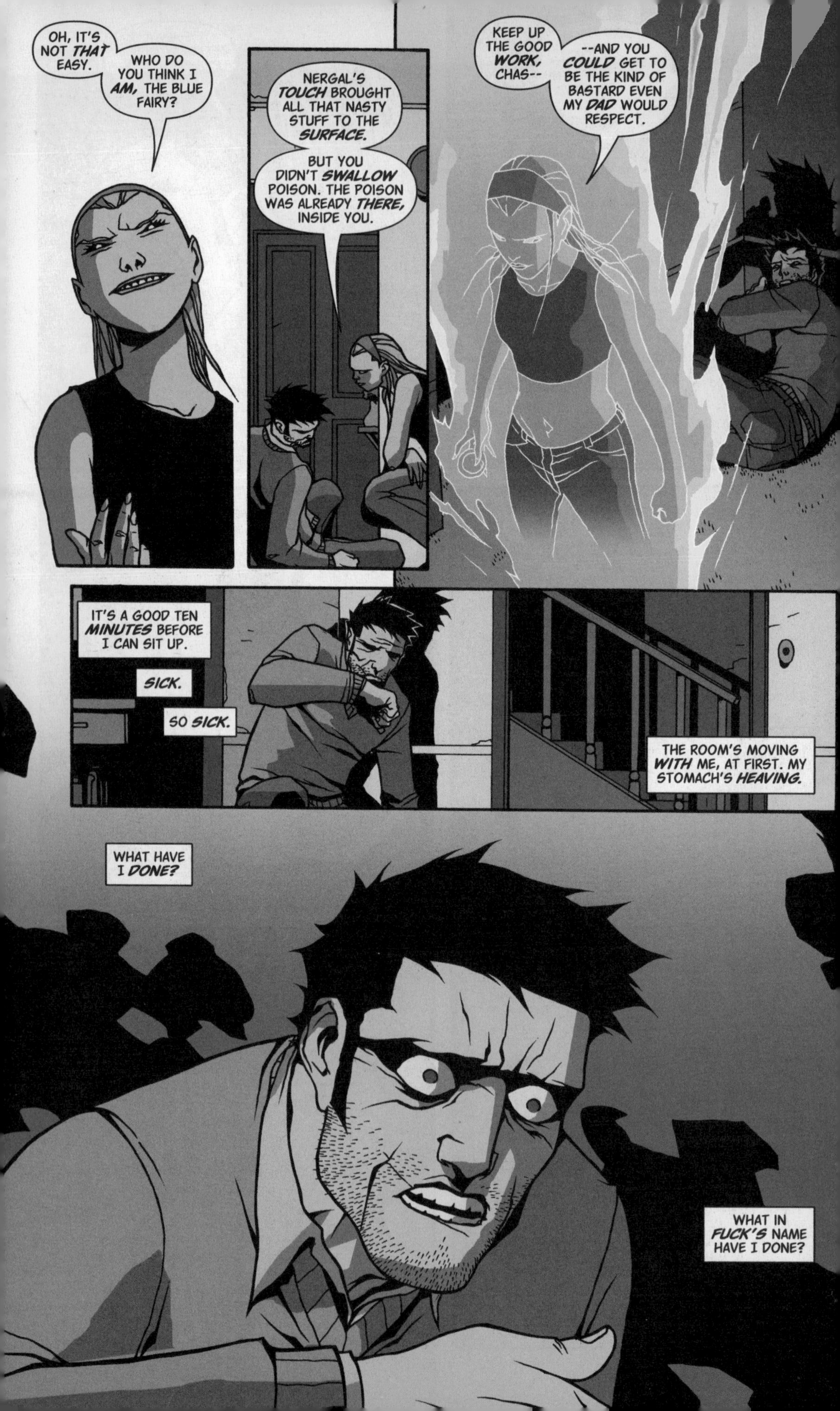
OH, IT'S NOT THAT EASY.
WHO DO YOU THINK I AM, THE BLUE FAIRY?
NERGAL'S TOUCH BROUGHT ALL THAT NASTY STUFF TO THE SURFACE.
BUT YOU DIDN'T SWALLOW POISON. THE POISON WAS ALREADY THERE, INSIDE YOU.
KEEP UP THE GOOD WORK, CHAS--
--AND YOU COULD GET TO BE THE KIND OF BASTARD EVEN MY DAD WOULD RESPECT.
IT'S A GOOD TEN MINUTES BEFORE I CAN SIT UP.
SICK.
SO SICK.
THE ROOM'S MOVING WITH ME, AT FIRST. MY STOMACH'S HEAVING.
WHAT HAVE I DONE?
WHAT IN FUCK'S NAME HAVE I DONE?

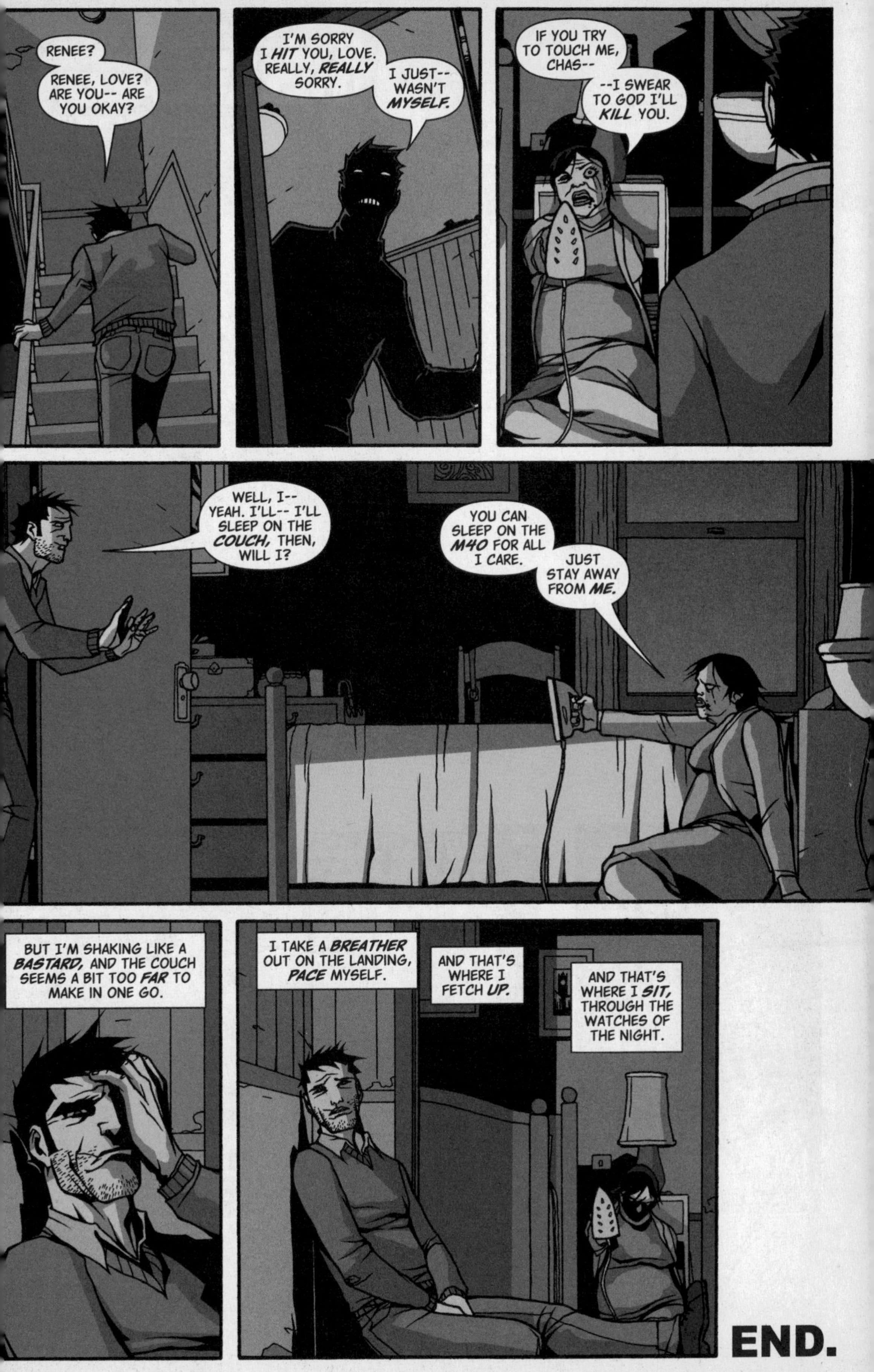
RENEE?
RENEE, LOVE? ARE YOU-- ARE YOU OKAY?
I'M SORRY I HIT YOU, LOVE. REALLY, REALLY SORRY.
I JUST-- WASN'T MYSELF.
IF YOU TRY TO TOUCH ME, CHAS--
--I SWEAR TO GOD I'LL KILL YOU.
WELL, I-- YEAH. I'LL-- I'LL SLEEP ON THE COUCH, THEN, WILL I?
YOU CAN SLEEP ON THE M40 FOR ALL I CARE.
JUST STAY AWAY FROM ME.
BUT I'M SHAKING LIKE A BASTARD, AND THE COUCH SEEMS A BIT TOO FAR TO MAKE IN ONE GO.
I TAKE A BREATHER OUT ON THE LANDING, PACE MYSELF.
AND THAT'S WHERE I FETCH UP.
AND THAT'S WHERE I SIT, THROUGH THE WATCHES OF THE NIGHT.

END.